THOREAU
THE POET-NATURALIST

WILLIAM·ELLERY·CHANNING

THOREAU
THE POET-NATURALIST

WITH MEMORIAL VERSES

BY WILLIAM ELLERY CHANNING

NEW EDITION, ENLARGED
EDITED BY F. B. SANBORN

MY GREATEST SKILL HAS BEEN TO WANT BUT LITTLE. FOR
JOY I COULD EMBRACE THE EARTH. I SHALL DELIGHT TO BE
BURIED IN IT. AND THEN I THINK OF THOSE AMONG MEN, WHO
WILL KNOW THAT I LOVE THEM, THOUGH I TELL THEM NOT.
H. D. T.

BIBLO and TANNEN
NEW YORK
1966

First Published 1902

Reprinted 1966 by

Biblo & Tannen Booksellers & Publishers, Inc.
63 Fourth Ave.   New York, N. Y. 10003

Library of Congress Catalog Card Number: 65-27095

Printed in U.S.A. by
NOBLE OFFSET PRINTERS, INC.
NEW YORK 3, N. Y.

DEDICATION

Silent and serene,
The plastic soul emancipates her kind.
She leaves the generations to their fate,
Uncompromised by grief. She cannot weep:
She sheds no tears for us,—our mother, Nature!
She is ne'er rude nor vexed, not rough or careless;
Out of temper ne'er, patient as sweet, though winds
In winter brush her leaves away, and time
To human senses breathes through frost.
      My friend!
Learn, from the joy of Nature, thus to be
Not only all resigned to thy worst fears,
But, like herself, superior to them all,
Nor merely superficial in thy smiles!
And through the inmost fibres of thy heart
May goodness constant flow, and fix in that
The ever-lapsing tides, that lesser depths
Deprive of half their salience. Be, throughout,
True as the inmost life that moves the world,
And in demeanor show a firm content,
Annihilating change.
    Thus Henry lived,
Considerate to his kind. His love bestowed
Was not a gift in fractions, half-way done;
But with some mellow goodness, like a sun,
He shone o'er mortal hearts, and taught their buds

[v]

DEDICATION

To blossom early, thence ripe fruit and seed.
Forbearing too much counsel, yet with blows
By pleasing reason urged, he touched their thought
As with a mild surprise, and they were good,
Even if they knew not whence that motive came;
Nor yet suspected that from Henry's heart—
His warm, confiding heart—the impulse flowed.

These lines were not originally addrest to Mr. Thoreau, nor, indeed, describe literally whatever character. But were meant for Mr. Emerson. w. e. c.

HENRY DAVID THOREAU

"Si tibi pulchra domus, si splendida mensa, quid inde?
Si species auri, argenti quoque massa, quid inde?
Si tibi sponsa decens, si sit generosa, quid inde?
Si tibi sunt nati, si prædia magna, quid inde?
Si fueris pulcher, fortis, dives ve, quid inde?
Si doceas alios in quolibet arte, quid inde?
Si longus servorum inserviat ordo, quid inde?
Si faveat mundus, si prospera cuncta, quid inde?
Si prior, aut abbas, si dux, si papa, quid inde?
Si felix annos regnes per mille, quid inde?
Si rota fortunæ se tollit ad astra, quid inde?
Tam cito, tamque cito fugiunt hæc ut nihil, inde.
Sola manet virtus: nos glorificabimur, inde.
Ergo Deo pare, bene nam provenit tibi inde."

> LAURA BASSI. *Sonnet on the gate of the Specola at Bologna.*

"From sea and mountain, city and wilderness,
Earth lifts its solemn voice; but thou art fled;
Thou canst no longer know or love the shapes
Of this phantasmal scene, who have to thee
Been purest ministers, who are, alas!
Now thou art not. Art and eloquence,
And all the shows of the world, are frail and vain
To weep a loss that turns their light to shade!
It is a woe too deep for tears when all
Is reft at once, when some surpassing spirit,
Whose light adorned the world around it, leaves
Those who remain behind nor sobs nor groans,
But pale despair and cold tranquillity,
Nature's vast frame, the web of human things,
Birth and the grave, that are not as they were."

> SHELLEY.

"The memory, like a cloudless sky,
The conscience, like a sea at rest."

> TENNYSON.

"Espérer ou craindre pour un autre est la seule chose qui donne
à l'homme le sentiment complet de sa propre existence."

> EUGÉNIE DE GUÉRIN.

"For not a hidden path, that to the shades
Of the beloved Parnassian forest leads,
Lurked undiscovered by him; not a rill
There issues from the fount of Hippocrene,
But he had traced it upward to its source,
Through open glade, dark glen, and secret dell,
Knew the gay wild-flowers on its banks, and culled
Its med'cinable herbs; yea, oft alone,
Piercing the long-neglected holy cave,
The haunt obscure of old Philosophy."

COLERIDGE.

"Such cooling fruit
As the kind, habitable woods provide."

MILTON.

"My life is but the life of winds and tides,
No more than winds and tides can I avail."

KEATS.

"Is this the mighty ocean?—is this all?"

LANDOR.

"Then bless thy secret growth, nor catch
At noise, but thrive unseen and dumb;
Keep clean, bear fruit, earn life, and watch,
Till the white-winged reapers come."

VAUGHAN.

"No one hates the sea and danger more than I do; but I fear
more not to do my duty to the utmost."

SIR ROBERT WILSON.

"The joyous birds shrouded in cheerful shade,
Their notes unto the voice attempted sweet;
Th' angelical soft trembling voices made
To th' instruments divine respondence meet,
With the low murmurs of the water's fall;
The water's fall with difference discreet,
Now soft, now loud, unto the wind did call;
The gentle warbling wind low answerèd to all."

SPENSER.

INTRODUCTION

ELLERY CHANNING's biography of his most intimate friend, Thoreau, had a peculiar history. Soon after Thoreau's death in May, 1862, Channing began to write his life, for which he had long been making preparation, both consciously and unconsciously. In 1853, when a plan was formed, which never was fully carried out, for collecting into a book under Channing's editing a series of walks and talks about Concord and its region, in which Emerson, Thoreau, Channing, and Alcott should be the recorders and interlocutors, Mr. Channing, who had then been for ten years a resident of Concord, with occasional absences in New York and Europe, had access to the journals of Thoreau, and made various copies therefrom. Later, and during Thoreau's last illness, he copied from them still more specifically; and the books, now in my possession, in which these extracts were entered, were borrowed by Emerson in revising for publication his funeral eulogy of Thoreau, which now appears as an introduction to the volume called "Excursions." Other portions were copied while Channing was assisting Sophia Thoreau to edit the "Maine Woods"; so that the manuscript volume finally contained many pages from Thoreau's journals for the last ten or twelve years of his life. In 1863 very few of these had been published, although a few appeared in Thoreau's contributions to the "Atlantic Monthly," and in Emerson's eulogy. Had the book appeared then, early in 1864, as Channing expected, it would have been a fresh and varied addition to what the public had of Thoreau's original and carefully written observations on nature and man.

With all this preparation, Channing in 1863 composed a hundred and thirty-four large manuscript pages in a book now lying before me, his first draft of "Thoreau, the Poet-Naturalist"; copied it out, with omissions and additions, and sent me the first half of the copy for publication, week by week, in the "Boston Commonwealth" newspaper, which I had begun to edit in February, 1863, and to which Miss Thoreau had contributed several of her brother's unprinted poems. I copyrighted the work in my own name, as Mr. Channing desired, and began to publish it early in 1864. After several weeks, I omitted the weekly chapter of Thoreau (whose readers were much fewer forty years ago than now), in order to give my limited space for literary matter to other contributors for a fortnight. At this omission my friend took offence, and recalled his manuscript, so that the work remained a fragment for nearly ten years, during which time much of the unprinted manuscript of Thoreau found its way into print, and stimulated the desire of readers to know more of the author. This suggested to me and to Channing that he might issue his work in a volume, as he had "The Wanderer" (1871), which proved in some degree popular. I made an arrangement with the late Thomas Niles, then the head of the house of Roberts Brothers, by which an edition of fifteen hundred copies of the biography should be published in the autumn of 1873; and the volume known to libraries and collectors as "Thoreau, the Poet-Naturalist" made its appearance, and sold moderately well. Indeed, it was the most popular of all Channing's nine volumes, published by him at intervals from 1843 to 1886. It escaped the Boston fires which had destroyed the unsold copies of "The Wanderer," and in twenty years was so completely sold out that it was with difficulty the publishers procured for me a single copy for presentation to our Plymouth friend, Marston Watson of Hillside, to whom Channing had omitted to send it, or who may have given away his copy. A copy now and then coming to market at present sells for five dollars.

But the volume of 1873 (now out of print and its copyright expired) was very different from that composed in 1863. With the perversity of genius Channing had gone over his first draft, omitting much, making portions of the rest obscure and enigmatical, but enriching it with the treasures

[xi]

of his recondite learning in mottoes, allusions, and number-
less citations,—the whole without much method, or with a
method of his own, not easily followed by the reader, who
had not the guide-board of an index to help him out. Withal,
Channing had inserted here and there matchless passages of
description, his own or Thoreau's, which made the book then,
and ever since, a mine of citations for every biographer of
the poet-naturalist who succeeded him,—beginning with the
Scotch litterateur who called himself "H. A. Page," and
whose little volume was soon reprinted in Boston by Thoreau's publishers.

In my new edition, based upon a copy with the author's
revision and notes, I have inserted here and there passages
of no great length which I find in the original sketch, and
which make the meaning plainer and the story more con-
secutive. At the end of this volume will be found some additions to the "Memorial Poems" which evidently belong there.

But a still more singular peculiarity marked the volume of
1873. As its printing went on, the publisher (Mr. Niles) consulted me in regard to it, finding Mr. Channing not always
responsive to his suggestions; and finally said to me, for the
author's information, that the volume was about fifty pages
smaller than he had expected to make it. Could not Mr.
Channing, then, who seemed to have much material at his

disposal, add the requisite pages to the work? Certainly, was
the reply; and how was it done? From the long-deferred
manuscript of 1853, "Country Walking" by name, containing
long passages from the journals of Emerson and Thoreau,
with bits of actual conversation; sketches and snatches of
character by Channing himself, and here and there a poem
or fragment by Channing or Emerson,—from this medley of
records, meant for another purpose, Channing selected the
required number of pages,—cut the original book open in
the midst, and inserted the new-old matter. It makes the
bulk of sixty-seven pages (old edition), from the hundred and
twentieth to the hundred and eighty-seventh, inclusive, and
is so printed that the authors themselves could hardly pick
out their own share in this olio. In the revision Channing
has indicated with some clearness (to my eyes) who is the
spokesman in each colloquy, and I have prefixed or affixed
the names of the interlocutors in most cases. This matter,
though improperly given to the world thirty years ago, and
occasioning Mr. Emerson, and possibly Miss Thoreau, some
vexation, has now been public property so long that I reprint
it without hesitation, but sometimes changing its order. I
have also inserted occasionally passages out of Thoreau's
journals or papers which have not yet been published, perhaps, but the printing of which will only add to the value

of that great store of unprinted manuscript which Mr. E. H. Russell of Worcester now holds, and is preparing to publish in a more methodical form than Thoreau's good friend Blake did.

I have felt a strong personal interest in this biography, not only from my long friendship both with Thoreau and Channing, but because I have been so conversant, for nearly forty years, with the contents of the volume, and with the manuscripts out of which they were condensed. And I have prefixed to this edition a portrait, not of Thoreau, but Ellery Channing himself, taken as a photograph by that excellent artist, Mr. Henry Smith of the Studio Building, Boston, not long after the publication of the first edition in 1873. At the time, three sittings were given by Mr. Channing, all in one day, but presenting different views of the sitter. That chosen for this book is not his most poetic aspect, — which is reserved for the volume of Channing's "Poems of Sixty-five Years," now in press at Philadelphia, — but rather the shrewd, humorous face, with its ancestral resemblances and reminders of kinship, which seems most fitting for this prose volume. Those who remember Mr. Channing's cousin, the late John Murray Forbes, at the age (about fifty-six) when this portrait was made, will be struck, as I was, with a certain resemblance, — as also to the interesting Perkins family of Boston, from whom both Mr. Forbes and Ellery Channing derived many traits. Intellectually, the cousinship of John Forbes and Ellery Channing showed itself in that surprising quickness and perspicacity which, in the elder, the Merchant, was directed towards the secrets of Fortune and the management of men,—and in the younger, the Poet, towards every aspect of Man and of Nature, imaginatively transcribed in that volume which Shakespeare studied, saying,

"In Nature's infinite book of secrecy
A little I can read."

Channing read much therein: had his gift of expression been coequal with his extraordinary insight, none would ever think of denying to him the title which he modestly claimed for himself,—the high name of Poet. He had, in fact, more completely than any man since Keats, the traditional poetical temperament, intuitive, passionate, capricious, with by turns the most generous and the most exacting spirit. One other trait he had, never seen by me in such force in any other,— the power to see and the impulse to state all sides of any matter which presented itself to his alert and discriminating intellect. He would utter an opinion, in itself pertinent, but partial; in a moment, if not disputed, he would bring forth the complementary opinion, and so go round his subject until its qualities had been exhausted; and this not with the formality of syllogisms or enthymemes, but as the poet's eye, in Shakespeare's phrase,

"Doth glance from heaven to earth, from earth to heaven."

The "Memorial Verses" at the end of the biography are here printed with some alterations and additions. Their connection with his friend Thoreau is sometimes slight, but the connection existed in his enduring memory and his tender heart, and among them are some of his best lines. The Cape poems, commemorative in part of his walks along the sands with Thoreau, and in part of earlier joys and sorrows at Truro, were, I believe, regarded by Emerson as the best of his middle-age verses, except the Ode at the consecration of the Cemetery, in 1855, where his ashes now repose. The "Still River" deals with a walk from Ayer to Lancaster, passing by a village or two, and the lonely farmhouse of "Fruitlands," where Alcott and his friends in 1843–44 played out their idyll of an ascetic community. I have added to this poem, which was written before 1853, a concluding passage describing the winter landscape in the valley of the Nashua, into which, not far from Fruitlands, the stream called Still River quietly flows.

F. B. SANBORN.

Concord, April 15, 1902.

CONTENTS

CONTENTS

ILLUSTRATIONS

Engraved and etched by Sidney L. Smith

PREFACE

GRAY says that "Hermes" Harris is what he "calls the shallow-profound." Dr. Johnson says that in the dedication to Harris's "Hermes," of fourteen lines, there are six grammatical faults. This is as much as we could expect in an English pedant whose work treats of grammar: we trust our prologue will prove more drop-ripe, even if the whole prove dull,—dull as the last new comedy.

In a biographic thesis there can hardly occur very much to amuse, if of one who was reflective and not passionate, and who might have entered like Anthony Wood in his journal, "This day old Joan began to make my bed,"—an entry not fine enough for Walpole. At the same time the account of a writer's stock in trade may be set off like the catalogues of George Robins, auctioneer, with illustrations even in Latin or, as Marlowe says—

> "The learned Greek, rich in fit epithets,
> Blest in the lovely marriage of pure words."

Byron's bath at Newstead Abbey is described as a dark and cellar-like hole. The halos about the brows of authors tarnish with time. Iteration, too, must be respected,—that law of Nature. Authors carry their robes of state not on their backs, but, like the Indians seen by Wafer, in a basket behind them, —"the times' epitome." But as the cheerful host says:—

[xix]

PREFACE

"I give thee all, I can no more,
If poor the offering be,"

the best scraps in the larder, like Pip's pork-pie.

A literary life may acquire value by contrast. Goldsmith in the "Good-Natured Man" says, "Never mind the world, my dear: you were never in a pleasanter place in your life. Tenderness is a virtue, Mr. Twitch." Like the Lady Brilliana Harley, authors can say of their servants: "I take it as a speciall providence of God, that I have so froward a made aboute me as Mary is, sence I love peace and quietnes so well: she has bene extremely froward since I have bine ill; I did not think that any would have bine so colericke. I would I could put a little water in her wine."

Claude Lorraine used to say, "I sell you my landscapes: the figures I give away." So there are patch-work quilts made by the saints where bits of fine silk are sewed on pieces of waste paper,—that seems, madam, not that is. But recall the trope that "very near to admiration is the wish to admire," and permit the excellence of the subject to defray in a measure the meanness of the treatment:—

"Stars now vanish without number,
Sleepy planets set and slumber." [1]

[1] *Vaughan.*

[xx]

EARLY LIFE

"Wit is the Soul's powder."

DAVENANT.

CHAPTER I

EARLY LIFE

THE subject of this sketch was born in the town of Concord, Massachusetts, on the twelfth day of July, 1817. The old-fashioned house on the Virginia road, its roof nearly reaching to the ground in the rear, remains as it was[1] when Henry David Thoreau first saw the light in the easternmost of its upper chambers. It was the residence of his grandmother, and a perfect piece of our New England style of building, with its gray, unpainted boards, its grassy, unfenced door-yard. The house is somewhat isolate and remote from thoroughfares; the Virginia road, an old-fashioned, winding, at-length-deserted pathway, the more smiling for its forked orchards, tumbling walls, and mossy banks. About the house are pleasant, sunny meadows, deep with their beds of peat, so cheering with its homely, hearth-like fragrance; and in front runs a constant stream through the centre of that great tract sometimes called "Bedford levels,"—this brook, a source of the Shawsheen River. It was lovely he should draw his first breath in a pure country air, out of crowded towns, amid the pleasant russet fields. His parents were active, vivacious people; his grandfather by the father's side coming from the Isle of Jersey, a Frenchman and Churchman at home, who married in Boston a Scotch woman called Jeanie Burns. On his mother's side the descent is from the well-known Jones

[1] No longer so in 1902. F. B. S.

[3]

family of Weston, Massachusetts, and from Rev. Asa Dunbar, a graduate of Harvard College, who preached in Salem, and at length settled in Keene, New Hampshire. As variable an ancestry as can well be afforded, with marked family characters on both sides.

About a year and a half from Henry's birth, the family removed to the town of Chelmsford, thence to Boston, coming back however to Concord, when he was of a very tender age. His earliest memory almost of the town was a ride by Walden Pond with his grandmother, when he thought that he should be glad to live there. Henry retained a peculiar pronunciation of the letter *r*, with a decided French accent. He says, "September is the first month with a *burr* in it"; and his speech always had an emphasis, a *burr* in it. His great-grandmother's name was Marie le Galais; and his grandfather, John Thoreau, was baptized April 28, 1754, and took the Anglican sacrament in the parish of St. Helier (Isle of Jersey), in May, 1773. Thus near to old France and the Church was our Yankee boy.

As Henry is associated with Concord especially, I pass over several of his years after he left the Virginia road, for they were spent in Chelmsford and Boston. When he was fourteen months old, his family removed to Chelmsford, where they were settled for two years, and thence to Boston (his grandfather's town), where they lived three years before returning to Concord. At Chelmsford he was tossed by a cow, and again, by getting at an axe without advice, he cut off a good part of one of his toes; and once he fell from a stair. After

CHAPTER II

MANNERS

WE hear complaint that he set up for a reformer; and what capital, then, had he to embark in that line? How was it he knew so much more than the rest, as to correct abuses, to make over church and state? He had no reform theories, but used his opinions in literature for the benefit of man and the glory of God. Advice he did not give. His exhortations to young students and poor Christians who desired to know his economy never meant to exclude the reasonable charities. Critics have eagerly rushed to make this modest citizen and "home-body" one of the travelling conversational Shylocks, who seek their pound of flesh in swallowing humanity, each the special savior on his own responsibility. As he says of some reformers, "They addressed each other continually by their Christian names, and rubbed you continually with the greasy cheek of their kindness. They would not keep their distance, but cuddle up and lie spoon-fashion with you, no matter how hot the weather or how narrow the bed. . . . It was difficult to keep clear of the slimy benignity with which H. C. Wright sought to cover you, before he took you fairly into his bowels. He addressed me as Henry, within one minute from the time I first laid eyes on him; and when I spoke, he said, with drawling, sultry sympathy: 'Henry, I know all you would say, I understand you perfectly: you need not explain anything to me.'" Neither did he belong to the "Mutual

Admiration" society, where the dunce passes for gold by rubbing his fractional currency on pure metal. His was not an admiring character.

The opinion of some of his readers and lovers has been that, in his "Week," the best is the discourse of Friendship. It is certainly a good specimen of his peculiar style, but it should never be forgot that the treatment is poetical and romantic. No writer more demands that his reader, his critic, should look at his writing as a work of art. Because Michel Angelo painted the Last Judgment, we do not accuse him of being a judge: he is working as artist. So our author, in his writing on Friendship, treats the topic in a too distant fashion. Some might call it a lampoon: others say, "Why! this watery, moonlit glance and glimpse contains no more of the flesh and blood of friendship than so much lay-figure; if this was all the writer knew of Friendship, he had better have sheared off and let this craft go free." When he says, "One goes forth prepared to say 'Sweet friends!' and the salutation is, 'Damn your eyes!'"—to read this literally would be to accuse him of stupidity. The meaning is plain: he was romancing with his subject, playing a strain on his theorbo like the bobolink.

The living, actual friendship and affection which makes time a reality, no one knew better. He gossips of a high, imaginary world, giving a glance of that to the inhabitants of this world; bringing a few mother-of-pearl tints from the skies to refresh us in our native place. He did not wish for a set of cheap friends to eat up his time; was rich enough to go

without a train of poor relations,—the menagerie of dunces
with open mouths. In the best and practical sense, no one had
more friends or was better loved. He drew near him simple,
unlettered Christians, who had questions they wished to dis-
cuss; for, though nothing was less to his mind than chopped
logic, he was ready to *accommodate* those who differed from
him with his opinion; and never too much convinced by op-
position. To those in need of information—to the farmer-
botanist naming the new flower, the boy with his puzzle of
birds or roads, or the young woman seeking for books—he
was always ready to give what he had.

Literally, his views of friendship were high and noble.
Those who loved him never had the least reason to regret it.
He made no useless professions, never asked one of those
questions which destroy all relation; but he was on the spot
at the time, and had so much of human life in his keeping,
to the last, that he could spare a breathing place for a friend.
When I said that a change had come over the dream of life,
and that solitude began to peer out curiously from the dells
and wood-roads, he whispered, with his foot on the step of the
other world, "It is better some things should end." Having
this unfaltering faith, and looking thus on life and death
(after which, the poet Chapman says, a man has nothing to
fear), let it be said for ever that there was no affectation or
hesitancy in his dealing with his friends. He meant friendship,
and meant nothing else, and stood by it without the slightest
abatement; not veering as a weathercock with each shift of a
friend's fortune, or like those who bury their early friendships

in order to gain room for fresh corpses. If he was of a Spartan mould, in a manner austere, if his fortune was not vast, and his learning somewhat special, he yet had what is better, —the old Roman belief which confided there was more in this life than applause and the best seat at the dinner-table: to have a moment to spare to thought and imagination, and to the *res rusticæ* and those who need you;

> "That hath no side at all
> But of himself."

A pleasant account of this easy assimilation is given in his visit to Canton, where in his Sophomore year (1834–35) he kept a school of seventy pupils, and where he was consigned to the care of Rev. O. A. Brownson, then a Unitarian clergyman, for examination. The two sat up talking till midnight, and Mr. Brownson informed the School Committee that Mr. Thoreau was examined, and would do, and would board with him. So they struck heartily to studying German, and getting all they could of the time together, like old friends. Another early experience was the town school in Concord, which he took after leaving college, announcing that he should not flog, but would talk morals as a punishment instead. A fortnight sped glibly along, when a knowing deacon, one of the School Committee, walked in and told Mr. Thoreau that he must flog and use the ferule, or the school would spoil. So he did,—feruling six of his pupils after school, one of whom was the maid-servant in his own house. But it did not suit well with his conscience, and he reported to the committee that he should no longer keep their school, if they interfered with his arrangements; and they could keep it.

A moment may be spent on a few traits of Thoreau, of the personal kind. In height, he was about the average; in his build, spare, with limbs that were rather longer than usual, or of which he made a longer use. His face, once seen, could not be forgotten. The features were marked: the nose aquiline or very Roman, like one of the portraits of Cæsar (more like a beak, as was said); large, overhanging brows above the deepest set blue eyes that could be seen,—blue in certain lights, and in others gray,—eyes expressive of all shades of feeling, but never weak or near-sighted; the forehead not unusually broad or high, full of concentrated energy and purpose; the mouth with prominent lips, pursed up with meaning and thought when silent, and giving out, when open, a stream of the most varied and unusual and instructive sayings. His hair was a dark brown, exceedingly abundant, fine and soft; and for several years he wore a comely beard. His whole figure had an active earnestness, as if he had no moment to waste. The clenched hand betokened purpose. In walking, he made a short cut if he could, and when sitting in the shade or by the wall-side, seemed merely the clearer to look forward into the next piece of activity. Even in the boat he had a wary, transitory air, his eyes on the outlook, —perhaps there might be ducks, or the Blanding turtle, or an otter or sparrow.

He was a plain man in his features and dress, one who could not be mistaken. This kind of plainness is not out of keeping with beauty. He sometimes went as far as homeliness; which again, even if there be a prejudice against it, shines out at times beyond a vulgar sense. Thus, he alludes to those who pass the night on a steamer's deck, and see the mountains in moonlight; and he did this himself once on the Hudson, at the prow, when, after a "hem" or two, the passenger who stood next inquired in good faith: "Come, now, can't ye lend me a chaw o' baccy?" He looked like a shipmate. It was on another Albany steamboat that he walked the deck hungrily, among the fine gentlemen and ladies, eating upon a half-loaf of bread, his dinner for the day, and very late. A plain man could do this heartily: in an ornamental, scented thing it looks affected.

That was before the pedestrian disease. In that, once, as he came late into a town devoid of a tavern, on going to the best-looking house in the place for a bed, he got one in the entry, within range of the family, his speech and manners being those of polite society. In some of our retired towns there are traditions of lodgers who arise before light and depart with the feather bed, or the origin of feathers in the hencoop. Once walking in old Dunstable, he much desired the town history by C. J. Fox of Nashua; and, knocking, as usual, at the best house, he went in and asked a young lady who made her appearance whether she had the book in question. She had,—it was produced. After consulting it, Thoreau in his sincere way inquired very modestly whether she "would not *sell* it to him." I think the plan surprised her, and have heard that she smiled; but he produced his wallet, gave her the pis-

tareen, and went his way rejoicing with the book, which remained in his small library.

He did his stint of walking on Cape Cod, where a stranger
attracts a partial share of criticism, and "looked despairingly
at the sandy village whose street he must run the gauntlet
of; there only by sufferance, and feeling as strange as if he
were in a town in China." One of the old Cod could not believe that Thoreau was not a pedler; but said, after explanations failed, "Well, it makes no odds what else it is you
carry, so long as you carry truth along with you." One of
those idiots who may be found in some Cape Cod houses,
grim and silent, one night mumbled he would get his gun,
"and shoot that damned pedler." And, indeed, he might have
followed in the wake of a spectacle pedler who started from
the inn of *Meg Dods* in Wellfleet, the same morning, both of
them looking after and selling spectacles. He once appeared
in the mist, in a remote part of the Cape, with a bird tied to
the top of his umbrella, which he shouldered like a gun: the
inhabitants of the first cottage set the traveller down for a
"crazy fellow." At Orleans he was comforted by two Italian
organ-boys who had ground their harmonies from Provincetown, for twoscore miles in the sand, fresh and gay. He once
stopped at a hedge-tavern where a large white bull-dog was
kept in the entry: on asking the bar-tender what Cerberus
would do to an early riser, he replied, "Do?—why, he would
tear out the substance of your pantaloons." This was a good
notice not to quit the premises without meeting the rent.

Whatever was suitable he did: as lecturing in the basement

of an Orthodox church in Amherst, New Hampshire, when he hoped facetiously he "contributed something to upheave and demolish the structure." He once lectured in a Boston reading-room, the subscribers sniffing their chloroform of journals, not awoke by the lecture. A simple person can thus find easy paths. In the course of his travels, he sometimes met with a character that inspired him to describe it. He drew this Flemish sketch of a citizen of New York.

"Getting into Patchogue late one night, there was a drunken Dutchman on board, whose wit reminded me of Shakespeare. When we came to leave the beach our boat was aground, and we were detained waiting for the tide. In the mean while, two of the fishermen took an extra dram at the Beach House. Then they stretched themselves on the seaweed by the shore in the sun, to sleep off the effects of their debauch. One was an inconceivably broad-faced young Dutchman, but oh! of such a peculiar breadth and heavy look, I should not know whether to call it more ridiculous or sublime. You would say that he had humbled himself so much that he was beginning to be exalted. An indescribable Mynheerish stupidity. I was less disgusted by their filthiness and vulgarity, because I was compelled to look on them as animals, as swine in their stye. For the whole voyage they lay flat on their backs in the bottom of the boat, in the bilge-water, and wet with each bailing, half-insensible and wallowing in their filth. But ever and anon, when aroused by the rude kicks of the skipper, the Dutchman, who never lost his wits nor equanimity, though snoring and rolling in the reek produced by his debauch, blurted forth some happy repartee like an illuminated swine. It was the earthliest, slimiest wit I ever heard.

"The countenance was one of a million. It was unmistakable Dutch. In the midst of a million faces of other races it could not be mistaken. It told of Amsterdam. I kept racking my brains to conceive how he had been born in America, how lonely he must feel, what he did for fellowship. When we were groping up the narrow creek of Patchogue at ten o'clock at night, keeping our boat now from this bank, now from that, with a pole, the two inebriates roused themselves betimes. For in spite of their low estate they seemed to have all their wits as much about them as ever, ay, and all the self-respect they ever had. And the Dutchman gave wise directions to the steerer, which were not heeded (told where eels were plenty, in the dark, etc.). At last he suddenly stepped on to another boat which was moored to the shore, with a divine ease and sureness, saying, 'Well, good-night, take care of yourselves, I can't be with you any longer.' He was one of the few remarkable men I have met. I have been inspired by one or two men in their cups. There was really a divinity stirred within them, so that in their case I have reverenced the drunken, as savages do the insane man. So stupid that he could never be intoxicated; when I said, 'You have had a hard time of it to-day,' he answered with indescribable good-humor out of the very midst of his debauch, with watery eyes, 'It doesn't happen every day.' It was happening then."

With these plain ways, no person was usually easier misapplied by the cultivated class than Thoreau. Some of those afflicted about him have started with the falsetto of a void estimate on his life, his manners, sentiments, and all that in him was. His two books, "Walden" and the "Week," are so excellent and generally read, that a commendation of their easy, graceful, yet vigorous style and matter is superfluous. Singular traits run through his writing. His sentences will bear study; meanings appear not detected at the first glance, subtle hints which the writer himself may not have foreseen. It is a good English style, growing out of choice reading and familiarity with the classic writers, with the originality adding a piquant humor, and unstudied felicities of diction. He was not in the least degree an imitator of any writer, old or new, and with little of his times or their opinions in his books.

Never eager, with a pensive hesitancy he steps about his native fields, singing the praises of music and spring and morning, forgetful of himself. No matter where he might have lived, or in what circumstance, he would have been a writer: he was made for this by all his tendencies of mind and temperament; a writer because a thinker, and even a philosopher, a lover of wisdom. No bribe could have drawn him from his native fields, where his ambition was—a very honorable one—to fairly represent himself in his works, accomplishing as perfectly as lay in his power what he conceived his business. More society would have impaired his designs; and a story from a fisher or hunter was better to him than an evening of triviality in shining parlors where he was misunderstood. His eye and ear and hand fitted in with the special task he undertook,—certainly as manifest a destiny as any man's ever was. The best test of the worth of character,—whether the person lived a contented, joyous life, filled his hours agreeably, was useful in his way, and on the whole achieved his purposes,—this he possessed.

The excellence of his books and style is identical with the excellence of his private life. He wished to write living books that spoke of out-of-door things, as if written by an out-of-door man; and thinks his "Week" had that *hypæthral* character he hoped for. In this he was an artist. The impression of the "Week" and "Walden" is single, as of a living product, a perfectly jointed building; yet no more composite productions could be cited. The same applies to the lectures on "Wild Apples" or "Autumnal Tints," which possess this unity of treatment; yet the materials were drawn from the utmost variety of resources, observations made years apart, so skilfully woven as to appear a seamless garment of thought. This constructive, combining talent belongs with his adaptedness to the pursuit. Other gifts were subsidiary to his literary gift. He observed nature; but who would have known or heard of that except through his literary effort? He observed nature, yet not for the sake of nature, but of man; and says, "If it is possible to conceive of an event outside to humanity, it is not of the slightest importance, though it were the explosion of the planet."

Success is his rule. He had practised a variety of arts with many tools. Both he and his father were ingenious persons (the latter a pencil-maker) and fond of experimenting. To show the excellence of their work, they resolved to make as good a pencil out of plumbago paste as those sawed from black lead in London. The result was accomplished and the certificate obtained, Thoreau himself claiming a good share of the success, as he found the means to cut the plates. After his father's death in 1859, he carried on the pencil and plumbago business; had his own mill, and used the same punctuality and prudence in these affairs as had ever distinguished him.

In one or two of his later articles, expressions crept in which might lead the reader to suspect him of moroseness, or that his old trade of schoolmaster stuck to him. He rubbed out as perfectly as he could the more humorous part of those articles, originally a relief to their sterner features, and said, to me, "I cannot bear the levity I find." To which I replied, that it was hoped he would spare them, even to the puns, which he sometimes indulged. When a farmer drove up with a strange pair of long-tailed ponies, his companion asked whether such a person would not carry a Colt's revolver to protect him in the solitude? Thoreau replied that "he did not know about that, but he saw he had a pair of revolving colts before him." A lady once asked whether he ever laughed. She was well acquainted with him halfway, but did not see him, unless as a visitor; and he never became versed in making formal visits, nor had much success with first acquaintance. As to his laughing, no one did that more or better. One was surprised to see him dance,—he had been well taught, and was a vigorous dancer; and any one who ever heard him sing "Tom Bowline" will agree that, in tune and in tone, he answered, and went far beyond, all expectation. His favorite songs were Mrs. Hemans's "Pilgrim Fathers," Moore's "Evening Bells" and "Canadian Boat Song," and Wolfe's "Burial of Sir John Moore,"—precisely the most tender and popular songs. And oh, how sweetly he played upon his flute! Not unfrequently he sang that brave catch of Izaak Walton's,—

> "In the morning when we rise,.
> Take a cup to wash our eyes,"—

his cup being cold water. The Indians loved to drink at running brooks which were warm, but he loved ice-cold water. Summer or winter he drank very little, and would sometimes try to recollect when he drank last.

Before he set out on a foot journey, he collected every information as to the routes and the place to which he was going, through the maps and guide-books. For Massachusetts he had the large State map divided in portions convenient, and carried in a cover such parts as he wanted: he deemed this map, for his purposes, excellent. Once he made for himself a knapsack, with partitions for his books and papers,— india-rubber cloth, strong and large and spaced (the common knapsacks being unspaced). The partitions were made of stout book-paper. His route being known, he made a list of all he should carry,—the sewing materials never forgotten (as he was a vigorous walker, and did not stick at a hedge

more than an English racer), the pounds of bread, the sugar,
salt, and tea carefully decided on. After trying the merit
of cocoa, coffee, water, and the like, tea was put down as
the felicity of a walking "*travail*,"—tea plenty, strong, with
enough sugar, made in a tin pint cup; thus it may be said
the walker will be refreshed and grow intimate with tea-
leaves. With him the botany must go too, and the book for
pressing flowers (an old "Primo Flauto" of his father's), and
the guide-book, spy-glass, and measuring-tape. Every one
who has carried a pack up a mountain knows how every
fresh ounce tells. He would run up the steepest place as
swiftly as if he were on smooth land, and his breath never
failed. He commended every party to carry "a junk of heavy
cake" with plums in it, having found by long experience that
after toil it was a capital refreshment.

He made three journeys into the Maine wilderness, two
from Moosehead Lake in canoes, accompanied by Indians,
another to Katahdin Mountain. These taught him the art
of camping out; and he could construct in a short time a
convenient camp sufficient for permanent occupancy. His
last excursion of this kind was to Monadnoc Mountain in
August, 1859. He spent five nights in camp with me, having
built two huts to get varied views. On a walk like this he
always carried his umbrella; and on this Monadnoc trip,
when about one mile from the station, a torrent of rain came
down, the day being previously fine. Without his well-used
umbrella his books, blankets, maps, and provisions would all
have been spoiled, or the morning lost by delay. On the

mountain, the first plateau being reached perhaps at about
3 P.M., in a thick, rather soaking fog, the first object was to
camp and make tea. Flowers, birds, lichens, and the rocks
were carefully examined, all parts of the mountain visited,
and as accurate a map as could be made by pocket-compass
carefully sketched and drawn out, in the five days spent
there; with notes of the striking aërial phenomena, inci-
dents of travel and natural history. Doubtless he directed
such work with a view to writing on this and other mountains, and his collections were of course in his mind. Yet all
this was incidental to the excursion itself, the other things
collateral.

The capital in use was the opportunity of the wild, free
life, the open air, the new and strange sounds by night and
day, the odd and bewildering rocks, among which a person
can be lost within a rod of camp; the strange cries of visitors
to the summit; the great valley over to Wachusett, with its
thunder-storms and battles in the cloud (to look at, not fear);
the farmers' back-yards in Jaffrey, where the family cotton
can be seen bleaching on the grass, but no trace of the
pygmy family; the rip of night-hawks after twilight, putting
up dor-bugs, and the dry, soft air all the night; the lack of
dew in the morning; the want of water, a pint being a good
deal,—these and similar things make up some part of such
an excursion. It is all different from anything else, and
would be so if you went a hundred times. The fatigue, the
blazing sun, the face getting broiled, the pint cup never
scoured, shaving unutterable; your stockings dreary, having

taken to peat,—not all the books in the world, as Sancho says, could contain the adventures of a week in camping.

A friendly coincidence happened on his last excursion (July, 1858), to the White Mountains. Two of his friends, Harrison Blake and Theo. Brown, thought they might chance upon him there; and, though he dreamed little of seeing them, he left a note at the Mountain House which said where he was going, and told them if they looked "they would see the smoke of his fire." This came to be true, the brush taking the flame, and a smoke rising to be seen over all the valley. Meantime, Thoreau, in leaping from one mossy rock to another (after nearly sliding down the snow-crust on the side of Tuckerman's Ravine, but saved by digging his nails into the snow), had fallen and severely sprained his foot. Before this, he had found the *Arnica mollis*, a plant famous for its healing properties; but he preferred the ice-cold water of the mountain stream, into which he boldly plunged his tortured limb to reduce the swelling; had the tent spread, and then, the rain beginning to come down, there came his two friends down the mountain as well, their outer integuments decimated with their tramp in the scrub. They had seen the smoke; and here they were in his little tent made for two, the rain falling all the while, and five full-grown men to be packed in for five days and nights. Thoreau was unable to move on, but he sat and entertained them heartily.

He admired the rose-colored linnæas lining the side of the narrow horse-track through the fir-scrub, and the leopard-spotted land below the mountains. He had seen the pines in Fitzwilliam in a primeval wood-lot, and "their singular beauty made such an impression that I was forced to turn aside and contemplate them. They were so round and perpendicular that my eyes slid off." The rose-breasted grosbeaks sang in a wonderful strain on Mount Lafayette. He ascended such hills as Monadnoc or Saddle-back Mountain by his own path; would lay down his map on the summit and draw a line to the point he proposed to visit below (perhaps forty miles away in the landscape), and set off bravely to make the short-cut. The lowland people wondered to see him scaling the heights as if he had lost his way, or at his "jumping over their cow-yard fences," asking if he had fallen from the clouds.

READING

"'I know not' is one word; 'I know' is ten words."

CHINESE PROVERB.

CHAPTER III

READING

THOREAU considered his profession to be literature, and his business the building up of books out of the right material, — books which should impress the reader as being alive. As he loved not dead birds, so neither loved he dead books; he had no care for scattered fragments of literature. His aim was to bring his life into the shape of good and substantial literary expression; and to this end he armed himself with all the aids and appliances usual to literature. A good and sufficient academic and college training had made him a Latin and Greek scholar, with good knowledge of French, and some acquaintance with Italian, Spanish, and German. Allusion has been made to his faithful reading of English poetry at Harvard College, where he graduated in 1837. Besides what are usually called the "old English poets," such as Chaucer, even such stout hacklogs as Davenant's "Gondibert" did not discourage him, a sagacious and resolute reader. If there was the one good line, he took it. In New York in 1843, while residing in the family of Mr. William Emerson, he extended these English and Scotch readings at the great libraries. He neglected no culture, left nothing undone that could aid him in the preparation of his first books, the "Week" and "Walden." That he was familiar with the classics, and kept up the acquaintance, is shown by his translations from Homer, Æschylus, Pindar, Anacreon, Aristotle, Pliny, Cato, Columella,

[49]

and other ancient authors. His "Prometheus Bound," since included in his posthumous "Miscellanies," is said to have been reprinted and used as a "pony" at Harvard College; his version of the "Seven against Thebes" may have disappeared. Homer and Virgil were his favorites, like the world's; in English, Chaucer, Milton, Ossian, the Robin Hood Ballads; the "Lycidas," never out of his mind, for he had the habit, more than usual among scholars, of thinking in the language of another, in an unstudied way.

Of his favorites, he has written a pleasant account in his "Week." But he used these and all literature as aids, and did not stop in a book; rarely or never read them over. His reading was done with a pen in his hand: he made what he calls "Fact-books,"—citations which concerned his studies. He had no favorite among modern writers save Carlyle. Stories, novels (excepting the History of Froissart and the grand old Pelion on Ossa of the Hindoo Mythology), he did not read. His East Indian studies never went deep, technically: into the philological discussion as to whether ab, ab, is Sanscrit, or "what is Om?" he entered not. But no one relished the Bhagvat Geeta better, or the good sentences from the Vishnu Purana. He loved the Laws of Menu, the Vishnu Sarma, Saadi, and similar books. After he had ceased to read these works, he received a collection of them as a present, from his English friend Cholmondeley in 1855. Plato and Montaigne and Goethe were all too slow for him: the hobbies he rode dealt with realities, not shadows, and he philosophized *ab initio.* Metaphysics was his aversion. He believed and lived in his senses loftily. Speculations on the special faculties of the mind, or whether the Not Me comes out of the "I," or the All out of the infinite Nothing, he could not entertain. Like the Queen of Prussia, he had heard of *les infiniments petits.* In his way, he was a great reader and eagerly perused books of adventure, travel, or fact; and never could frame a dearer wish than spending the winter at the North pole: "could eat a fried rat with a relish," if opportunity commanded.

The "Week" is a mine of quotations from good authors, the proof of careful reading and right selection. Such knotty writers as Quarles and Donne here find a place in lines as fresh and sententious as the fleetest wits. Here we have the best lines from many of the most remarkable English writers, and all the best lines from many not as remarkable, or who only exist by virtue of such spare passages. Many authors have only their one line of merit; and many more are wanting even in this. Giles and Phineas Fletcher contain but a small portion of glory in all their high-sounding verse; yet the former afforded him that great passage from his "Christ's Victory and Triumph" beginning, —

> "How may a worm that crawls along the dust
> Clamber the azure mountains, thrown so high?"

as well as that, —

> "And now the taller sons whom Titan warms
> Of unshorn mountains, blown with easy winds,
> Dandle the Morning's childhood in their arms,
> And if they chanced to slip the prouder pines,

The under corylets did catch the shines
　　To gild their leaves."

From Phineas Fletcher's "Purple Island" he brings a splendid tribute to the Muses, —

"By them went Fido marshal of the field,
　Weak was his mother when she gave him day," etc.

Two stanzas not excelled in Milton or in Shakespeare. And what can be more subtle than these lines from Quarles's "Divine Fancies"?

"He that wants faith, and apprehends a grief,
　Because he wants it, hath a true belief;
　And he that grieves because his grief's so small,
　Has a true grief, and the best Faith of all."

"The laws of Nature break the rules of art."

Then, Samuel Daniel, another example of admirable English, he had read well; and his "Musophilus" "containing a general defence of learning" was a favorite, addressed as it was "to the Right Worthy and Judicious Favourer of Virtue Mr. Fulke Greville"—a patron after Thoreau's own heart, and whom he would have been only too glad to have met. This fine stanza is from that poem, —

"Men find that action is another thing
　From what they in discoursing papers read:
　The world's affairs require in managing
　More arts than those wherein you clerks proceed."

I quote this stanza and others as a better expression of Thoreau's opinion on men and things, as collected and approved

by himself, than I could find elsewhere. And this, too, is from
Daniel,—his "Epistle to the Lady Margaret, Countess of
Cumberland,"—

> "Unless above himself he can
> Erect himself, how poor a thing is man!"

Which perhaps was the most frequent verse he repeated. This
is followed in the common-place book, by that opinion from
Quarles (his "Emblems," Book IV. 11) which represents the
result of many queries:—

> "I asked the Schoolman; his advice was free,
> But scored me out too intricate a way."

Quarles was always a favorite of Thoreau; he relished the
following lines:—

> " Be wisely worldly, but not worldly wise."

> "The ill that's wisely feared is half withstood."

> " An unrequested star did gently slide
> Before the wise men to a greater light."

> " Lord, if my cards be bad yet grant me skill
> To play them wisely, and make the best of ill."

The astonishing Dean of St. Paul's, the learned Dr. Donne,
was another poet whom he treated with. From him comes
this in the "Week,"—

> "Although we with celestial bodies move
> Above the earth,—the earth we till and love."

And also,—

> "Why Love among the virtues is not known,
> Is, that Love is them all, contract in one."

Elsewhere he took from this cabalistical poet, —

> "Who are a little wise, the best fools be."

> " Only he who knows
> Himself, knows more."

He might also, in alluding (if he had chosen to do so) to his prevailing magnanimity, have used this sententious verse of Donne: —

> "For me (if there be such a thing as I),
> Fortune (if there be such a thing as she),
> Spies that I bear so well her tyranny,
> That she thinks nothing else so fit for me."

Here is one of Thoreau's early favorites, who copied it so far back as 1837: —

> "O, how feeble is man's power!
> That, if good fortune fall,
> Cannot add another hour,
> Nor a lost hour recall;
> But come bad chance,
> And we add to 't our strength,
> And we teach it art and length,
> Itself o'er us t' advance."

In Charles Cotton, the friend of Izaak Walton, he found two or three bits which pleased him; one of them in the "Week" gave him a motto for "Morning."

> "And round about 'Good morrows' fly,
> As if Day taught humanity."

Which is capital morals. But another motto for "Evening" is equally fortunate in its descriptive rarity:—

> "A very little, little flock
> Shades half the ground that it would stock,
> Whilst the small stripling following them
> Appears a mighty Polypheme."

Virgil would have appreciated this (*Et jam summa procul,* etc.) and Turner the painter should have had it. And though Ruskin, his critic, has fallen on Scott and Tennyson for picturesque description, Turner never found anything better than this in the landscape department. Cotton also afforded the fine definition of Contentment,—

> "Thou bravest soul's terrestrial Paradise."

Another of his favorites was Michael Drayton, who wrote something about the English rivers; but his Sonnets and other pieces are (many of them) in the best Shakespeare style. He refers to Drayton's Elegy, "To my dearly beloved friend, Henry Reynolds,—of Poets and Poesy," where he says:—

> "Next Marlowe, bathed in the Thespian springs,
> Had in him those brave translunary things
> That your first poets had: his raptures were
> All air and fire, which made his verses clear;
> For that fine madness still he did retain
> Which rightly should possess a poet's brain."

Drummond's Sonnet "Icarus" pleased him with its stirring line,—

> "For still the shore my brave attempt resounds,"

and was hinted at in "Walden." In hardly any instance does

Thoreau give, in his published works, the author for his verses. He supposed those who read him would either know the poets he quoted, or else admire his good things heartily enough, without knowing on what bough the apple grew that made the tart. Yet few persons would credit Spenser (in the "Ruines of Rome") with the modernness of these lines:—

> "Rome living was the world's sole ornament,
> And dead is now the world's sole monument.
> .   .   .   .
> With her own weight down-pressèd now she lies,
> And by her heaps her hugeness testifies."

Or that Francis Quarles, in his "Hieroglyphics of the Life of Man," could be thus plain:—

> "And now the cold autumnal dews are seen
>   To cobweb every green;
> And by the low-shorn rowens doth appear
>   The fast declining year."

Or this:—

> "To Athens gowned he goes, and from that school
> Returns unsped, a more instructed fool;"

or this, from the same Quarles, which (begging Shakespeare's pardon) might have been done by Shakespeare,—the account of a beggar, from the "Emblems":—

> "That bold adopts each house he views his own,
> Makes every purse his checquer, and at pleasure
> Walks forth and taxes all the world, like Cæsar."

Ever alive to distinction, he admired that verse of Habington's,—

> "Let's set so just
> A rate on knowledge, that the world may trust
> The poet's sentence, and not still aver
> Each art is to itself a flatterer."

The poem of the same author, with that nonpareil title, "*Nox nocti indicat scientiam*," drew the Eskimo race,—

> "Some nation yet shut in
> With hills of ice."

He hears Daniel again, discoursing of learning,—

> "How many thousand never heard the name
> Of Sidney or of Spenser, or their books!
> And yet, brave fellows, and presume of fame,—
> And seem to bear down all the world with looks."

He also loved William Browne's "Pastorals,"—of all England's books, one richest in out-door sympathies. These citations may serve to show Thoreau's taste in English, which I cannot but think very exquisite; and this will be still more of account as George Peele says,—

> "When Fame's great double doors fall to, and shut."

To Thoreau may be applied what John Birkenhead said in his tribute to Beaumont the dramatist,—

> "Thy ocean fancy knew nor banks nor dams;
> We ebb down dry to pebble anagrams;"

putting the word "labor" in the place of "fancy."

He valued Homer for his nature, Virgil for his beauty, the Robin Hood Ballads and Chaucer for their health, Ossian for his grandeur, Persius for his philosophy, Milton for his elegance. Perhaps the "Lycidas" was his favorite short poem; at least I have heard it most often from his mouth; but he knew the Robin Hood Ballads remarkably well.

He was by no means one of those crotchety persons who believe, because they set up Plato or Goethe or Shakespeare as the absolute necessities of literary worship, that all other students must so make idols of them. I never knew him say a good word for Plato, and I fear he had never finished Shakespeare. His was a very uncompleted reading; there being with him a pressure of engrossing flowers, birds, snow-storms, swamps, and seasons. He had no favorites among the French or Germans and I do not recall a modern writer except Carlyle and Ruskin whom he valued much. In fact, the pointed and prismatic style now so common, and the chopped-hay fashion of writing, suited not with his homely, long-staple vein. For novels, stories, and such matters, he was devoid of all curiosity; and for the works of Dickens had a hearty contempt. Usually, all the popular books were sealed volumes to him. But no labor was too onerous, no material too costly, if expended on the right enterprise. His working up the Indians corroborates this.

Everything has its price. These books form a library by themselves. Extracts from reliable authorities from De Bry to poor Schoolcraft, with the early plates and maps accurately copied, and selections from travellers the world over; for his notes embraced all that bears on his "list of subjects,"— wherever scalps, wampum, and the Great Spirit prevail,—in all uncivilized people. Indian customs in Natick are savage customs in Brazil, the Sandwich Islands, or Timbuctoo. With the Indian vocabularies he was familiar, and in his Maine excursions tested his knowledge by all the words he could get from the savages *in puris naturalibus*. Personally these living red men were not charming; and he would creep out of camp at night to refresh his olfactories, damped with uncivilized perfumes, which it seems, like musquash and other animals, they enjoy. After the toughest day's work, when even *his* bones ached, the Indians would keep awake till midnight, talking eternally all the while. They performed valiant feats as trencher-men, "licked the platter clean," and for all answer to many of his questions grunted; which did not discourage him, as he could grunt himself. Their knowledge of the woods, the absolutisms of their scent, sight, and appetite, amazed him. He says, "There is always a slight haze cr mist in the brow of the Indian." He read and translated the Jesuit relations of the first Canadian missions, containing "the commodities and discommodities" of the Indian life, such as the roasting of a fresh parson. He read that romantic book, "Faite par le Sieur de la Borde," upon the origin, manners, customs, wars, and voyages of the Caribs, who were the Indians of the Antilles of America; how these patriots will sell their beds in the morning (their memories too short for night), and in their heaven, *Ouicou*, the Carib beer runs all the while. The children eat dirt and the mothers work. If the dead man own a negro, they bury him with his master to wait on him in paradise, and despatch the doctor to be sure of one

[59]

in the other state. The men and women dress alike, and they have no police or civility; everybody does what he pleases.

> "Lo, the poor Indian, whose untutored mind
> Brews beer in heaven, and drinks it for mankind."
>
> Pope [*altered*].

Another faithful reading was those old Roman farmers, Cato and Varro, and musically named Columella, for whom he had a liking. He is reminded of them by seeing the farmers so busy in the fall carting out their compost. "I see the farmer now on every side carting out his manure, and sedulously making his compost-heap, or scattering it over his grass-ground and breaking it up with a mallet, and it reminds me of Cato's advice. He died 150 years before Christ. Indeed, the farmer's was pretty much the same routine then as now. '*Sterquilinium magnum stude ut habeas. Stercus sedulo conserva, cum exportatis purgato et comminuito. Per autumnum evehito.*' Study to have a great dungheap. Carefully preserve your dung. When you carry it out, make clean work of it, and break it up fine. Carry it out during the autumn." Just such directions as you find in the Farmers' Almanac to-day. As if the farmers of Concord were obeying Cato's directions, who but repeated the maxims of a remote antiquity. Nothing can be more homely and suggestive of the every-day life of the Roman agriculturists, thus supplying the usual deficiencies in what is technically called Roman history; *i.e.*, revealing to us the actual life of the Romans, the "how they got their living," and "what they did from day to day." Rome and the Romans commonly are a piece of rhetoric, but we have here their "New England Farmer," or the very manual those Roman farmers read, as fresh as a dripping dishcloth from a Roman kitchen.

His study of old writers on Natural History was careful: Aristotle, Ælian, and Theophrastus he sincerely entertained, and found from the latter that neither the weather nor its signs had altered since his day. Pliny's *magnum opus* was his last reading in this direction, a work so valuable to him, with the authors just named, that he meant probably to translate and write on the subject as viewed by the ancients. As illustrations, he carefully noted many facts from modern travellers, whose writing hatches Jack-the-Giant-Killers as large as Pliny's. He observed that Aristotle was furnished by the king with' elephants and other creatures for dissection and study: his observations on the habits of fish and their nests especially interested Thoreau, an expert in spawn. In continuing this line of study, he was aided by the perusal of St. Pierre, Gerard, Linnæus, and earlier writers. The "Studies of Nature" he admired, as written with enthusiasm and spirit, —qualities in his view essential to all good writing. The old English botanist pleased him by his affectionate interest in plants, with something quaint, like Evelyn, Tusser, and Walton. Recent scientific *pâté-de-foie-gras*—a surfeit of microscope and "dead words with a tail"—he valued for what it is worth—the stuffing. For the Swede, his respect was transcendent. There is no better explanation of his love for botany than the old—"Consider the lilies of the field, how they

[61]

grow; they toil not, neither do they spin: and yet I say unto you, that even Solomon in all his glory was not arrayed like one of these." His pleasant company, during so many days of every year, he wished he was better acquainted with. The names and classes change, the study of the lovely flower persists. He wished to know willow and grass and sedge, and there came always with the new year the old wish renewed: a carex, a salix, kept the family secret.

NATURE

" For this present, hard
    Is the fortune of the bard
    Born out of time."
                    EMERSON.

CHAPTER IV

NATURE

His habit was to go abroad a portion of each day, to fields or woods or the Concord River. "I go out," he said, "to see what I have caught in my traps which I set for facts." He looked to fabricate an epitome of creation, and give us a homœopathy of Nature. During many years he used the afternoon for walking, and usually set forth about half-past two, returning at half-past five; this (three hours) was the average length of his walk. As he got over the ground rapidly, if desirable (his step being very long for so short a man), he had time enough to visit all the ordinary points of interest in his neighborhood. In these walks, two things he must have from his tailor: his clothes must fit, and the pockets, especially, must be made with reference to his out-door pursuits. They must accommodate his note-book and spy-glass; and so their width and depth was regulated by the size of the note-book. It was a cover for some folded papers, on which he took his out-of-door notes; and this was never omitted, rain or shine. It was his invariable companion, and he acquired great skill in conveying by a few lines or strokes a long story, which in his written Journal might occupy pages. Abroad, he used the pencil, writing but a few moments at a time, during the walk; but into the note-book must go all measurements with the foot-rule which he always carried, or the surveyor's tape that he often had with him. Also all observations with his spy-glass (another invariable companion for years), all conditions of plants, spring, summer, and fall, the depth of snows, the strangeness of the skies,—all went down in this note-book. To his memory he never trusted for a fact, but to the page and the pencil, and the abstract in the pocket, not the Journal. I have seen bits of this note-book, but never recognized any word in it; and I have read its expansion in the Journal, in many pages, of that which occupied him but five minutes to write in the field. "Have you written up your notes in your Journal?" was one of his questions. Such was the character of his mind,—to make what is called little become grand and noble, and thus to dignify life. "To have some one thing to do, and do it perfectly,"—many times have I heard this maxim for students fall from his lips.

In his Journal for November 9, 1851, I found this entry describing an incident which I could recall: "In our walks, Channing takes out his note-book sometimes, and tries to write as I do, but all in vain. He soon puts it up again, or contents himself with scrawling some sketch of the landscape. Observing me still scribbling, he will say that he confines himself to the ideal,—purely ideal remarks,—he leaves the facts to me. Sometimes he will say, a little petulantly, 'I am universal; I have nothing to do with the particular and definite.'"

The particular and definite were much to Thoreau. His pockets were large to hold and keep not only his implements, but the multitude of objects which he brought home from his walks; objects of all kinds,—pieces of wood or stone, lichens, seeds, nuts, apples, or whatever he had found for his

uses. For he was a vigorous collector, never omitting to get
and keep every possible thing in his direction of study.

He did not walk with any view to health, or exercise, or
amusement. His diet was spare enough to have been digested
if he had never stirred an inch; usually thin and in capital
health,—as elastic as an Indian,—he needed no artificial
prop to keep him vital; and he might have slept, as Harrison
says of the old English, with a block of wood for a pillow.
No, the walk, with him, was for work; it had a serious purpose; witness the thirty volumes of Journals left by him,—
and only going back to 1850. As I walk for recreation and
variety, after reading, these walks of Thoreau were something
aside from my habits; and, unlike my own, had a local aim.
While he was not, in the usual sense, a scientific man,'—his
talent (as he always thought and said) being literary,—he was,
though in no narrow view, a naturalist. The idea he conceived
was, that he might, upon a small territory,—such a space as
that filled by the town of Concord,—construct a chart or
calendar which should chronicle the phenomena of the seasons
in their order, and give their general average for the year.
This was only one of the various plans he had in view during
his walks; but his habit of mind demanded complete accuracy,
the utmost finish, and that nothing should be taken on hear-
say; believing that Nature would only so in perfection, and
truly could no otherwise be reported. It is obvious how vast
a work this is, and that he could only have completed some
portion of it in a long lifetime. His calendar embraced cold
and heat, rain and snow, ice and water; he had his gauges

on the river, which he consulted winter and summer; he knew the temperature of all the springs in the town; he measured the snows when remarkable. All unusual changes of weather, with novel skies, storms, views, find place in his notes.

All must get included. "No fruit grows in vain. The red squirrel harvests the fruit of the pitch-pine." He wanted names. "I never felt easy till I got the name for the *Andropogon scoparius* (a grass): I was not acquainted with my beautiful neighbor, but since I knew it was the Andropogon I have felt more at home in my native fields." He had no trace of that want of memory which infests some amiable beings. He loved the world and could not pass a berry, nor fail to ask his question, I fear—leading. Men who had seen the partridge drum, caught the largest pickerel, and eaten the most swamp apples, did him service; and he long frequented one who, if not a sinner, was no saint,—Goodwin the gunner. The Farmer who could find him a hawk's egg or give him a fisher's foot, he would wear in his heart of hearts, whether called Jacob Farmer or not. He admired our toil-crucified farmers, conditioned like granite and pine, slow and silent as the seasons,—"like the sweetness of a nut, like the toughness of hickory. He, too, is a redeemer for me. How superior actually to the faith he professes! He is not an office-seeker. What an institution, what a revelation is a man! We are wont foolishly to think the creed a man professes a more significant fact than the man he is. It matters not how hard the conditions seemed, how mean the world, for a man is a prevalent force and a new law himself. He is a system whose law is to be observed. The old farmer still condescends to countenance this nature and order of things. It is a great encouragement that an honest man makes this world his abode. He rides on the sled drawn by oxen, world-wise, yet comparatively so young as if he had not seen scores of winters. The farmer spoke to me, I can swear, clear, cold, moderate as the snow where he treads. Yet what a faint impression that encounter may make on me after all. Moderate, natural, true, as if he were made of stone, wood, snow."[1]

No hour tolled on the great world-horologe must be omitted, no movement of the second-hand of this patent lever that is so full-jewelled. He wrote,

"Behold these flowers, let us be up with time,
Not dreaming of three thousand years ago."

He drinks in the meadow, at Second Division Brook; "then sits awhile to watch its yellowish pebbles, and the cress in it and the weeds. The ripples cover its surface as a network, and are faithfully reflected on the bottom. In some places, the sun reflected from ripples on a flat stone looks like a golden comb. The whole brook seems as busy as a loom: it is a woof and warp of ripples; fairy fingers are throwing the shuttle at every step, and the long, waving brook is the fine product. The water is so wonderfully clear,—to have a hut here and a foot-path to the brook. For roads, I think that a poet cannot tolerate more than a foot-path through the field. That is wide enough, and for purposes of winged poesy suffices. I would fain travel by a foot-path round the world."

[1] From the Journal of 1851.

So might he say in that mood, yet think the wider wood-path was not bad, as two could walk side by side in it in the ruts,—ay, and one more in the horse-track. He loved in the summer to lay up a stock of these experiences "for the winter, as the squirrel, of nuts,—something for conversation in winter evenings. I love to think then of the more distant walks I took in summer. Might I not walk further till I hear new crickets, till their creak has acquired some novelty as if they were a new species whose habitat I had discovered?"

Night and her stars were not neglected friends. He saw

> "The wandering moon
> Riding near her highest noon,"

and sings in this strain:—

"My dear, my dewy sister, let thy rain descend on me. I not only love thee, but I love the best of thee; that is to love thee rarely. I do not love thee every day, commonly I love those who are less than thee; I love thee only on great days. Thy dewy words feed me like the manna of the morning. I am as much thy sister as thy brother; thou art as much my brother as my sister. It is a portion of thee and a portion of me which are of kin. Thou dost not have to woo me. I do not have to woo thee. O my sister! O Diana! thy tracks are on the eastern hill. Thou merely passed that way. I, the hunter, saw them in the morning dew. My eyes are the hounds that pursued thee. Ah, my friend, what if I do not know thee? I hear thee. Thou canst speak; I cannot; I fear and forget to answer; I am occupied with hearing. I awoke and thought of thee, thou wast present to my mind. How cam'st thou there? Was I not present to thee likewise?"

Thou couldst look down with pity on that mound,—some silver beams faintly raining through the old locust boughs, for thy lover, thy Endymion, is watching there! He was abroad with thee after the midnight mass had tolled, and the consecrated dust of yesterdays "each in its narrow cell for ever laid," which he lived to hive in precious vases for immortality,—tales of natural piety, bound each to each. He said once

> "Now chiefly is my natal hour,
>   And only now my prime of life.
>
> I will not doubt the love untold,
>   Which not my worth nor want hath bought,
>   Which wooed me young and wooes me old,
>   And to this evening hath me brought."

Thus conversant was he with great Nature. Perchance he reached the wildness for which he longed, "a nature which I cannot put my foot through, woods where the wood-thrush for ever sings, where the hours are early morning ones and the day is for ever improved, where I might have a fertile unknown for a soil about me."

Always suggestive (possibly to some, unattractive) themes lay about him in this Nature. Even "along the wood-paths, wines of all kinds and qualities, of noblest vintages, are bottled up in the skins of countless berries, for the taste of men and animals. To men they seem offered, not so much

for food as for sociality, that they may picnic with Nature.
Diet drinks, cordial wines, we pluck and eat in remembrance
of her. It is a sacrament, a communion. The *not* Forbidden
Fruits, which no Serpent tempts us to taste."

I never heard him complain that the plants were too
many, the hours too long. As he said of the crow, "If he
has voice, I have ears." The flowers are furnished, and he can
bring his note-book.

> "As if by secret sight, he knew
>   Where, in far fields, the orchis grew."

He obeyed the plain rule,—

> "Take the goods the gods provide thee,"

and having neither ship nor magazine, gun nor javelin,
horse nor hound, had conveyed to him a property in many
things equal to the height of all his ambition. What he did
not covet was not forced on his attention. What he desired
lay at his feet. The breath of morning skies with the saffron
of Aurora beautifully dight; children of the air wafting the
smiles of spring from the vexed Bermoothes; fragrant life-
everlasting in the dry pastures; blue forget-me-nots along
the brook,—were his: ice piled its shaggy enamel for him,
where coral cranberries yesterday glowed in the grass; and
forests whispered loving secrets in his ear. For is not the
earth kind?

"We are rained and snowed on with gems. I confess that
I was a little encouraged, for I was beginning to believe
that Nature was poor and mean, and I now was convinced

that she turned off as good work as ever. What a world we live in! Where are the jewellers' shops? There is nothing handsomer than a snow-flake and a dew-drop. I may say that the Maker of the world exhausts his skill with each snow-flake and dew-drop that He sends down. We think that the one mechanically coheres, and that the other simply flows together and falls; but in truth they are the product of *enthusiasm*, the children of an ecstasy, finished with the artist's utmost skill."

. . . "The first humble-bee, that prince of hummers,—he follows after flowers. To have your existence depend on flowers, like the bee and humming-birds. . . . I expect that the lichenist will have the keenest relish for Nature in her every-day mood and dress. He will have the appetite of the worm that never dies, of the grub. This product of the bark is the essence of all times. The lichenist loves the tripe of the rock, that which eats and digests the rock: he eats the eater. A rail is the fattest and sleekest of coursers for him. . . . The blue curls and fragrant everlasting, with their ripening aroma, show themselves now pushing up on dry fields, bracing to the thought; I need not *smell* the calamint,—it is a balm to my mind to remember its fragrance. The pontederia is in its prime, alive with butterflies,—yellow and others. I see its tall blue spikes reflected beneath the edge of the pads on each side, pointing down to a heaven beneath as well as above. Earth appears but a thin crust or pellicle.

"It is a leaf,—that of the green-briar,—for poets to sing about: it excites me to a sort of autumnal madness. They are

[73]

leaves for satyrs and fauns to make their garlands of. My
thoughts break out like them, spotted all over, yellow and
green and brown,—the freckled leaf. Perhaps they should
be poison to be thus spotted. . . . I have now found all the
Hawk-weeds. Singular are these genera of plants,—plants
manifestly related, yet distinct. They suggest a history to
nature, a *natural* history in a new sense. . . . Any anomaly
in vegetation makes Nature seem more real and present in
her working, as the various red and yellow excrescences on
young oaks. I am affected as if it were a different nature that
produced them. As if a poet were born, who had designs in
his head. . . . I perceive in the Norway cinque-foil (*Potentilla
Norvegica*), now nearly out of blossom, that the alternate six
leaves of the calyx are closing over the seeds to protect them.
This evidence of forethought, this simple *reflection*, in a
double sense of the term, in this flower is affecting to me, as
if it said to me, 'Not even when I have blossomed and have
lost my painted petals, and am preparing to die down to its
root, do I forget to fall with my arms around my babe, faithful to the last, that the infant may be found preserved in
the arms of the frozen mother.' There is one door closed of the
closing year. I am not ashamed to be contemporary with the
cinque-foil. May I perform my part as well! We love to see
Nature fruitful in whatever kind. I love to see the acorns
plenty on the scrub-oaks, ay, and the night-shade berries. It
assures us of her vigor, and that she may equally bring forth
fruits which we prize. I love to see the potato-balls numerous and large, as I go through a low field; the plant thus

bearing fruit at both ends, saying ever and anon, 'Not only these tubers I offer you for the present, but if you will have new varieties (if these do not satisfy you), plant these seeds, fruit of the strong soil, containing potash; the vintage is come, the olive is ripe. Why not for my coat-of-arms, for device, a drooping cluster of potato-balls in a potato field?'

> "I come to pluck your berries harsh and crude,
> And with forced fingers rude,
> Shatter your leaves before the mellowing year."

These glimpses at the life of the lover of Nature admonish us of the richness, the satisfactions in his unimpoverished districts. Man needs an open mind and a pure purpose, to become receptive. His interest in animals equalled that in flowers. At one time he carried his spade, digging in the galleries and burrows of field-mice. "They run into their holes, as if they had exploded before your eyes." Many voyages he made in cold autumn days and winter walks on the ice, to examine the cabins of the muskrat and discover precisely how and of what they were built,—the suite of rooms always damp, yet comfortable for the household, dressed in their old-fashioned waterproofs. He respected the skunk as a human being in a very humble sphere.

In his western tour of 1861, when he went to Minnesota and found the crab-apple and native Indians, he pleased himself with a new friend,—the gopher with thirteen stripes. Rabbits, woodchucks, red, gray, and "chipmunk" squirrels, he knew by heart; the fox never came amiss. A Canada lynx was killed in Concord, whose skin he eagerly obtained and preserved. It furnished a proof of wildness intact, and the nine lives of a wildcat. He mused on the change of habit in domestic animals, and recites a porcine epic, — the adventures of a fanatic pig. He was a debtor to the cows like other walkers.

"When you approach to observe them, they mind you just enough. How wholesome and clean their clear brick red! No doubt man impresses his own character on the beasts which he tames and employs. They are not only humanized, but they acquire his particular human nature. . . . The farmer acts on the ox, and the ox reacts on the farmer. They do not meet half way, it is true; but they do meet at a distance from the centre of each, proportionate to each one's intellectual power."

Let us hasten to his lovely idyl of the "Beautiful Heifer":—

"One more confiding heifer, the fairest of the herd, did by degrees approach as if to take some morsel from our hands, while our hearts leaped to our mouths with expectation and delight. She by degrees drew near with her fair limbs (progressive), making pretence of browsing; nearer and nearer, till there was wafted to us the bovine fragrance, — cream of all the dairies that ever were or will be: and then she raised her gentle muzzle towards us, and snuffed an honest recognition within hand's reach. I saw it was possible for his herd to inspire with love the herdsman. She was as delicately featured as a hind. Her hide was mingled white and fawn color, and on her muzzle's tip there was a white spot not bigger than a daisy; and on her side turned toward me, the map of Asia plain to see.[1]

"Farewell, dear heifer! Though thou forgettest me, my prayer to heaven shall be that thou mayst not forget thyself. There was a whole bucolic in her snuff. I saw her name was Sumac. And by the kindred spots I knew her mother, more sedate and matronly with full-grown bag, and on her sides was Asia great and small, the plains of Tartary, even to the pole; while on her daughter's was Asia Minor. She was not disposed to wanton with the herdsman. And as I walked she followed me, and took an apple from my hand, and seemed to care more for the hand than the apple. So innocent a face as I have rarely seen on any creature, and I have looked in the face of many heifers. And as she took the apple from my hand I caught the apple of her eye. She smelled as sweet as the clethra blossom. There was no sinister expression. And for horns, though she had them, they were so well disposed in the right place, but neither up nor down, I do not now remember she had any. No horn was held towards me."

Seeing a flock of turkeys, the old faintly gobbling, the half-grown young peeping, they suggest a company of "turkey-men." He loves a cricket or a bee: —

"As I went through the Deep Cut before sunrise [*August 23, 1851*], I heard one or two early humble-bees come out on the damp sandy bank, whose low hum sounds like distant horns from far in the horizon, over the woods. It was long

[1] In much that Mr. Thoreau wrote, there was a *philological* side, — this needs to be thoughtfully considered. W. E. C.

before I detected the bees that made it,—so far-away musical it sounded, like the shepherds in some distant eastern vale, greeting the king of day. [*September 3.*] Why was there never a poem on the cricket? Its creak seems to me to be one of the most obvious and prominent facts in the world, and the least heeded. In the report of a man's contemplations I look to see something answering to this sound,—so serene and cool, the iced-cream of song. It is modulated shade: the incessant cricket of the fall is heard in the grass, chirping from everlasting to everlasting; no transient love-strain, hushed when the incubating season is past. They creak hard now, after sunset; no word will spell it. The humming of a dor-bug drowns all the noise of the village. So roomy is the universe."

No class of creatures he found better than birds. With these mingled his love for sound: "Listen to music religiously, as if it were the last strain you might hear. Sugar is not as sweet to the palate as sound to the healthy ear. Is not all music a hum more or less divine?" His concert was the bluebird, the robin, and song-sparrow, melting into joy after the silent winter. "Do you know on what bushes a little peace, faith, and contentment grow? Go a-berrying early and late after them." The color of the bluebird seemed to him "as if he carried the sky on his back. And where are gone the bluebirds whose warble was wafted to me so lately like a blue wavelet through the air, warbling so innocently to inquire if any of its mates are within call? The very grain of the air seems to have undergone a change, and is ready to split into the form of the bluebird's warble. The air over these fields is a foundry full of moulds for casting bluebirds' warbles. Methinks if it were visible or I could cast up some fine dust which would betray it, it would take a corresponding shape."

LITERARY THEMES

"No tidings come to thee
  Not of thy very neighbors,
  That dwellen almost at thy doors,
  Thou hearest neither that nor this;
  For when thy labor all done is,
  And hast made all thy reckonings,
  Instead of rest and of new things,
  Thou goest home to thy house anon."

CHAUCER.

"To hill and cloud his face was known, —
  It seemed the likeness of their own."

EMERSON.

"His short parenthesis of life was sweet."

STORER'S LIFE OF WOLSEY.

CHAPTER V

LITERARY THEMES

"MEN commonly exaggerate the theme. Some themes they think are significant, and others insignificant. I feel that my life is very homely, my pleasures very cheap. Joy and sorrow, success and failure, grandeur and meanness, and indeed most words in the English language, do not mean for me what they do for my neighbors. I see that my neighbors look with compassion on me, that they think it is a mean and unfortunate destiny which makes me to walk in these fields and woods so much, and sail on this river alone. But so long as I find here the only real elysium, I cannot hesitate in my choice. My work is writing, and I do not hesitate though I know that no subject is too trivial for me, tried by ordinary standards; for, ye fools! the theme is nothing, the life is everything. All that interests the reader is the depth and intensity of the life exerted. We touch our subject but by a point which has no breadth; but the pyramid of our experience, or our interest in it, rests on us by a broader or narrower base. What is man is all in all, Nature nothing but as she draws him out and reflects him. Give me simple, cheap, and homely themes."

These words from Thoreau partially illustrate his views upon the subjects he proposed to treat and how they should be treated, with that poetic wealth he enjoyed; and no one need look for prose. He never thought or spoke or wrote that. In the same spirit he says of his first book, which had a

[83]

slow sale: "I believe that this result is more inspiring and better for me than if a thousand had bought my wares. It affects my privacy less, and leaves me freer. Men generally over-estimate their praises."

Of his themes, the following is one view among others:—

"As I walked I was intoxicated with the slight, spicy odor of the hickory-buds and the bruised bark of the black-birch, and in the fall with the pennyroyal. The sight of budding woods intoxicates me like diet-drink. I feel my Maker blessing me. For years my appetite was so strong that I fed, I browsed on the pine-forest's edge seen against the winter horizon,—the silvery needles of the pine straining the light; the young aspen-leaves like light green fires. The young birch-leaves, very neatly plaited, small, triangular, light green leaves, yield an agreeable, sweet fragrance (just expanded and sticky), sweet-scented as innocence. To the sane man the world is a musical instrument. Formerly methought Nature developed as I developed, and grew up with me. My life was ecstasy. In youth, before I lost any of my senses, I can remember that I was all alive and inhabited my body with inexpressible satisfaction; both its weariness and its refreshment were sweet to me. This earth was the most glorious musical instrument, and I was audience to its strains. To have such sweet impressions made on us, such ecstasies begotten of the breezes, I can remember I was astonished. I said to myself, I said to others, there comes into my mind such an indescribable, infinite, all-absorbing, divine, heavenly pleasure, a sense of salvation and expansion. And I have had naught to do with it; I perceive that I am dealt with by superior powers. By all manner of bounds and traps threatening the extreme penalty of the divine law, it behooves us to preserve the purity and sanctity of the mind. That I am innocent to myself, that I love and reverence my life."

To make these themes into activities, he considered, —

"The moods and thoughts of man are revolving just as steadily and incessantly as Nature's. Nothing must be postponed; take time by the forelock, now or never. You must live in the present, launch yourself on any wave, find your eternity in each moment. Fools stand on their island opportunities, and look toward another land. There is no other land, there is no other life but this or the like of this. Where the good husbandman is, there is the good soil. Take any other course, and life will be a succession of regrets."

If writing is his business, to do this well must be sought. August 21, 1851, he wrote:—

"What a faculty must that be which can paint the most barren landscape and humblest life in glorious colors! It is pure and invigorated sense reacting on a sound and strong imagination. Is not this the poet's case? The intellect of most men is barren. They neither fertilize nor are fertilized. It is the marriage of the soul with Nature that makes the intellect fruitful, that gives birth to imagination. When we were dead and dry as the highway, some sense which has been healthily fed will put us in relation with Nature, in sympathy with her, some grains of fertilizing pollen floating in the air fall on us, and suddenly the sky is all one rainbow, is full of music and

[85]

fragrance and flavor. The man of intellect only, the prosaic man, is a barren and staminiferous flower; the poet is a fertile and perfect flower. Men are such confirmed arithmeticians and slaves of business, that I cannot easily find a blank-book that has not a red line or a blue one for dollars and cents. The poet must keep himself unstained and aloof. Let him perambulate the bounds of Imagination's provinces, the realms of poesy and not the insignificant boundaries of towns. How many faculties there are which we have never found! Some men methinks have found only their hands and feet. At least I have seen some who appeared never to have found their heads, but used them only instinctively as the negro butts with his.

"It is wise to write on many subjects, to try many themes, that so you may find the right and inspiring one. Be greedy of occasions to express your thoughts; improve the opportunity to draw analogies; there are innumerable avenues to a perception of the truth. Improve the suggestion of each object, however humble, however slight and transient the provocation; what else is there to be improved? Who knows what opportunities he may neglect? It is not in vain that the mind turns aside this way or that: follow its leading, apply it whither it inclines to go. Probe the universe in a myriad points. Be avaricious of these impulses. Nature makes a thousand acorns to get one oak. He is a wise man and experienced who has taken many views, to whom stones and plants and animals, and a myriad objects have each suggested something, contributed something. We cannot write well or truly but what we write with gusto. The body and senses must conspire with the mind. Experience is the act of the whole man, — that our speech may be vascular. The intellect is powerless to express thought without the aid of the heart and liver and of every member. Often I feel that my head stands out too dry when it should be immersed. A writer, a man writing, is the scribe of all nature; he is the corn and the grass and the atmosphere writing. It is always essential that we *live* to do what we are doing, do it with a heart. •There are flowers of thought and there are leaves of thought, and most of our thoughts are merely leaves to which the thread of thought is the stem. Whatever things I perceive with my entire man, those let me record and it will be poetry. The sounds which I hear with the consent and coincidence of all my senses, those are significant and musical; at least, they only are heard. [*September 2.*] I omit the unusual, the hurricanes and earthquakes, and describe the common. This has the greatest charm, and is the true theme of poetry. You may have the extraordinary for your province if you will; let me have the ordinary. Give me the obscure life, the cottage of the poor and humble, the work-days of the world, the barren fields; the smallest share of all things but poetical perception. Give me but the eyes to see the things which you possess.

"How watchful we must be to keep the crystal well clear, that it be not made turbid by our contact with the world, so that it will not reflect objects. If I would preserve my relation to Nature, I must make my life more moral, more

[87]

pure and innocent. The problem is as precise and simple as a mathematical one. I must not live loosely, but more and more continently. How can we expect a harvest of thought who have not had a seed-time of character? Already some of my small thoughts, fruit of my spring life, are ripe, like the berries which feed the first broods of birds; and some others are prematurely ripe and bright like the lower leaves of the herbs which have felt the summer's drought. Human life may be transitory and full of trouble, but the perennial mind whose survey extends from that spring to this, from Columella to Hosmer, is superior to change. I will identify myself with that which did not die with Columella and will not die with Hosmer."

As the song of the spring birds makes the richest music of the year, it seems a fit overture to have given a few of Thoreau's spring sayings upon his life and work. Few men knew better, or so well, what these were. In some senses he was a scientific man, in others not. I do not think he relished science in long words, or the thing Wordsworth calls—

> "Philosopher! a fingering slave,
> One that would peep and botanize
> Upon his mother's grave."

He loved Nature as a child,—reverenced her veils, that we should not conceitedly endeavor to raise. He did not believe the study of anatomy helped the student to a practical knowledge of the human body, and replied to a doctor's suggested prescription, "How do you know that his pills will go down?" Nor that the eggs of turtles to be, seen through a glass darkly, were turtles; and he said to the ornithologist who wished to hold his bird in his hand, that "he would rather hold it in his affections." So he saw the colors of his with a kind heart, and let the spiders slide. Yet no man spent more labor in making out his bird by Wilson or Nuttall.

His was a broad catholic creed. He thought of the Hindoo Mythology, "It rises on me like the full moon after the stars have come out, wading through some far summer stratum of sky." From Homer, who made a "corner" with Grecian mythology, to his beloved Indian, whose life of scalping and clam-bakes was a religion, he could appreciate the good of creeds and forms and omit the scruples. He says:—

"If I could, I would worship the paring of my nails. He who discovers two gods where there was only known to be one, and such a one! I would fain improve every opportunity to wonder and worship, as a sunflower welcomes the light." "God could not be unkind to me if he should try. I love best to have each thing in its season, doing without it at all other times. It is the greatest of all advantages to enjoy no advantage at all. I have never got over my surprise that I should have been born into the most estimable place in all the world, and in the very nick of time too. I heard one speak to-day of his sense of awe at the thought of God, and suggested to him that *awe* was the *cause* of the potato-rot."

He again expressed himself in a lively way about these matters: "Who are the religious? They who do not differ much from mankind generally, except that they are more conservative and timid and useless, but who in their conver-

sation and correspondence talk about kindness and Heavenly
Father, instead of going bravely about their business, trusting God ever." He once knew a minister, and photographs
him: "Here's a man who can't butter his own bread, and he
has just combined with a thousand like him to make a dipt
toast for all eternity."

Of a book published by Miss Harriet Martineau, that
Minerva mediocre, he observes: "Miss Martineau's last book
is not so bad as the timidity which fears its influence. As if
the popularity of this or that book could be so fatal, and man
would not still be man in the world. Nothing is so much to
be feared as fear. Atheism may, comparatively, be popular
with God." Religion, worship, and prayer were words he
studied in their history; but *out-of-doors* (which can serve
for the title of much of his writing) is his creed. He used this
expression: "May I love and revere myself above all the gods
that man has ever invented; may I never let the vestal fire
go out in my recesses."

He thought the past and the men of the past, as they crop
out in institutions, were not as valuable as the present and
the individual alive. "They who will remember only this kind
of right, do as if they stood under a shed and affirmed that
they were under the unobscured heavens. The shed has its
use, but what is it to the heavens above." The institution of
American slavery was a filthy and rotten shed which Thoreau
used his utmost strength to cut away and burn up. From first
to last he loved and honored abolitionism. Not one slave alone
was expedited to Canada by Thoreau's personal assistance.

SPRING AND AUTUMN

"Methinks I hear the sound of time long past,
  Still murmuring o'er us in the lofty void
  Of these dark arches, like the ling'ring voice
  Of those who long ago within their graves have slept."

ORRA, A TRAGEDY.

CHAPTER VI

SPRING AND AUTUMN

As he is dropping beans in the spring, he hears the bay-wing:—

"I saw the world through a glass as it lies eternally. It reminded me of many a summer sunset, of many miles of gray rails, of many a rambling pasture, of the farmhouse far in the fields, its milk-pans and well-sweep, and the cows coming home at twilight; I correct my Human views by listening to their Volucral. I ordinarily plod along a sort of white-washed prison entry, subject to some indifferent or even grovelling mood; I do not distinctly seize my destiny; I have turned down my light to the merest glimmer, and am doing some task which I have set myself. I take incredibly narrow views, live on the limits, and have no recollection of absolute truth. But suddenly, in some fortunate moment, the voice of eternal wisdom reaches *me* even, in the strain of the sparrow, and liberates me; whets and clarifies my own senses, makes me a competent witness."

He says elsewhere of the same sparrow: "The end of its strain is like the ring of a small piece of steel wire dropped on an anvil." How he loved Aurora! how he loved the morning! "You must taste the first glass of the day's nectar if you would get all the spirit of it. Its fixed air begins to stir and escape. The sweetness of the day crystallizes in the morning coolness." The morning was the spring of the day, and spring the morning of the year. Then he said, musing: "All Nature *revives* at this season. With her it is really a new life, but with these church-goers it is only a revival of religion or hypocrisy; they go down stream to still muddier waters. It cheers me more to behold the mass of gnats which have revived in the spring sun. If a man do not revive with Nature in the spring, how shall he revive when a white-collared priest prays for him?" This dash at theological linen is immediately followed by "Small water-bugs in Clematis Brook."

Of the willow fish-creel in Farrar's Brook, near the Nine-acre Corner Bridge, he says:—

"It was equal to a successful stanza whose subject was spring. I see those familiar features, that large type with which all my life is associated, unchanged. We too are obeying the laws of all Nature. Not less important are the observers of the birds than the birds themselves. This rain is good for thought, it is especially agreeable to me as I enter the wood and hear the rustling dripping on the leaves. It domiciliates me in nature. The woods are more like a house for the rain; the few slight noises resound more hollow in them, the birds hop nearer, the very trees seem still and pensive. We love to sit on and walk over sandy *tracts* in the spring, like cicindelas. These tongues of russet land, tapering and sloping into the flood, do almost speak to me. One piece of ice, in breaking on the river, rings when struck on another, like a trowel on a brick. The loud *peop* of a pigeon woodpecker is heard in our rear, and anon the prolonged and shrill cackle calling the thin wooded hillsides and pastures to life. You doubt if the season will be long enough for such oriental and luxurious slowness. I think that my senses made the truest report the first time.

"There is a time to watch the ripples on Ripple Lake, to look for arrow-heads, to study the rocks and lichens, a time to walk on sandy deserts, and the observer of nature must improve these seasons as much as the farmer his. Those ripple lakes[1] lie now in the midst of mostly bare, brown, or tawny dry woodlands, themselves the most living objects. They may say to the first woodland flowers,—'We played with the North winds here before ye were born!' When the playful breeze drops on the pool, it springs to right and left, quick as a kitten playing with dead leaves.

"This pine warbler impresses me as if it were calling the trees to life; I think of springing twigs. Its jingle rings through the wood at short intervals, as if, like an electric spark, it imparted a fresh spring life to them. The fresh land emerging from the water reminds me of the isle which was called up from the bottom of the sea, which was given to Apollo. Or, like the skin of a pard,—the great mother leopard that Nature is,—where she lies at length, exposing her flanks to the sun. I feel as if I could land to kiss and stroke the very sward, it is so fair. It is homely and domestic to my eyes like the rug that lies before my hearth-side. As the walls of cities are fabled to have been built by music, so my pines were established by the song of the field-sparrow. I heard the

---

[1] Near Goose Pond. Emerson greatly admired these ripples, and I have visited these places with him in breezy autumn days. w. e. c.

jingle of the blackbird,—some of the most liquid notes, as if produced by some of the water of the Pierian spring flowing through some kind of musical water-pipe, and at the same moment setting in motion a multitude of fine vibrating metallic springs,—like a shepherd merely meditating most enrapturing tunes on such a water-pipe. The robin's song gurgles out of all conduits now,—they are choked with it.

"I hear at a distance in the meadow, still at long intervals, the hurried commencement of the bobolink's strain: the bird is just touching the strings of his theorbo, his glassichord, his water-organ, and one or two notes globe themselves and fall in liquid bubbles from his teeming throat. . . . Beginning slowly and deliberately, the partridge's beat sounds faster and faster far away under the boughs and through the aisle of the wood, until it becomes a regular roll. How many things shall we not see and be and do, when we walk there where the partridge drums. The rush-sparrow jingles her small change,—pure silver,—on the counter of the pasture. How sweet it sounds in a clear, warm morning, in a wood-side pasture, amid the old corn-hills, or in sprout-lands, clear and distinct like 'a spoon in a cup,' the last part very clear and ringing. I hear the king-bird twittering or chattering like a stout-chested swallow, and the sound of snipes winnowing the evening air. The cuckoo reminds me of some silence among the birds I had not noticed. I hear the squirrel chirp in the wall, like a spoon.[1] Times and seasons

---

[1] Sound and scent: in considering Thoreau you must constantly associate these senses with his way of looking after things. W. E. C.

may perhaps be best marked by the notes of reptiles; they express, as it were, the very feelings of the earth or nature. About May-day the ring of the first toad leaks into the general stream of sound,—a bubbling ring; I am thrilled to my very spine, it is so terrene a sound; as crowded with protuberant bubbles as the rind of an orange: sufficiently considered by its maker, in the night and the solitude. I hear the dumping sound of frogs, that know no winter. It is like the tap of a drum when human legions are mustering. It reminds me that Summer is now in earnest gathering her forces, and that ere long I shall see their waving plumes and hear the full bands and steady tread. What lungs! what health! what terrenity [1] (if not serenity) it suggests! How many walks I take along the brooks in the spring! What shall I call them? Lesser riparial [1] excursions? prairial rivular? If you make the least correct observation of nature this year, you will have occasion to repeat it with illustrations the next, and the season and life itself is prolonged. Days are long enough and fair enough for the worthiest deeds. The day is an epitome of the year. I think that a perfect parallel may be drawn between the seasons of the day and of the year.

"If the writer would interest readers, he must report so much life, using a certain satisfaction always as a *point d'appui*. However mean and limited, it must be a genuine and contented life that he speaks out of. They must have the essence and oil of himself, tried out of the fat of his experience and joy."

[1] Note the philology. w. e. c.

[97]

THOREAU

"The Titan heeds his sky affairs,
  Rich rents and wide alliance shares;
  Mysteries of color daily laid
  By the sun in light and shade;
  And sweet varieties of chance."

Color was a treat to Thoreau. He saw the seasons and the landscapes through their colors; and all hours and fields and woods spoke in varied hues which impressed him with sentiment. "Nature does not forget beauty and outline even in a mud-turtle's shell." Is it winter?—he "loves the few homely colors of Nature at this season, her strong, wholesome browns, her sober and primeval grays, her celestial blue, her vivacious green, her pure, cold, snowy white. The mountains look like waves in a blue ocean tossed up by a stiff gale." In early spring he thinks,—

"The white *saxifrage* is a response from earth to the increased light of the year, the yellow *crowfoot* to the increased light of the sun. Why is the pollen of flowers commonly yellow? The pyramidal pine-tops are now seen rising out of a reddish, permanent mistiness of the deciduous trees just bursting into leaf. The sorrel begins to redden the fields with ruddy health. The sun goes down red again like a high-colored flower of summer. As the white and yellow flowers of the spring are giving place to the rose and will soon to the red lily, so the yellow sun of spring has become a red sun of June drought, round and red like a midsummer flower, productive of torrid heats. Again, I am attracted by the deep scarlet of the wild rose, half open in the grass, all glowing with rosy light."

SPRING AND AUTUMN

"The soft, mellow, fawn-colored light of the July sunset
seemed to come from the earth itself. My thoughts are drawn
inward, even as clouds and trees are reflected in the smooth,
still water. There is an inwardness even in the musquito's hum
while I am picking blueberries in the dark wood. The landscape is fine as behind glass, the horizon-edge distinct. The
distant vales towards the north-west mountains lie up open
and clear and elysian like so many Tempes. The shadows of
trees are dark and distinct; the din of trivialness is silenced.
The woodside after sunset is cool as a pot of green paint, and
the moon reflects from the rippled surface like a stream of
dollars. The shooting stars are but fireflies of the firmament.
Late in September, I see the whole of the red-maple,—bright
scarlet against the cold, green pines. The clear, bright scarlet
leaves of the smooth sumac in many places are curled and
drooping, hanging straight down, so as to make a funereal
impression, reminding me of a red sash and a soldier's funeral.
They impress me quite as black crape similarly arranged,—
the bloody plants. In mid-December the day is short; it seems
to be composed of two twilights merely, and there is sometimes a peculiar, clear, vitreous, greenish sky in the west, as
it were a molten gem."

"In this January thaw I hear the pleasant sound of running water; here is my Italy, my heaven, my New England.
I can understand why the Indians hereabouts placed heaven
in the south-west, the soft south. The delicious, soft, spring-
suggesting air! The sky, seen here and there through the
wrack, bluish and greenish, and perchance with a vein of red

[99]

in the west seems like the inside of a shell deserted by its tenant, into which I have crawled. What beauty in the running brooks! What life! What society! The cold is merely superficial; it is summer still at the core, far, far within. It is in the cawing of the crow, the crowing of the cock, the warmth of the sun on our backs. I hear faintly the cawing of a crow far, far away, echoing from some unseen woodside, as if deadened by the spring-like vapor which the sun is drawing from the ground. It mingles with the slight murmur from the village, the sound of children at play, as one stream gently empties into another, and the wild and tame are one. What a delicious sound! It is not merely crow calling to crow. If he has voice, I have ears. . . . I think I never saw a more elysian blue than my shadow. I am turned into a tall, blue Persian from my cap to my boots, such as no mortal dye can produce, with an amethystine hatchet in my hand.

"The holes in the pasture on Fairhaven Hill where rocks were taken out are now converted into perfect jewels. They are filled with water of crystalline transparency, through which I see to their emerald bottoms, paved with emerald. Even these furnish goblets and vases of perfect purity to hold the dews and rains; and what more agreeable bottom can we look to than this, which the earliest sun and moisture had tinged green? I see an early grasshopper drowning in one; it looks like a fate to be envied: April wells call them: vases clean, as if enamelled. What wells can be more charming? You almost envy the wood-frogs and toads that hop amid such gems as fungi, some pure and bright enough for a breast-pin. Out of every crevice between the dead leaves oozes some vehicle of color, the unspent wealth of the year which Nature is now casting forth, as if it were only to empty herself. And, now to your surprise, these ditches are crowded with millions of little stars (*Aster Tradescanti*). Call them travellers' thoughts. What green, herbaceous, graminivorous thoughts the wood-frog must have! I wish that my thoughts were as reasonable as his."

"I notice many little, pale-brown, dome-shaped puff-balls, puckered to a centre beneath, which emit their dust: when you pinch them, a smoke-like, brown dust (snuff-colored) issues from the orifice at their top, like smoke from a chimney. It is so fine and light that it rises into the air and is wafted away like smoke. They are low, oriental domes or mosques, sometimes crowded together in nests like a collection of humble cottages on the moor, in the coal-pit or Numidian style. For there is suggested some humble hearth beneath, from which this smoke comes up; as it were, the homes of slugs and crickets. Amid the low and withering grass, their resemblance to rude, dome-shaped cottages where some humble but everlasting life is lived, pleases me not a little, and their smoke ascends between the legs of the herds and the traveller. I imagine a hearth and pot, and some snug but humble family passing its Sunday evening beneath each one. I locate there at once all that is simple and admirable in human life; there is no virtue which these roofs exclude. I imagine with what faith and contentment I could come home to them at evening."

[101]

Thus social is Nature, if her lover bring a friendly heart. The love of beauty and truth which can light and cheer its possessor, not only in youth and health, but to the verge of the abyss, walked abroad with our Walden naturalist; for "Nature never did betray the heart that loved her." To be faithful in few things, to possess your soul in peace and make the best use of the one talent, is deemed an acceptable offering,—*omne devotum pro significo.*

"I am a stranger in your towns; I can winter more to my mind amid the shrub-oaks; I have made arrangements to stay with them. The shrub-oak, lowly, loving the earth and spreading over it, tough, thick-leaved; leaves firm and sound in winter, and rustling like leather shields; leaves firm and wholesome, clear and smooth to the touch. Tough to support the snow, not broken down by it, well-nigh useless to man, a sturdy phalanx hard to break through, product of New England's surface, bearing many striped acorns. Well-tanned leather-color on the one side, sun-tanned, color of colors, color of the cow and the deer; silver-downy beneath, turned toward the late bleached and russet fields. What are acanthus leaves and the rest to this, emblem of my winter condition? I love and could embrace the shrub-oak with its scaly garment of leaves rising above the snow, lowly whispering to me, akin to winter thoughts and sunsets and to all virtue. Rigid as iron, clear as the atmosphere, hardy as virtue, innocent and sweet as a maiden, is the shrub-oak. I felt a positive yearning to one bush this afternoon. There was a match found for me at last,—I fell in love with a shrub-oak. Low, robust, hardy, indigenous, well-known to the striped squirrel and the partridge and rabbit, what is Peruvian bark to your bark? How many rents I owe to you, how many eyes put out, how many bleeding fingers! How many shrub-oak patches I have been through, winding my way, bending the twigs aside, guiding myself by the sun over hills and valleys and plains, resting in clear grassy spaces. I love to go through a patch of shrub-oaks in a bee line,—where you tear your clothes and put your eyes out."

"Sometimes I would rather get a transient glimpse, a side view of a thing, than stand fronting to it, as these polypodys. The object I caught a glimpse of as I went by, haunts my thought a long time, is infinitely suggestive, and I do not care to front it and scrutinize it; for I know that the thing that really concerns me is not there, but in my relation to *that*. That is a mere reflecting surface. Its influence is sporadic, wafted through the air to me. Do you imagine its fruit to stick to the back of its leaf all winter? At this season, polypody is in the air. My thoughts are with them a long time after my body has passed. It is the cheerful community of the polypodys: are not wood-frogs the philosophers who walk in these groves?"

In winter: "How completely a load of hay revives the memory of past summers. Summer in us is only a little dried, like it." The foul flanks of the cattle remind him how early it still is in the spring. He knows the date by his garment, and says on the twenty-eighth of April, "The twenty-seventh and to-day are weather for a half-thick single coat. This first

off-coat warmth." The first week of May, "The shadow of the
cliff is like a dark pupil on the side of the hill. That cliff and
its shade suggests dark eyes and eyelashes and overhanging
brows. It is a leafy mist throughout the forest." And with a
rare comparison, "The green of the new grass, the last week
in April, has the regularity of a parapet or rampart to a fortress. It winds along the irregular lines of tussocks like the
wall of China over hill and dale. As I was measuring, along
the Marlboro' road, a fine little blue-slate butterfly fluttered
over the chain. Even its feeble strength was required to fetch
the year about. How daring, even rash, Nature appears, who
sends out butterflies so early. Sardanapalus-like, she loves ex-
tremes and contrasts." (It was this day, April 28, 1856, that
Thoreau first definitely theorized the succession of forest
trees.) The sight and sound of the first humming-bird made
him think he was in the tropics, in Demerara or Maracaibo.

Shall we take an autumn walk, the first September week?

"Nature improves this, her last opportunity, to empty her
lap of flowers. I turn Anthony's corner. It is an early September afternoon, melting, warm, and sunny; the thousand of
grasshoppers leaping before you, reflect gleams of light. A
little distance off, the field is yellowed with a Xerxean army
of *Solidago nemoralis* (gray golden-rod) between me and the
sun. It spreads its legions over the dry plains now, as soldiers
muster in the fall,—fruit of August and September sprung
from the sun-dust. The fields and hills appear in their yellow
uniform (its recurved standard, a little more than a foot high),
marching to the holy land, a countless host of crusaders. The

earth-song of the cricket comes up through all, and ever and
anon the hot *z-ing* of the locust is heard. The dry, deserted
fields are one mass of yellow, like a color shoved to one side
on Nature's palette. You literally wade in flowers knee-deep,
and now the moist banks and low bottoms are beginning to
be abundantly sugared with the *Aster Tradescanti*. How ineffectual is the note of a bird now! We hear it as if we heard
it not and forget it immediately. The blackbirds were prun-
ing themselves and splitting their throats in vain, trying to
sing as the other day; all the melody flew off in splinters. By
the first week of October, the hue of maturity has come even
to that fine, silver-topped, feathery grass, two or three feet
high in clumps, on dry places; I am riper for thought too.
Every thing, all fruits and leaves, even the surfaces of stone
and stubble, are all ripe in this air. The chickadees of late
have winter ways, flocking after you." "Birds generally wear
the russet dress of nature at this season [*November 7*], they
have their fall no less than the plants; the bright tints depart from their foliage of feathers, and they flit past like
withered leaves in rustling flocks. The sparrow is a withered
leaf. When the flower season is over, when the great company
of flower-seekers have ceased their search, the fringed gentian
raises its blue face above the withering grass beside the brooks
for a moment, having at the eleventh hour made up its mind
to join the planet's floral exhibition. Pieces of water are now
reservoirs of dark indigo; as for the dry oak-leaves, all winter
is their fall."

"The tinkling notes of goldfinches and bobolinks which we

hear in August are of one character, and peculiar to the season. They are not voluminous flowers, but rather nuts of sound, ripened seeds of sound. It is the tinkling of ripened grains in Nature's basket; like the sparkle on water, a sound produced by friction on the crisped air. The cardinals (*Lobelia cardinalis*) are fluviatile, and stand along some river or brook like myself. It is the three o'clock of the year when the *Bidens Beckii* (water marigold) begins to prevail. By mid-October, the year is acquiring a grizzly look from the climbing mikania, golden-rods, and *Andropogon scoparius* (purple wood-grass).

> And painted ducks, too, often come to sail,
> And float amid the painted leaves.

Surely, while geese fly overhead, we can live here as contentedly as they do at York Factory or Hudson's Bay. We shall perchance be as well provisioned and have as good society as they. Let us be of good cheer then, and expect the annual vessel which brings the spring to us, without fail.

"Goodwin, the one-eyed Ajax, and other fishermen, who sit thus alone from morning to night at this season, must be greater philosophers than the shoemakers. The streets are thickly strewn with elm and button-wood and other leaves, *feuille-morte* [1] color. And what is acorn color? Is it not as good as chestnut? Now (the second November week) for twinkling light, reflected from unseen windows in the horizon in early twilight. The frost seems as if the earth was letting off steam after the summer's work is over. If you do feel any fire

[1] Fawn color, dry-leaf color. w. e. c.

at this season out of doors, you may depend upon it, it is your own. November, eat-heart,—is that the name of it? A man will eat his heart in this, if in any month. The old she-wolf is nibbling at your very extremities. The frozen ground eating away the soles of your shoes is only typical of the Nature that gnaws your heart. Going through a partly frozen meadow near the river, scraping the sweet-gale, I am pleasantly scented with its odoriferous fruit. The smallest (*Asplenium*) ferns under a shelving rock, pinned on rosette-wise, looked like the head of a breast-pin. The rays from the bare twigs across the pond are bread and cheese to me. . . . I see to the bone. See those bare birches prepared to stand the winter through on the bare hill-side. They never sing, ' What's this dull town to me?' The maples skirting the meadow (in dense phalanxes) look like light infantry advanced for a swamp fight. Ah! dear November, ye must be sacred to the Nine, surely."

"If you would know what are my winter thoughts, look for them in the partridge's crop. The winter, cold and bound out as it is, is thrown to us like a bone to a famishing dog. I go budding like a partridge. Some lichenous thoughts still adhere to us, our cold immortal evergreens. Even our experience is something like wintering in the pack, and we assume the spherical form of the marmot. We have peculiarly long and clear silvery twilights, morn and eve, with a stately withdrawn after-redness,—it is *indigo-ey* along the horizon. . . . Wachusett looks like a right whale over our bow, ploughing the continent with his flukes well down. He has a vicious look, as if he had a harpoon in him. All waters now seen through the leafless trees are blue as indigo, reservoirs of dark indigo among the general russet, reddish-brown, and gray.

"I rode home on a hay rigging with a boy who had been collecting a load of dry leaves for the hog-pen,—this, the third or fourth; two other boys asked leave to ride, with four large, empty box-traps, which they were bringing home from the woods. They had caught five rabbits this fall, baiting with an apple. Some fine straw-colored grasses, as delicate as the down on a young man's cheek, still rise above this crusted snow. I look over my shoulder upon an arctic scene. . . . The winters come now as fast as snow-flakes; there is really but one season in our hearts. The snow is like a uniform white napkin in many fields. I see the old, pale-faced farmer walking beside his team (in the sled), with contented thoughts, for the five thousandth time.[1] This drama every day in the streets. This is the theatre I go to."

[1] This was old Hayden, a farm-laborer.

PHILOSOPHY

"La génie c'est la patience."

BUFFON.

"As he had kyked on the newe mone."

CHAUCER.

CHAPTER VII

PHILOSOPHY

"IT was summer, and now again it is winter. Nature loves this
rhyme so well that she never tires of repeating it. So sweet
and wholesome is the winter, so simple and moderate, so satis-
factory and perfect, that her children will never weary of it.
What a poem! an epic, in blank verse, inscribed with uncounted tinkling rhymes. It is solid beauty. It has been sub-
jected to the vicissitudes of a million years of the gods, and
not a single superfluous ornament remains. The severest and
coldest of the immortal critics shot their arrows at and pruned
it, till it cannot be amended. We might expect to find in the
snows the footprint of a life superior to our own; of which no
zoölogy takes cognizance; a life which pursued does not earth
itself. The hollows look like a glittering shield set round
with brilliants, as we go south-westward, through the Cassandra swamps, toward the declining sun, in the midst of
which we walked. That beautiful frost-work, which so fre-
quently in winter mornings is seen bristling about the throat
of every breathing-hole in the earth's surface, is the frozen
breath of the earth upon its beard. I knew what it was by my
own experience. Some grass culms eighteen inches or two feet
high, which nobody noticed, are an inexhaustible supply of
slender ice wands set in the snow. The waving lines within
the marsh-ice look sometimes just like some white, shaggy
wolf-skin. The fresh, bright chestnut fruit of some lichens,

glistening in moist winter days, brings life and immortality to light. The sight of the masses of yellow hastate leaves and flower-buds of the yellow lily, already four or six inches long at the bottom of the river, reminds me that Nature is prepared for an infinity of springs yet. How interesting a few clean, dry weeds on the shore a dozen rods off, seen distinctly against the smooth reflecting water between ice!

"The surface of the snow everywhere in the fields, where it is hard blown, has a fine grain with low shelves, like a slate stone that does not split well; also, there are some shell-like drifts, more than once round. Over the frozen river only the bridges are seen peeping out from time to time like a dry eyelid. The damp, driving snow-flakes, when we turned partly round and faced them, hurt our eyeballs as if they had been dry scales: there are plenty of those shell-like drifts along the south sides of the walls now, and countless perforations, sometimes like the prows of vessels, or the folds of a white napkin or counterpane dropped over a bonneted head. Snow-flakes are the wheels of the storm chariots, the wreck of chariot wheels after a battle in the skies; these glorious spangles, the sweeping of heaven's floor. And they all sing, melting as they sing, of the mysteries of the number six, six, six. He takes up the water of the sea in his hand, leaving the salt; he disperses it in mist through the skies; he recollects and sprinkles it like grain in six-rayed snowy stars over the earth, there to lie till it dissolves its bonds again.

"I see great thimbleberry bushes, rising above the snow with still a rich, rank bloom on them as in July,—hypæthral mildew, elysian fungus! To see the bloom on a thimbleberry thus lasting into mid-winter! What a salve that would make collected and boxed! I should not be ashamed to have a shrub-oak for my coat-of-arms; I would fain have been wading through the woods and fields and conversing with the sane snow. Might I aspire to praise the moderate nymph, Nature! I must be like her,—moderate. Who shall criticise that companion? It is like the hone to the knife. There I get my underpinnings laid and repaired, cemented and levelled. There is my country club; we dine at the sign of the shrub-oak, the new Albion House.

"A little flock of red-polls (*Linaria minor*) is busy picking the seeds of the pig-weed in the garden, this driving snow-storm. Well may the tender buds attract us at this season, no less than partridges, for they are the hope of the year, the spring rolled up; the summer is all packed in them. Again and again I congratulate myself on my so-called poverty. How can we spare to be abroad in the morning red; to see the forms of the leafless eastern trees against the clear sky, and hear the cocks crow, when a thin low mist hangs over the ice and frost in meadows? When I could sit in a cold chamber, muffled in a cloak, each evening till Thanksgiving time, warmed by my own thoughts, the world was not so much with me. When I have only a rustling oak-leaf, or the faint metallic cheep of a tree-sparrow, for variety in my winter walk, my life becomes continent and sweet as the kernel of a nut. Show me a man who consults his genius, and you have shown me a man who cannot be advised. . . . Going along the Nut Meadow, or Jimmy Miles road, when I see the sulphur lichens on the rails brightening with the moisture, I feel like studying them again as a relisher or tonic, to make life go down and digest well, as we use pepper and vinegar and salads. They are a sort of winter greens, which we gather and assimilate with our eyes. The flattened boughs of the white-pine rest stratum above stratum like a cloud, a green mackerel-sky, hardly reminding me of the concealed earth so far beneath. They are like a flaky crust to the earth; my eyes nibble the piney sierra which makes the horizon's edge, as a hungry man nibbles a cracker. . . . That bird (the hawk) settles with confidence on the white-pine top, and not upon your weather-cock; that bird will not be poultry of yours, lays no eggs for you, for ever hides its nest. Though willed or *wild*, it is not wilful in its wildness. The unsympathizing man regards the wildness of some animals, their strangeness to him, as a sin. No hawk that soars and steals our poultry is wilder than genius; and none is more persecuted, or above persecution. It can never be poet-laureate, to say 'pretty Poll,' and 'Poll want a cracker.'"

In these sayings may his life best be sought. It is an autobiography with the genuine brand,—it is unconscious. How he was affected by the seasons, who walked with them as a familiar friend! thinking thus aloud the thoughts which they brought; associations in linked sweetness long drawn out; dear and delightful as memories or hopes! He had few higher sources of inspiration than night, and having given a prayer of his to the moon, and now a saying, "The moon comes out of the mackerel cloud,[1] and the traveller rejoices"; let us see what one evening furnishes: it is that of September 7, 1851.

"The air is very still; a fine sound of crickets, but not loud. The woods and single trees are heavier masses than in the spring; night has more allies. I hear only a tree-toad or song-sparrow singing at long intervals, as in spring. The most beautiful thing in Nature is the sun reflected from a tearful cloud. Now in the fields I see the white streak of the Neottia in the twilight: The whippoorwill sings far off. I hear the sound from time to time of a leaping fish or a frog, or a muskrat or a turtle. I know not how it is that this universal cricket's creak should sound thus regularly intermittent, as if for the most part they fell in with one another and creaked in time, making a certain pulsing sound, a sort of breathing or panting of all Nature. You sit twenty feet above the still river, see the sheeny pads and the moon and some bare tree-tops in the distant horizon. Those bare tree-tops add greatly to the wildness.

"Lower down I see the moon in the water as bright as in the heavens, only the water-bugs disturb its disk, and now I catch a faint glassy glare from the whole river surface, which before was simply dark. This is set in a frame of double darkness in the east; *i.e.*, the reflected shore of woods and hills and the reality, the shadow and the substance bi-partite, answering to each. I see the northern lights over my shoulder

[1] The mackerel-sky is named from the peculiar bluish-whitish tint of the shutter-leaved clouds that spread like vast mother-of-pearl blinds over heaven. W. E. C.

[115]

to remind me of the Esquimaux, and that they are still my contemporaries on this globe; that they, too, are taking their walks on another part of the planet, in pursuit of seals perchance. It was so soft and velvety a light as contained a thousand placid days recently put to rest in the bosom of the water. So looked the North-twin Lake in the Maine woods. It reminds me of placid lakes in the mid-noon of Indian summer days, but yet more placid and civilized, suggesting a higher cultivation, as wildness ever does, which æons of summer days have gone to make, like a summer day seen far away. All the effects of sunlight, with a softer tone, and all the stillness of the water and air superadded, and the witchery of the hour. What gods are they that require so fair a vase of gleaming water to their prospect in the midst of the wild woods by night?

"Else why this beauty allotted to night, a gem to sparkle in the zone of *Nox?* They are strange gods now out; methinks their names are not in any mythology. The light that is in night, a smile as in a dream on the face of the sleeping lake, enough light to show what we see, any more would obscure these objects. I am not advertised of any deficiency of light. The faint sounds of birds dreaming aloud in the night, the fresh cool air and sound of the wind rushing over the rocks remind me of the tops of mountains. In this faint, hoary light all fields are like a mossy rock and remote from the cultivated plains of day. It is all one with Caucasus, the slightest hill-pasture.

"Now the fire in the north increases wonderfully, not shoot-

ing up so much as creeping along, like a fire on the mountains of the north, seen afar in the night. The Hyperborean
gods are burning brush, and it spread, and all the hoes in
heaven could n't stop it. It spread from west to east, over the
crescent hill. Like a vast fiery worm it lay across the northern sky, broken into many pieces; and each piece, with rainbow colors skirting it, strove to advance itself towards the
east, worm-like on its own annular muscles. It has spread into
the choicest wood-lots of Valhalla; now it shoots up like a
single, solitary watch-fire, or burning brush, or where it ran
up a pine-tree like powder, and still it continues to gleam
here and there like a fat stump in the burning, and is reflected
in the water. And now I see the gods by great exertions have
got it under, and the stars have come out without fear in
peace. Though no birds sing, the crickets vibrate their shrill
and stridulous cymbals in the alders of the causeway, those
minstrels especially engaged for night's quire."

He saw the great in the little: the translucent leaves of the
Andromeda calyculata seemed in January, with their soft red,
more or less brown, as he walked towards the sun, like cathedral windows; and he spoke of the cheeks and temples of the
soft crags of the sphagnum. The hubs on birches are regular
cones, as if they might be volcanoes in outline; and the small
cranberries occupy some little valley a foot or two over, between two mountains of sphagnum (that dense, cushion-like
moss that grows in swamps). He says distant lightning is like
veins in the eye. Of that excellent nut, the chestnut, "the
whole upper slopes of the nuts are covered with the same

hoary wool as the points." A large, fresh stone-heap, eight or ten inches above water, is quite sharp, like Teneriffe. These comparisons to him were realities, not sports of the pen: to elevate the so-called little into the great, with him, was genius.[1] In that sense he was no humorist. He sees a gull's wings, that seem almost regular semicircles, like the new moon. Some of the bevelled roofs of the houses on Cape Ann are so nearly flat that they reminded him of the low brows of monkeys. The enlarged sail of the boat suggests a new power, like a Grecian god . . . Ajacean. The boat is like a plough drawn by a winged bull. He asks, "Are there no purple reflections from the culms of thought in my mind?" thinking of the colors of the poke-stem. In a shower he feels the first drop strike the right slope of his nose, and run down the ravine there, and says, "Such is the origin of rivers," and sees a wave whose whole height, "from the valley between to the top," was fifteen inches. He thus practically illustrates his faith,—how needless to travel for wonders; they lie at your feet; the seeing eye must search intently. The Wayland bird-stuffer shoots a meadow-hen, a Virginia rail, a *stormy petrel* and the *little auk*, in Sudbury meadows.

He wished so to live as to derive his satisfactions and inspirations from the commonest events, every-day phenomena; so that what his senses hourly perceived, his daily walk, the conversation of his neighbors, might inspire him; and he wished to dream of no heaven but that which lay about him.

[1] I remember the exact spot where he spoke of this. He was then in his last sickness, and said that he could never feel warm. w. e. c.

Seeing how impatient, how rampant, how precocious were the
osiers in early spring, he utters the prayer, "May I ever be
in as good spirits as a willow. They never say die." The charm
of his journal must consist in a certain greenness, thorough
freshness, and not in maturity. "Here, I cannot afford to be
remembering what I said, did, my scurf cast off,—but what
I am and aspire to become." Those annoyed by his hardness
should remember that "the flowing of the sap under the dull
rinds of the trees is a tide which few suspect." The same object is ugly or beautiful according to the angle from which
you view it. He went to the rocks by the pond in April to
smell the catnep, and always brought some home for the cat,
at that season. To truly see his character, you must "see with
the unworn sides of your eye." Once he enlarges a little on an
offer he did not accept of a passenger. He had many: genial
gentlemen of all sizes felt ready to walk or sail with him, and
he usually accepted them, sometimes two in one. On this occasion he declines:—

"This company is obliged to make a distinction between
dead freight and passengers: I will take almost any amount
of freight for you cheerfully,—anything, my dear sir, but
yourself. You are a heavy fellow, but I am well disposed. If
you could go without going, then you might go. There 's the
captain's state-room, empty to be sure, and you say you
could go in the steerage: I know very well that only your
baggage would be dropped in the steerage, while you would
settle down into that vacant recess. Why, I am *going*, not
staying; I have come on purpose to sail, to paddle away from

such as you, and you have waylaid me on the shore. . . . If I remember aright it was only on condition *that you were asked*, that you were to go with a man one mile or twain. I could better carry a heaped load of meadow mud and sit on the thole-pins."

He believed that "we must not confound man with man. We cannot conceive of a greater difference than that between the life of one man and that of another."

"It is possible for a man wholly to disappear and be merged in his manners." *He thought a man of manners was an insect in a tumbler.* But genius had evanescent boundaries like an altar from which incense rises.

"Our stock in life, our real estate, is that amount of thought which we have had, and which we have thought out. The ground we have thus created is for ever pasturage for our thoughts. I am often reminded that, if I had bestowed on me the wealth of Crœsus, my aims must still be the same and my means essentially the same. The art of life, of a poet's life, is, not having anything to do, to do something. Improve the suggestion of each object however humble, however slight and transient the provocation; what else is there to be improved? You must try a thousand themes before you find the right one, as nature makes a thousand acorns to get one oak. Both for bodily and mental health court the present. Embrace health wherever you find her. None but the kind gods can make me sane. If only they will let their south wind blow on me: I ask to be melted. You can only ask of the metals to be tender to the fire that melts them. To naught else can they be tender. Only he can be trusted with gifts, who can present a face of bronze to expectations."

At times, he asked: "Why does not man sleep all day as well as all night, it seems so very easy. For what is he awake?" "Do lichens or fungi grow on you? The luxury of wisdom! the luxury of virtue! are there any intemperate in these things?" "Oh such thin skins, such crockery as I have to deal with! Do they not know that I can laugh?" "Why do the mountains never look so fair as from my native fields?" "Who taught the oven-bird to conceal her nest?" He states a familiar fact, showing that the notion of a thing can be taken for the thing, literally: "I have convinced myself that I saw smoke issuing from the chimney of a house, which had not been occupied for twenty years,—a small bluish, whitish cloud, instantly dissipated." Like other scribes, he wishes he *"could buy at the shops some kind of India-rubber that would rub out at once all that in my writing which it now costs me so many perusals, so many months, if not years, and so much reluctance to erase."* His temperament is so moral, his least observation will breed a sermon, or a water-worn fish rear him to Indian heights of philosophy: "How many springs shall I continue to see the common sucker (*Catostomus Bostoniensis*) floating dead on our river? Will not Nature select her types from a new font? The vignette of the year. This earth which is spread out like a map around me is but the lining of my inmost soul exposed. In me is the sucker that I see. No wholly extraneous object can compel me to recognize it. I am guilty of suckers. . . . The red-bird which I saw on my companion's string on election-days, I thought but the outmost sentinel of the wild immortal camp, of the wild and dazzling infantry of the wilderness. The red-bird which is the last of nature is but the first of God. We condescend to climb the crags of earth."

He believes he is soothed by the sound of the rain, because he is allied to the elements. The sound sinks into his spirit as the water into the earth, reminding him of the season when snow and ice will be no more. He advises you to be not in haste amid your private affairs. Consider the turtle: a whole summer, June, July, and August are not too good, not too much to hatch a turtle in. Another of his questions is: "What kind of understanding was there between the mind that determined these leaves of the black willow should hang on during the winter, and that of the worm that fastened a few of these leaves to its cocoon in order to disguise it?" As an answer may be found the following: "It was long ago in a full senate of all intellects determined how cocoons had best be suspended; kindred mind with mind that admires and approves decided it so. *The mind of the universe which we share has been intended on each particular point.*" Thus persevering, —and, as he says of a dwelling on the Cape, he knocked all round the house at five doors in succession,—so he at the great out-doors of nature, where he was accommodated.

"Chide me not, laborious band,
    For the idle flowers I brought;
Every aster in my hand
    Goes home loaded with a thought."

[122]

PHILOSOPHY

His fineness of perceiving, his delicacy of touch, has rarely been surpassed with pen or pencil, a fineness as unpremeditated as successful. For him the trout glances like a film from side to side and under the bank. The pitch oozing from pine logs is one of the beautiful accidents that attend on man's works, instead of a defilement. Darby's oak stands like an athlete, it is an agony of strength. Its branches look like gray lightning stereotyped on the sky. The lichens on the pine remind him of the forest warrior and his shield adhering to him.

In spring he notices pewee days and April showers. The mountains are the pastures to which he drives his thoughts, on their 20th of May. So the storm has its flashing van followed by the long dropping main body, with at very long intervals an occasional firing or skirmishing in the rear, or on the flank. "The lightning, like a yellow spring-flower, illumines the dark banks of the clouds. Some æstrum stings the cloud that she darts headlong against the steeples, and bellows hollowly, making the earth tremble. It is the familiar note of another warbler echoing amid the roofs." He compares the low universal twittering of the chip-birds, at daybreak in June, to the bursting bead on the surface of the uncorked day. If he wishes for a hair for his compass-sight, he must go to the stable; but the hair-bird, with her sharp eyes, goes to the road. He muses over an ancient muskrat skull (found behind the wall of Adams's shop), and is amused with the notion of what grists have come to this mill. Now the upper and nether stones fall loosely apart, and the brain chamber where the miller lodged is now empty (passing under the portcullis of the incisors), and the windows are gone. The opening of the first asters, he thinks, makes you fruitfully meditative; helps condense your thoughts like the mildews in the afternoon. He is pretty sure to find a plant which he is shown from abroad, or hears of, or in any way becomes interested in. The cry of hounds he lists to, as it were a distant natural horn in the clear resonant air. He says that fire is the most tolerable third party. When he puts the hemlock boughs on the blaze, the rich salt crackling of its leaves is like mustard to the ear; dead trees love the fire. The distant white-pines over the Sanguinetto [1] seem to flake into tiers; the whole tree looks like an open cone. The pond reminds him, looking from the mill-dam, of a weight wound up; and when the miller raised the gate, what a smell of gun-wash or sulphur! "I who never partake of the sacrament made the more of it." The solitude of Truro is as sweet as a flower. He drank at every cooler spring in his walk in a blazing July, and loved to eye the bottom there, with its pebbly Caddis-worm cases, or its white worms, or perchance a luxurious frog cooling himself next his nose. The squirrel withdraws to his eye by his aërial turnpikes. "The roof of a house at a distance, in March, is a mere gray scale, diamond shape, against the side of a hill." "If I were to be a frog-hawk for a month, I should soon have known something about the frogs." He thinks most men can keep a horse, or keep up a certain fashionable style of living,

[1] A name given by Mr. Emerson to the little brook running under the railroad and to Baker Farm, from his woodland meadow or swamp. w. e. c.

but few indeed can keep up great expectations. He improves every opportunity to go into a grist-mill, any excuse to see its cobweb-tapestry, such as putting questions to the miller, while his eye rests delighted on the cobwebs above his head and perchance on his hat.

So he walked and sang his melodies in the pure country, in the seclusion of the field. All forms and aspects of night and day were glad and memorable to him, whose thoughts were as pure and innocent as those of a guileless maiden. Shall they not be studied?

> "I will give my son to eat
> Best of Pan's immortal meat,
> Bread to eat, and juice to drink;
> So the thoughts that he shall think
> Shall not be forms of stars, but stars,
> Not pictures pale, but Jove and Mars.
> .   .   .   .
> The Indian cheer, the frosty skies,
> Rear purer wits, inventive eyes.
>
> In the wide thaw and ooze of wrong
> Adhere like this foundation strong,
> The insanity of towns to stem
> With simpleness for stratagem."

EMERSON'S MONADNOC.

If it is difficult (to some) to credit, it is no less certain that Thoreau would indulge himself in a rhapsody,—given the right topic, something the writer *cordially* appreciated. In speech or with the pen, the eloquent vein being touched, the spring of discourse flowed rapidly, as on this subject of the Corner-road:—

"Now I yearn for one of those old, meandering, dry, uninhabited roads which lead away from towns, which lead us away from temptation, which conduct to the outside of the earth over its uppermost crust; where you may forget in what country you are travelling; where no farmer can complain that you are treading down his grass; no gentleman who has recently constructed a seat in the country that you are trespassing; on which you can go off at half-cock and wave adieu to the village; along which you may travel like a pilgrim going no-whither; where travellers are not often to be met, where my spirit is free, where the walls and flowers are not cared for, where your head is more in heaven than your feet are on earth; which have long reaches, where you can see the approaching traveller half a mile off, and be prepared for him; not so luxuriant a soil as to attract men; some stump and root fences, which do not need attention; where travellers have no occasion to stop, but pass along and leave you to your thoughts; where it makes no odds which way you face, whether you are going or coming, whether it is morning or evening, mid-noon or midnight; where earth is cheap enough by being public; where you can walk and think with least obstruction, there being nothing to measure progress by; where you can pace when your breast is full, and cherish your moodiness; where you are not in false relations with men, are not dining or conversing with them; by which you may go to the uttermost parts of the earth.

"Sometimes it is some particular half-dozen rods which I wish to find myself pacing over; as where certain airs blow, there my life will come to me; methinks, like a hunter, I lie in wait for it. When I am against this bare promontory of a huckleberry hill, then forsooth my thoughts will expand. Is it some influence, as a vapor which exhales from the ground, or something in the gales which blow there, or in all things there brought together, agreeably to my spirit? The walls must not be too high, imprisoning me, but low, with numerous gaps. The trees must not be too numerous nor the hills too near, bounding the view; nor the soil too rich, attracting attention to the earth. It must simply be the way and the life, —a way that was never known to be repaired, nor to need repair, within the memory of the oldest inhabitant. I cannot walk habitually in those ways that are likely to be repaired, for sure it was the devil only that wore them; never by the heel of thinkers (of thought) were they worn. The saunterer wears out no road, even though he travel on it, and therefore should pay no highway (or rather *lowway*) tax; he *may* be taxed to construct a higher way than that men travel. A way which no geese defile or hiss along it, but only sometimes their wild brethren fly far overhead; which the kingbird and the swallow twitter over, and the song-sparrow sings on its rails; where the small red butterfly is at home on the yarrow, and no boy threatens it with imprisoning hat,—there I can walk and stalk and plod. Which nobody but Jonas Potter travels beside me; where no cow but his is tempted to linger for the herbage by its side; where the guideboard is fallen, and now the hand points to heaven significantly, to a Sudbury and Marlboro' in the skies. That's a road I can travel,

[127]

that the particular Sudbury I am bound for, six miles an hour, or two, as you please; and few there be that enter therein. Here I can walk and recover the lost child that I am, without any ringing of a bell. Where there was nothing ever discovered to detain a traveller, but all went through about their business; where I never 'passed the time of day' with any,—indifferent to me were the arbitrary divisions of time; where Tullus Hostilius might have disappeared, at any rate has never been seen,—the road to the Corner!

"The ninety and nine acres you go through to get there, —I would rather see it again, though I saw it this morning, than Gray's Churchyard. The road whence you may hear a stake-driver, or whippoorwill, or quail, in a midsummer day. Oh, yes! a quail comes nearest to the Gum-c bird [1] heard there. Where it would not be sport for a sportsman to go. The Mayweed looks up in my face there, the pale lobelia and the Canada snap-dragon; a little hardhack and meadow-sweet peep over the fence; nothing more serious to obstruct the view, and thimbleberries are the food of thought (before the drought), along by the walls. A road that passes over the Height-of-land, between earth and heaven, separating those streams which flow earthward from those which flow heavenward.

"It is those who go to Brighton and to market that wear out all the roads, and they should pay all the tax. The deliberate pace of a walker never made a road the worse for travelling on,—on the promenade deck of the world, an out-

[1] One of Thoreau's names for some bird, so named by the farmers. w. e. c.

side passenger; where I have freedom in my thought, and in my soul am free. Excepting the omnipresent butcher with his calf-cart, followed by a distracted and anxious cow; or the inattentive stranger baker, whom no weather detains, that does not bake his bread in this hemisphere, and therefore it is dry before it gets here! Ah! there is a road where you might adventure to fly, and make no preparations till the time comes; where your wings will sprout if anywhere, where your feet are not confined to earth. An airy head makes light walking, when I am not confined and baulked by the sight of distant farmhouses, which I have not gone past. I must be fancy free; I must feel that, wet or dry, high or low, it is the genuine surface of the planet, and not a little chip-dirt or a compost heap, or made land, or redeemed. A thinker's weight is in his thought, not in his tread; when he thinks freely, his body weighs nothing. He cannot tread down your grass, farmers!"

> "Thus far to-day your favors reach,
> O fair appeasing presences!
> Ye taught my lips a single speech
> And a thousand silences." [1]

[1] From Emerson's "Merops,"—the unspoken, perhaps, or unspeakable.
W. E. C.

WALKS AND TALKS

"Absents within the line conspire."

VAUGHAN.

"What I have reaped in my journey is, as it were, a small contentment in a never-contenting subject ; a bitter-pleasant taste of a sweet-seasoned sour.[1] All in all, what I found was more than ordinary rejoicing in an extraordinary sorrow of delights."

LITHGOW.

"What is it to me that I can write these Table-Talks? Others have more property in them than I have; they may reap the benefit, I have had only the pain. Nor should I have known that I had ever thought at all, but that I am reminded of it by the strangeness of my appearance, and my unfitness for anything else."

HAZLITT.

"Not mine the boast of countless herds,
    Nor purple tapestries, nor treasured gold;
        But mine the peaceful spirit,
    And the dear Muse, and pleasant wine
        Stored in Bœotian urns."

BACCHYLIDES. *(Translated by Percival.)*

EDITOR'S NOTE. We have now come to the extraneous matter introduced by Channing while his book was printing, to increase its size,— literal padding, yet of no common quality. Introducing it, he framed these mottoes to fit his "Country Walking," from which it was taken, and to fit his own case as he understood it. The quotations from Vaughan and Hazlitt show this more particularly; the "absents" in 1873 being Thoreau, who had cheerfully contributed to the suppressed book. The quotation from Hazlitt applies rather closely to Channing's conception of his own character and fortunes in 1853, when the "Country Walking" was written. To the paradoxical quotation from Lithgow, Channing added the note given below. Only about half the original manuscript of "Country Walking" was used in this book. I have the original draft in pencil. It was all carefully copied out by Channing and the copy submitted to Mr. Emerson, from whose collection of manuscripts it came to me, but only in part. What became of the rest I know not; but suppose it remained in Channing's hands, and was used by him to print from in 1873. He communicated to me then the general fact that he had taken the walks described, with Emerson and Thoreau, and that his description of them passed from hand to hand among the three for revision. I suppose this was strictly true, so long as the plan remained to print the whole as a book; but when that was given up, for what reason I cannot say, the details of the affair seem to have been forgotten by Mr. Emerson. At least, he never spoke of them to me, although he complained that Channing had done ill to print things from his manuscript which he had not yet given to the world. Perhaps he may have fancied — his memory even then being somewhat impaired — that his friend had secretly copied them; but that cannot have been the case. F. B. S.

[1] *Emerson was never in the least contented. This made walking or company to him a penance. The Future,— that was the terrible Gorgon face that turned the Present into "a thousand bellyaches." "When shall I be perfect? when shall I be moral? when shall I be this and that? when will the really good rhyme get written?" Here is the Emerson colic. Thoreau had a like disease. Men are said never to be satisfied. W. E. C.*

CHAPTER VIII

WALKS AND TALKS

To furnish a more familiar idea of Thoreau's walks and talks with his friends and their locality, some reports of them are furnished for convenience in the interlocutory form.

A WALK TO SECOND DIVISION BROOK [1]

E. And so you are ready for a walk?

"Hence sand and dust are shak'd for witnesses."

VAUGHAN.

C. When was I ever not? Where shall we go? To Conantum or White Pond, or is the Second Division our business for this afternoon?

E. As you will. Under your piloting I feel partially safe; but not too far, not too much. Brevity is the sole of walking.

[1] The citations here made from Emerson's journal begin in May, 1843, but are mostly from that of 1848. The first one relates to a walk in early spring in the south-west direction from Concord village. The conversation is partly oral, and mostly a record of the years 1848–50, so far as Emerson's journal is the source; the citations from Thoreau's journals are from that of 1851 largely; but extend to and through 1853–54, and go on with occasional passages to 1860; after which Thoreau wrote but little in his completed journal. When it is possible to distinguish between the speakers, I have marked Emerson's passages "E." and Thoreau's "T.," while Channing's interpellations, poetic quotations, and descriptions go in under "C." The "Minott" here mentioned was the friend of the three walkers, George by name, who lived near Emerson and died a few months before Thoreau in 1862. He has been described by all three; by Channing under the fanciful name of "Angelo," and again in verse by his own Christian name. F. B. S.

T. And yet all true walking, all virtuous walking, is a *travail*. The season is proper to the Brook. I am in the mood to greet the Painted Tortoise; nor must I fail to examine the buds of the marsh-marigold, now, I think, somewhat swollen. But few birds have come in, though Minott says he has heard a bluebird.

C. Did he ask his old question,—"Seen a robin?"George Minott is native and to the manor born; was never away from home but once, when he was drafted as a soldier in the last war with England, and went to Dorchester Heights; and he has never ridden on a rail. What do you make of him?

E. He makes enough of himself. The railroad has proved too great a temptation to most of our farmers; the young men have a foreign air their fathers never had. We shall not boast of *Mors Ipse*, Grass-and-Oats, or Oats-and-Grass, and old Verjuice in the next generation. These rudimental Saxons have the air of pine-trees and apple-trees, and might be their sons got between them; conscientious laborers, with a science born within them, from out the sap-vessels of their savage sires. This savagery is native with man, and polished New England cannot do without it. That makes the charm of grouse-shooting and deer-stalking to these Lord Breadalbanes, walking out of their doors a hundred miles to the sea on their own property; or Dukes of Sutherland getting off at last their town coat, and donning their hunter's gear, exasperated by saloons and dress-boots.

C. Let me rest a fraction on this bridge.

E. I am your well-wisher in that. The manners of water are

beautiful. "As for beauty I need not look beyond my oar's length for my fill of it." I do not know whether you used the expression with design the other day; but my eye rested on the charming play of light on the water, which you were slowly striking with your paddle. I fancied I had never seen such color, such transparency, such eddies. It was the hue of Rhine wines, it was gold and green and chestnut and hazel, in bewildering succession and relief, without cloud or confusion. A little canoe with three men or boys in it put out from a creek and paddled down stream; and, afar or near, we paid homage to the Blessed Water, inviolable, magical, whose nature is Beauty; which instantly began to play its sweet games, all circles and dimples and lovely gleaming motions,—always Ganges, the Sacred River,—and which cannot be desecrated or made to forget itself.

C. "For marble sweats, and rocks have tears."

Hark! Was that the bluebird's warble?

E. I could not hear it, as now cometh the seventh abomination, the train. And yet it looks like a new phenomenon, though it has appeared at the same hour each day for these ten years since 1843.

C. Already the South Acton passengers squeeze their bundles, and the member of the legislature hastens to drain the last drop of vulgar gossip from the Ginger-beer paper before he leaves the cars to fodder and milk his kine. I trust that in heaven will be no cows. They are created, apparently, to give the farmer a sport between planting and harvest, the joy of haying, dust, grime, and tan, diluted by sunstrokes.

E. The cause of cows is, that they make good walking where they feed. In the paths of the thicket the best engineer is the cow.

T. We cross where the high bank will give us a view over the river at Clam-shell, and where I may possibly get an arrow-head from this Concord Kitchen-mödding.

C. A singular proclivity, thou worshipper of Indians! for arrow-heads; and I presume, like certain other worships, uncurable!

T. Apply thy Procrustes-bed to my action, and permit me to continue my search. They speak of Connecticuts and Hudsons: our slow little stream, in its spring overflow, draws on the surtout of greater rivers; a river,—fair, solitary path,— the one piece of real estate belonging to the walker, unfenced, undeeded, sacred to musquash and pickerel, and to George Melvin, gunner; more by the token he was drowned in it.

C. Are not those gulls, gleaming like spots of intense white light, far away on the dark bosom of the meadows?

T. Yes, indeed! they come from the sea each spring-overflow, and go a-fishing like Goodwin. See! I have got a quartz arrow-head,—and perfect. This bank is made of the clams baked by the Indians. Let us look a moment at the minnows as we cross the brook; I can see their shadows on the yellow sand much clearer than themselves, and can thus count the number of their fins. I wonder if the Doctor ever saw a minnow. In his report on reptiles, he says he has never seen but one *Hylodes Pickeringii*, in a dried state. It is well also to report upon what you have not seen. He never troubled himself with looking about in the country.

C. The poet more than the *savant* marries man to nature. I wish we had some fuller word to express this fine picture we see from Clam-shell bank: *kinde* was the old English word.

E. [*September 5, 1847.*] *Kinde* only filled half the range of our fine Latin word. But nothing designates that Power which seems to work for beauty alone; whilst man, as you say, works only for use.

C. See, O man of Nature, yon groups of weather-stained houses we now o'ertop. There live some Christians, put away on Life's plate like so many rinds of cheese; single women living out of all villages, in the quiet of fields and woods. There descend, like dew on flowers, the tranquillizing years into their prickly life-petals. Save the rats scrabbling along the old plastering, the sawing of pluvial pea-hens, or the low of the recuperating cow,—what repose! And in the midst such felons of destiny! What avails against hot-bread, cream-of-tartar, and Oriental-Company tea,—with an afternoon nap?

> "O mother Ida, hearken ere I die."

I have met Œnones whom I could have spared better than these horn-pouts of gossip. Is there a fixed sum of hyson allotted to each sibyl?

> E. "Only a learned and a manly soul
> I purposed her, that should with even powers
> The rock, the spindle, and the shears control
> Of Destiny,—and spin her own free hours."

C. The bluebird, sir! the first bluebird! there he sits and

warbles. Dear bird of Spring! first speech of the original Beauty,—first note in the annual concert of Love! why soundest thy soft and plaintive warble on my ear like the warning of a mournful Past? As the poet Crashaw sings, if not of the new birds:—

> "We saw thee in thy balmy nest,
>   Bright dawn of our eternal day!
> We saw thine eyes break from their East,
>   And chase the trembling shades away:
> We saw thee,—and we blest the sight,—
> We saw thee by thine own sweet light.
>
> She sings thy tears asleep, and dips
>   Her kisses in thy weeping eye;
> She spreads the red leaves of thy lips,
>   That in their buds yet blushing lie:
> She 'gainst those mother diamonds tries
> The points of her young eagle's eyes."

Excuse soliloquy.

E. Go on, go on: I can hear the bluebird just the same.

C. I am glad we are at the sand-bank. Radiantly here the brook parts across the shallows its ever-rippling tresses of golden light. It steals away my battered senses as I gaze therein; and, if I remember me, 't is in some murmuring line:—

> "Thus swam away my thoughts on thee,
>   And in thy joyful ecstasy
> Flowed with thy waters to thy sea."

E. Let us to the ancient woods![1] I say, let us value the

---

[1] The date of this walk in the woods was October, 1848.

woods,—they are full of solicitations. My wood-lot has no price; I could not think of selling it for the money I gave for it. Full of mysterious values,—what forms, what colors, what powers! null to our ignorance, but opening fast enough to wit. One thing our Concord wants,—a Berkshire brook, now beside the road and now under it, which cheers the traveller for miles with its loud voice.

C. But here is our Brook itself, a petted darling of the meadows—wild minstrel of an ancient song, poured through our vales for ever. The sands of Pactolus were not more golden than these: and black are the eddying pools where the old experienced trout sleeps on his oars. "As hurries the water to the Sea, so seeks the Soul its Universe." And this is our May-flower, sweet as Cytherea's breath; in yonder lowlands grows the climbing fern. Simple flowers! yet was not Solomon in all his glory arrayed like one of these. Soon come the water mouse-ear, typha or reed-mace; *Drosera rotundifolia,* Solomon's seal, violets of all sorts, bulbous *arethrum,* yellow lily, dwarf cornel, lousewort, yellow Star of Bethlehem, *Polygala paucifolia, Arum triphyllum,* cohosh,—

E. O hush! hush! what names! Hadst thou spoken to me of Violet, that child of beauty! of which your poet Street says,—

> "Where its long rings unwinds the fern,
> The violet, nestling low,
> Casts back the white lid of its urn,
> Its purple streaks to show."

C. Yes, and he adds,—

[139]

"Beautiful blossom! first to rise
And smile beneath Spring's wakening skies;
The courier of the band
Of coming flowers, — what feelings sweet
Flow as the silvery germ we meet
Upon its needle-wand!"

CONANTUM

C. Let us now go forward to Conantum, that wide tract named by our Henry from its owner, old Eben Conant, — as good as the domains of royalty, and yet the possession of that ancient New England farmer.

E. From the bridge I see only a simple field, with its few old apple-trees. It rises neatly to the west.

C. When we traverse the whole of the long seigniorage, I think you will agree that this is a good place for a better than Montaigne-chateau.

T. There is the stake-driver "pump-a-gawing" again. From this corner to Fairhaven Bay the domain extends, with not an ounce of cultivated soil. First a tract of woodland, with its pleasant wood-paths, its deep and mossy swamp, where owls and foxes have holes, and the long lichens sway their soft green tresses from the rotting spruce.[1]

C. Behind yon old barn stands the original farmhouse; the mouldering shell has ripened birth and death, marriage feasts and funeral tables, where now the careless flies only buzz and the century-old crow alights on the broad roof that almost touches the ground. The windows are gone, the door half

[1] Holden's Swamp, where grows *Kalmia glauca*.

ruined, the chimney down, the roof falling in,—sans eyes, sans ears, sans life, sans everything. Not even a contemplative cat shakes his irresponsive sides in this solitude, and the solid grass grows up to the edges of the enormous door-stone. Our ancestors took a pride in acquiring the largest and flattest rock possible to lay before the hospitable sill. We do get unscrupulously rid of the ancestral mansion, and the pot of beans of the careful grandson bakes upon the architectural desolation of "my grandpapa." Ascend this height, and you will see (part second) the lovely valley of the Concord at your feet,—

> "See where the winding vale its lavish stores irriguous spreads."
>
> THOMSON.

E. There is Musketaquit, the grass-ground river; a goodly view, and noble walking!

C. Let us continue on a few steps more, till we reach the little meadow,—a natural arboretum, where grow the black ash, the bass and the cohosh; cornels, viburnums, sassafras, and arethusas.

> E. "Each spot where lilies prank their state
> Has drunk the life-blood of the great;
> The violets yon field which stain
> Are moles of beauties Time hath slain."

So sings Omar Chiam. Sitting in this steep Park of Conantum, always the same regret. Is all this beauty to perish? shall none remake this sun and wind,—the sky-blue river, the river-blue sky?

[141]

C. How the earliest kiss of June will heap these trees with leaves, and make land and orchard, hillside and garden, verdantly attractive. This great domain, all but one meadow, is under the holding of one old prudent husbandman; and here is an old cellar-hole, where in front yet grows the vivacious lilac, soon to be in profuse flower,—a plant to set! It has outlived man and dog, hen and pig, house and wife; "all, all are gone" except the "old familiar face" of the delightsome lilac. And now we stand on the verge of broad Fairhaven, and below us falls the scaly frost-abraded precipice to the pitch-pines and walnuts that stand resigned to their lower avocations. There is about us here that breath of wildness, in whose patronage the good Indians dwelt; there is around us in these herbaceous odors, in these lustral skies, all that earthly life hath ever known of beauty or of joy. Thus sings the lark as he springs from his nest in the grassy meadow; thus in the barberry hedge, along the gray and precarious wall, the melodious song-sparrow chants in his brownish summer-suit and that *brevet* of honor on his breast, the black rosette, constituting him "Conantum's Malibran." It is Time's holiday, the festival of June, the leafy June, the flower-sped June, the bird-singing June,

"And sweeter than the lids of Juno's eyes."

T. Let us get a good look from these cliffs at Baker Farm that lies on that opposite shore. There is Clematis Brook, Blue Heron Pond, and Mount Misery.

WALKS AND TALKS

OLD SUDBURY INN[1]

C. There you have it, — Howe's Tavern, on the old Worcester turnpike! I was never here before, — *au revoir!* A new place is good property, if we have the prospect of owning it, — hey, Betty Martin? 'T is one of the ancient taverns of the noble old Commonwealth: observe the date, 1719, painted on the sign. From that to this the same family have had it in their keeping; and many a glass has been drunk and paid for at the bar, whose defence, you observe, moves curiously up and down like a portcullis; and the room is "ceiled" all round, instead of plastered.

E. There is a seigniorial property attached to it, — some hundred acres; and see the old buttresses of time-channelled oak along the road, in front, that must have been set at the same time with the inn. A spacious brook canters behind the house; yonder is a noble forest; and there above us, Nobscot, our nearest mountain. Indeed, the tract across to Boone's Pond and Sudbury is all a piece of wild wood. Come, away for Nobscot! taking the sandy path behind the barn. Do you see that strange, embowered roof, peeping out of its great vase of apple-blossoms? for this, O man of many cares! is the twenty-third of May, and just as much Blossom-day as ever was.

C. I see the peeping chimney, — romance itself. May I hope never to know the name of the remarkable genius who dwells therein?

T. Very proper, no doubt, — Tubs or Scrubs.

[1] The Wayside Inn.

[143]

C. Believe it not, enemy to Blossom-day romance. My soul whispers of a fair, peculiar region behind those embracing bouquets.

T. Where one should surely find an anxious cook and a critical family.

C. Hush! hush! traduce not the venerable groves. Here, or in some such devoted solitude, should dwell the Muse, and compose a treatise on the worship of Dryads.

T. Dry as powder-post. Have you seen the scarlet tanager?

C. No,—the Puseyite unmistakable among our birds,—true high-church scarlet. Hear! the pewee's soft, lisping *pee-a-wee!* Now as we rise, and leave the splendid chestnut forest, the view opens. Nobscot is a true but low mountain, and these small creatures give the best look-off. I love the broad, healthy, new-springing pastures, ornamented with apple-tree pyramids, the pastoral architecture of the cow; the waving saxifrage and delicate Houstonia, that spring-beauty; and the free, untrammelled air of the mountains,—it never swept the dusty plain. There's our Cliff and Meeting-house in Concord, and Barrett's Hill [1] and Anursnuc; next comes high Lincoln with its gleaming spires, and modest Wayland low in the grass; the Great Sudbury Meadows (sap-green) and Framingham and Natick. How many dark belts of pines stalk across this bosky landscape! like the traditions of the old Sagamores, who fished in yonder Long Pond (Lake Cochituate) that now colors Boston with reddish water that a country boy *might* bathe in, if hard pushed.

[1] What is now called Nashawtuc, by its Indian name, like Anursnuc.

E. I faintly hear the sound of the church-going bell,—I suppose, of Framingham.

T. As the country-wife beats her brass pan to collect her bees.

E. Our landscape is democratic; the buildings not gathered into one city or baronial town, but equally scattered, leading up to the white steeples, round which a town clusters in every place where six roads meet, or where a river branches or falls. In the landscape to-day is found the magic of color. The world is all opal, and these ethereal tints the mountains wear have the finest effects of music on us. Mountains are great poets, and one glance at this fine New Hampshire range of Watatic, Monadnoc, Peterboro', and Uncannoonnuk, undoes a deal of prose and reinstates poor, wronged men in their rights; life and society begin to be illuminated and transparent, and we generalize boldly and well. Space is felt as a privilege. There is some pinch and narrowness to the best. Here we laugh and leap to see the world; and what amplitudes it has of meadow, stream, upland, forest, and sea! which yet are but lanes and crevices to the great space in which the world swims like a cockboat on the ocean. There below are those farms, but the life of farmers is unpoetic. The life of labor does not make men, but drudges. 'T is pleasant, as the habits of all poets may testify, to think of great proprietors, to reckon this grove we walk in as a park of the noble; but a continent cut up into ten-acre lots is not attractive. The farmer is an enchanted laborer, who, after toiling his brains out, sacrificing thought, religion, love, hope, courage, to toil, turns out a bankrupt, as well as the shopman.

C. I see I must meditate an ode to be called, "Adieu, my Johnny-cake." Ay, ay; hasty-pudding for the masculine eye, chickens and jellies for girls.

E. Yonder, on that hill is Marlboro', a town (in autumn, at least, when I visited it) that wears a rich appearance of rustic plenty and comfort; ample farms, good houses, profuse yellow apple-heaps, pumpkin mountains in every enclosure, orchards left ungathered, and, in the Grecian piazzas of the houses, squashes ripening between the columns. Gates's, where Dr. Channing and Jonathan Phillips used to resort, is no longer a public house. At Cutting's were oats for the horse, but no dinner for men; so we went, you and I, to a chestnut grove and an old orchard for our fare.

C. So our Alcott might have dined in his retreat at Fruit-lands. But for an inscription upon our Wayside Inn, Howe's Tavern, here are lines: —

> Who set thine oaks
> Along the road?
> Was it not Nature's hand,
> Old Sudbury Inn? for here I stand
>   And wonder at the sight;
> Thy oaks are my delight:
>
> As are the elms,
> So boldly branching to the sky,
> And the interminable woods,
> Old Inn, that wash thee nigh,
>   On every side,
> With green and rustling tide.

Such oaks! such elms!
And the contenting woods,
And Nobscot near;
Old Inn! 't is here
That I, creature of moods,
A haunt could find
Well suited to the custom of my mind.

Old Sudbury Inn! most homely seat
Where Nature hath her frugal meals,
  And studies to outwit
What thy inside reveals;
Long mayst thou be
More than a match for her and me!

E. And so it comes every year, this lovely Blossom-day!

The cup of life is not so shallow
  That we have drained the best,
That all the wines at once we swallow,
  And lees make all the rest.

Maids of as soft a bloom shall marry,
  As Hymen yet hath blessed,
And fairer forms are in the quarry
  Than Angelo released.

C. And to-day the air is spotted with the encouraging rig-marole of the bobolink,—that buttery, vivacious, fun-may-take-me cornucopia of song. Once to hear his "larripee, larripee, buttery, scattery, wittery, pittery"; some yellow, some black feathers, a squeeze of air, and this summer warming song! The bobolink never knew cold, and never could,—the musician of blossoms. Hark! the veery's liquid strain, with trilling cadence; his holy brother, the wood-thrush, pitches his flute-notes in the pine alleys, where at twilight is heard the strange prophecy of the whippoorwill. The oven-bird beats his brass *witcher-twitcher* in the heated shades of noon, mixed with the feathery roll-call of the partridge. As we take our nooning, I will recall some lines on this famous bird.

THE PARTRIDGE

Shot of the wood, from thy ambush low, —
  Bolt off the dry leaves flying,
With a whirring spring like an Indian's bow,
  Thou speed'st when the year is dying;
And thy neat gray form darts whirling past,
So silent all, as thou fliest fast,
Snapping a leaf from the copses red;
Our native bird, in the woodlands bred.

I have trembled a thousand times,
  As thy bolt through the thicket was rending,
Wondering at thee in the autumn chimes,
  When thy brother's soft wings were bending
Swift to the groves of the spicy south;
Where the orange melts in the zephyr's mouth,
And the azure sunshine humors the air,
And Winter ne'er sleeps in his pallid chair.

And thy whirring wings I hear,
  When the colored ice is warming
The twigs of the forest sere,
  While the northern wind a-storming
Draws cold as death round the Irish hut,
That lifts its blue smoke in the railroad cut;

[148]

And the hardy chopper sits dreaming warm,
And thou and I are alone in the storm.

Brave bird of my woodland haunt,
  Good child of the autumn dreary!
Drum of my city and bass of my chaunt,
  With thy rushing music cheery!
Desert not my bowers for the southern flowers,
Nor my pale north woods for her ruby hours;
Let us bide the rude blast and the ringing hail,
Till the violets peep on the Indian's trail.

TO WHITE POND

T. Above our heads the night-hawk rips; and, soaring over the tallest pine, the fierce hen-harrier screams and hisses; *cow, cow, cow,* sounds the timorous cuckoo: thus our cheerful and pleasant birds do sing along else silent paths, strewn with the bright and bluest violets, with Houstonias, anemones, and cinque-foils. Academies of Music and Schools of Design, truly! and to-day on all the young oaks shall be seen their bright crimson leaves, each in itself as good as a rich and delicate flower; and the sky bends o'er us with its friendly face like Jerusalem delivered.

E. And Mrs. Jones and Miss Brown—

T. No, indeed: I declare it boldly, let us leave out man in such days; his history may be written at nearly any future period, in dull weather.

C. Yet hath the same toiling knave in yonder field a kind of grim advantage.

T. The grime I perceive, and hear the toads sing.

[149]

E. Yet the poet says,—

> "Not in their houses stand the stars,
> But o'er the pinnacles of thine."

T. And also listen to *my* poet:—

> "Go thou to thy learned task,
> I stay with the flowers of Spring;
> Do thou of the Ages ask,
> What to me the Hours will bring."

Oh, the soft, mellow green of the swamp-sides! Oh, the sweet, tender green of the pastures! Do you observe how like the colors of currant-jelly are the maple-keys where the sun shines through them? I suppose to please you I ought to be unhappy, but the contrast is too strong.

C. See the *Rana palustris* bellying the world in the warm pool, and making up his froggy mind to accept the season for lack of a brighter; and will not a gossiping dialogue between two comfortable brown thrashers cure the heartache of half the world? Hear the charming song-sparrow, the Prima-donna of the wall-side; and the meadow-lark's sweet, timid, yet gushing lay, hymns the praise of the Divine Beauty. And —were you ever in love?

T. Was that the squeak of a night-hawk?

C. Yes, flung beyond the thin wall of nature, whereon thy fowls and beasts are spasmodically plastered, and swamped so perfectly in one of thy own race as to forget this illusory showman's wax figures?

T. A stake-driver! *pump-a-gaw, pump-a-gaw*, like an old

wooden pump. They call the bittern *butter-bump* in some countries. Everything is found in nature, even the stuff of which thou discoursest thus learnedly.

C. I would it were not, O Epaminondas Holly!

T. What, sir! and have *you* had a touch of that chicken-pox?

C. I shall not let the cat out of the bag.

T. Go in peace! I must do my best and catch that green-throated gentleman. To take frogs handsomely requires a quick eye and a fine touch, like high art. They dive under the sludge; their colors are of the water and the grass, chameleon-like. How ridiculous is yonder colt, the color of sugar gingerbread, set upon four long legs and swishing a bald tail! and how he laughs at us men-folks nibbling our crackers and herring! May our wit be as dry as our *matinée*.

E. Yesterday was Spring: to-day beginneth the second lesson, what doth Summer typify?

C. Hot ovens, a baking-pan, the taking our turn at the spit. Grasshoppers creak over dry fields, and devil's-needles whizz across your hat as if they were scorched. Black snakes conclude it is pretty comfortable, considering January in the distance. Oh! the heat is like solid beds of feathers.

E. I think you said we were going to White Pond?

C. A favorable July afternoon's plunge; the river flashes in the sun like a candle. (This little forget-me-not of ours is as pure a blue as the German's.) Ants, bees, millers, June flies, horse flies, open shop; woodchucks *set up* at the mouths of their holes, and our learned advocate, the *Mephitis chinga,*

probes the wood-roads for beetles; robins, bull-frogs, bobolinks, Maryland yellow-throats, and oven-birds perform operas
all day long; the brave *senecio* spots the sides of ditches with
its dusky gold. How sweet its root smells!

E. This is a right pleasant stroll along the Assabet.

C. First-class! The caterpillars make minced-meat of the
wild cherries. Nature does so love to pet worms,—an odd
taste. The great iris is now perfect, and the maple-leaved viburnum,—two flower-belles; the turtles dream at their ease,
with but their noses above water among the floating-heart and
potamogetons,—a good investment in a blaze. Verdure, verdure,—meadows, copses, foregrounds and distances. Showers
raise up their heads in the west to catch the leafy prospect.

E. Is it not against the dignity of man that a little light
and heat can so despoil him?

C. See that nest of breams, the parents swimming over it,
—some fun now in being tickled by a cool stream. And there
lives a lordly baron, a great manorial seignior, with a private
road to his castle of Belvoir, as good a king as can be found
in Christendom. We had best stop at Duganne's spring and
get a drink: it is as cold as charity. The swallows dart away
over the river and Nut-meadow Brook, but a few feet above
the surface, taking insects; the turtles have writ their slow
history on this Duganne sand-bank. There stretches the old
Marlboro' road, and now, gleaming beneath the trees, you
may see the water of White Pond.

E. 'T is not as large as Walden: the water looks of the like
purity.

C. Yes, 't is a pretty little Indian basin, lovely as Walden once was, and no pen could ever purely describe its beauties. We can almost see the sachem in his canoe in the shadowy cove.

E. How wonderful, as we make the circuit of the shore, are the reflections! but once we saw them in autumn, and then the marvellous effect of the colored woods held us almost to the going down of the sun. The waters, slightly rippled, took their proper character from the pines, birches, and few oaks which composed the grove; and the submarine wood seemed made of Lombardy poplar, with such delicious green, stained by gleams of mahogany from the oaks, and streaks of white from the birches, every moment more excellent: it was the world through a prism. In walking with you we may see what was never before shown to the eye of man. And yet for how many ages has this pretty wilderness of White Pond received the clouds and sun into its transparency, and woven each day new webs of birch and pine; shooting out wilder angles, and more fantastical crossings of the coarse threads, which in the water have such momentary elegance!

C. What intolerable usurpations of the Past do we see! not in Nature, which never did oppress the heart that loved her, —but in literature. See how those great hoaxes, the Homers and Shakespeares, are hindering the books and the men of to-day! You people who have been pedagogues scarcely tolerate the good things in the moderns. There is a versifier of *ours* who has made some accurate notices of our native things, —Alfred Street. I fear you must let me give you a proof of

[153]

this,—nothing from Herrick. Mate me, if you will, these passages:—

> "Yon piny knoll, thick-covered with the brown
> Dead fringes, in the sunshine's bathing flood
> Looks like dark gold."

> "The thicket by the roadside casts its cool
> Black breadth of shade across the heated dust."

> "These thistle-downs, through the rich
> Bright blue, quick float, like gliding stars, and then
> Touching the sunshine, flash and seem to melt
> Within the dazzling brilliance."

> "Another sunset, crouching low
> Upon a rising pile of cloud,
> Bathes deep the island with its glow,
> Then shrinks behind its gloomy shroud."

E. He is a good colorist.

C. Not less acute and retentive is his ear:—

> "That flying harp, the honey-bee."

> "The spider's clock
> Ticked in some crevice of the rock."

> "The light click of the milk-weed's bursting pods."

> "The spider lurks
> A close-crouched ball; out-darting, as a hum
> Dooms its trapped prey, and, looping quick its threads,
> Chains into helplessness those buzzing wings."

> "The wood-tick taps its tiny muffled drum
> To the shrill cricket-fife."

E. He saw peculiarities no one else describes.

C. Yes,—exquisite touches of creation made for his insight:—

"The whizzing of the humming-bird's swift wings
Spinning grey, glittering circles round its shape."

"Yon aster, that displayed
A brief while since its lustrous bloom, has now,
Around the shells that multiply its life,
Woven soft downy plumes."

"The gossamer motionless hung from the spray
Where the weight of the dewdrops had torn it away,
And the seed of the thistle, that whisper could swing
Aloft on its wheel, as though borne on a wing,
When the yellow-bird severed it, dipping across,
Its soft plumes unruffled, fell down on the moss."

Does the mullein (*Thapsus verbascum*) grow in England?

E. I do not remember it there, but have heard that it grows on Mount Pelion, with its architectural spire, too conspicuous to be forgotten.

C. Street notices in one of his lines something

"Beside yon mullein's braided stalk;"

and he has a picture of the early fern, "uncrumpling" as somebody says,—

"From the earth the fern
Thrusts its green, close-curled wheel;"

and he has a movement to record:—

"The snail
Creeps in its twisted fortress."

[155]

Sometimes I have thought Herrick the best of English poets, —a true Greek in England. He was a much better Grecian than Milton, who is too much like my uncle, Dr. Channing.

E. The landscape before us would give Herrick all he needed. Leaving White Pond, and passing by that dismal dell recommended by you as a valuable preserve for shooting owls, and well adapted for self-murder, we have come over a hill of the right New Hampshire slope, and now are among good rude landscapes of the Okefenokee or Quinquinabosset type,—hitherto unwalked by our Saturday afternoon professors.

C. I once thought there were some occupations that could be taken up by amateurs; but no; even walking cannot be; it must be done by professors, as you say. But what say you of "Festus,"—Bailey's poem? I can repeat you a few of his lines, —classic, and as good as those of your old dramatists.

> "How can the beauty of material things
>   So win the heart and work upon the mind,
>   Unless like-natured with them?"

> "When the soul sweeps the future like a glass,
>   And coming things, full-freighted with our fates,
>   Jut out, dark, on the offing of the mind."

> "The shadow hourly lengthens o'er my brain,
>   And peoples all its pictures with thyself."

> "And lasses with sly eyes,
>   And the smile settling in their sun-flecked cheeks,
>   Like noon upon the mellow apricot."

"To the high air sunshine and cloud are one."

"Friendship has passed me like a ship at sea."

"The wave is never weary of the wind.
. . . .
For marble is a shadow weighed with mind.
. . . .
The last high, upward slant of sun upon the trees,
Like a dead soldier's sword upon his pall."

E. And that is a pretty little poem of Swedenborg's, the beginning of a book, written in prose: "The ship is in the harbor; the sails are swelling; the east wind blows; let us weigh anchor, and put forth to sea."

C. Which of us would not choose to be one of these insects, —rosebugs of splendid fate, living on grape-flowers, apple-trees and roses, and dying of an apoplexy of sweet sensations in these golden middle days of July? Hail, vegetable gods! What saith your Adshed of the melon? for criticism needs a sop to Cerberus:—

"Color, taste and smell, smaragdus, honey and musk,
Amber for the tongue, for the eye a picture rare;
If you cut the fruit in slices, every slice a crescent fair;
If you have it whole, the full harvest moon is there."

E. I could not find it in my heart to chide the man who should ruin himself to buy a patch of well-timbered oak-land; I admire the taste which makes the avenue to a house (were the house never so small) through a wood, as this disposes the mind of the host and guest to the deference due. We want deference; and when we come to realize that thing me-

chanically, we want acres. Scatter this hot and crowded popu-
lation at respectful distances each from each, over the vacant
world. The doctor and his friends fancied it was the cattle
made all this wide space necessary; and that if there were no
cows to pasture, less land would suffice. But a cow does not
require so much land as my eyes require betwixt me and my
neighbor.

C. Man fits into Nature like a seal in its ring. Clap down
in the middle of to-day's pudding and eat thereof. They whip
lads at school for looking off their books; despatch your
Sunday plate of broth. The poet asks, —

> "Where is Skymir, giant Skymir?
> Come, transplant the woods for me!
> Scoop up yonder aged ash,
> Centennial fir, old boundary pine,
> Beech by Indian warriors blazed,
> Maples tapped by Indian girls,
> Oaks that grew in the Dark Ages:
> Heedful bring them, set them straight
> In sifted soil before my porch!
> Now turn the river on their roots,
> That no leaf wilt, or leading shoot
> Drop his tall-erected plume."

E. I admire here the waving meadow, the iron-gray house,
just the color of the granite rock below, the paths of the
thicket, the wide, straggling, wild orchard, in which Nature
has deposited every possible flavor in the apples of different
trees, — whole zones and climates she has concentrated into
apples. We think of the old benefactors who have conquered

these fields; of the old man, who is just dying in these days,
who has absorbed such volumes of sunshine, like a huge melon
or pumpkin in the sun, who has owned in every part of Concord a wood-lot, until he could not find the boundaries of
them, and never saw their interiors.

But, we say, where is he who is to save the present moment, and cause that this beauty be not lost? Shakespeare
saw no better heaven or earth, but had the power and need
to sing, and seized the dull, ugly England (ugly to this), and
made it amiable and enviable to all reading men; and now
we are forced into likening this to that; whilst, if one of us
had the chanting constitution, that land would be no more
heard of. But let us have space enough; let us have wild
grapes, and rock-maples with tubs of sugar; let us have huge
straggling orchards; let us have the *Ebba Hubbard*[1] pear,
cider-mills with tons of pomace, — walnut and oak, peat,
cows, horses, Paddies, carts, and sleds.

C. That good Welsh poet, Henry Vaughan, said, —

"O knit me that am crumbled dust."

E. Oh, certainly! Oaks and horse-chestnuts are quite obso-
lete, and the Horticultural Society are about to recommend
the introduction of the cabbage as a shade-tree; so much
more comprehensible and convenient, all grown from the
seed upward to its extreme generous crumple, within thirty

[1] Ebenezer Hubbard was the old farmer who owned the house of the
Revolutionary miller by the village Mill-dam, and left by will a thousand dollars for the monument which is now the Minute-man. F. B. S.

days,—past contradiction the ornament of the modern world, and then good to eat,—choice good, as acorns and horse-chestnuts are not. We will have shade-trees for breakfast.

Then the effrontery of one man's exhibiting more wit or merit than another! Man of genius said you? man of virtue? I tell you both are malformations, dropsies of the brain or the liver, and shall be strictly punishable in the new Commonwealth. Nothing that is not extempore shall now be tolerated. Pyramids and cities shall give place to tents; the man—soul, sack, and skeleton, which many years or ages have built up—shall go for nothing; his dinner—the rice and mutton he ate two hours ago, now fast flowing into chyle—is all we consider. And the problem,—how to detach new dinner from old man,—what we respect from what we repudiate,—is the problem for the Academies.

WALKS AND TALKS CONTINUED

"Felix ille animi, divisque simillimus ipsis,
  Quem non mordaci resplendens gloria fuco
  Solicitat, non fastosi mala gaudia luxus,
  Sed tacitos sinit ire dies, et paupere cultu
  Exigit innocuæ silentia vitæ."

POLITIAN.

"If over this world of ours
  His wings my phœnix spread,
  How gracious o'er land and sea
  The soul-refreshing shade!

"Either world inhabits he,
  Sees oft below him planets roll;
  His body is all of air compact,
  Of Allah's love his soul.

    .   '   .   .   .   .   .

"Courage, Hafiz, though not thine
  Gold wedges and silver ore,
  More worth to thee thy gift of song,
  And thy clear insight more."

HAFIZ.

"The wretched pedlear more noise he maketh to cry his
soap than a rich merchant all his dear worth wares."

ANCREN RIWLE.

CHAPTER IX

WALKS AND TALKS CONTINUED

FLINT'S POND

T. Suppose we go to Flint's.

C. Agreed.

T. That country with its high summits in Lincoln is good for breezy days. I love the mountain view from the Three Friends' Hill beyond the pond, looking over Concord. It is worth the while to see the mountains in our horizon once a day. They are the natural temples, the elevated brows of the earth, looking at which the thoughts of the beholder are naturally elevated and sublime,—etherealized. I go to Flint's Pond, also, to see a rippling lake and a reedy island in its midst,—Reed Island. A man should feed his senses with the best the land affords. These changes in the weather,—how much they surprise men who keep no journal! but look back for a year, and you will most commonly find a similar change at the same time, like the dry capsules of the violets along this wood-road. Temperatures, climates, and even clouds, may be counted (like flowers, insects, animals, and reptiles) among the constants,—inevitable reappearances; and things yet further typify each other, like the breeze rushing over the waterfall.

C. Nay, do not pierce me with your regularity, though you might say, like Peter to the sentimental lady, "Madam, my pigs never squeal."

T. Not so: learn to see its philosophy in each thing. It is a significant fact, that though no man is quite well or healthy, yet every one believes, practically, that health is the rule, and disease the exception; and each invalid is wont to think himself in a minority, and to postpone somewhat of endeavor to another state of existence. But it may be some encouragement to men to know that in this respect they stand on the same platform, that disease is in fact the rule of our terrestrial life, and the prophecy of a *celestial* life. Where is the coward who despairs because he is sick? Seen in this light, our life with all its diseases will look healthy; and, in one sense, the more healthy as it is the more diseased.

C. Upon your principle: "I am thus wet, because I am thus dry."

T. Disease is not an accident of the individual, nor even of the generation, but of life itself. In some form, and to some degree or other, it is one of the permanent conditions of life. It is a cheering fact, nevertheless, that men affirm health unanimously, and esteem themselves miserable failures. Here was no blunder. They gave us life on exactly these conditions, and methinks we shall live it with more heart when we clearly perceive that these are the terms on which we have it. Life is a warfare, a struggle, and the diseases of the body answer to the troubles and defects of the spirit. Man begins by quarrelling with the animal in him, and the result is immediate disease. In proportion as the spirit is more ambitious and persevering, the more obstacles it will meet with. It is as a seer that man asserts his disease to be exceptional.

C. Your philosophers and their tax of explanations remind me of Donne's familiar Snail:—

> "Wise emblem of our politic world,
>   Sage snail, within thine own self curled;
> Instruct me swiftly to make haste,
>   Whilst thou my feet go slowly past.
> Compendious snail! thou seem'st to me
> Large Euclid's strict epitome,
> That big still with thyself dost go,
> And livest an aged embryo."

T. And I might make that other criticism upon society and its institutions:—

> "While man doth ransack man
>   And builds on blood, and rises by distress;
> And th' inheritance of desolation leaves
>   To great-expecting hopes."

C. Then mark how man and his affairs fall in rounds: the railroad keeps time like one of Simon Willard's clocks, saturated with insurance. How much the life of certain men goes to sustain, to make respected, the institutions of society! They are the ones who pay the heaviest tax. They are, in effect, supported by a fund which society possesses for that end, or they receive a pension; and their life *seems* to be a sinecure, but it is not. Unwritten laws are the most stringent. He who is twice erratic has become the object of custom:—

> "There are whom Heaven has blessed with store of wit,
>   Yet want as much again to manage it."

E. Then am I a customer, and a paying one. Montaigne

[165]

took much pains to be made a citizen of Rome: I should much prefer to have the freedom of a peach-orchard,—once a great part of this town of Lincoln was such,—or of some plantations of apples and pears I have seen,—to that of any city. "You do not understand values," said Sylvan. "I economize every drop of sap in my trees, as if it were wine. A few years ago these trees were whipsticks: now every one of them is worth a hundred dollars. Look at their form: not a branch nor a twig is to spare. They look as if they were arms and hands and fingers, holding out to you the fruit of the Hesperides. Come, see," said he, "what weeds grow behind this fence." And he brought me to a pear-tree. "Look," he said: "this tree has every property that should belong to a plant. It is hardy and almost immortal. It accepts every species of nourishment, and can live almost on none, like a date. It is free from every form of blight. Grubs, worms, flies, bugs, all attack it. It yields them all a share of its generous juices; but, when they left their eggs on its broad leaves, it thickened its cuticle a little, and suffered them to dry up and shook off the vermin." It grows like the ash Ygdrasil.—

C. A bushel of wood-ashes were better than a cart-load of mythology. If I did not love Carlyle for his worship of heroes, I should not forgive him for setting out that ash. There is the edge of the Forest Lake, like an Indian tradition, gleaming across the pale-face's moonshine. From this Three Friends' Hill [1] (when shall we three meet again?) the distant forests have a curiously rounded or bowery look, clothing the hills

[1] The friends were Emerson, Channing, and Thoreau.

quite down to the water's edge and leaving no shore; the ponds are like drops of dew, amid and partly covering the leaves.

T. So the great globe is luxuriously crowded without margin. The groundsel, or "fire-weed," which has been touched by frost, already is as if it had died long months ago, or a fire had run through it. The black birches, now yellow on the hill-sides, look like flames; the chestnut-trees are burnished yellow as well as green. It is a beautifully clear and bracing air, with just enough coolness; full of the memory of frosty mornings, through which all things are distinctly seen, and the fields look as smooth as velvet. The fragrance of grapes is on the breeze, and the red drooping barberries sparkle amid their leaves. The horned (*cornuta*) utricularia on the sandy pond-shores is not affected by the frost. The sumacs are among the reddest leaves; the witch-hazel is in bloom, and the crows fill the landscape with a savage sound. The mullein, so conspicuous with its architectural spire, the prototype of candelabrums, must be remembered.

E. If Herrick be the best of English poets, as sometimes, when in the vein, you say (a true Greek), this landscape again could give him all he needed,—he who sang a cherry, Julia's hair (we have plenty of that), Netterby's pimple (yes), his own hen Partlet, and Ben Jonson (we have all of these, excepting a large assortment of Ben Jonsons). We possess a wider variety here among the maples; but the poetry and the prose of that age was more solid and cordial.—

C. But hear Street once more:—

[167]

THOREAU

. . . "The little violet
Pencilled with purple on one snowy leaf.

.   .   .   .   .   .

And golden-rod and aster stain the scene
With hues of sun and sky.

.   .   .   .

                    The last butterfly
Like a winged violet, floating in the meek
Pink-colored sunshine, sinks his velvet feet
Within the pillared mullein's delicate down.

.   .   .   .   .   .

Here showers the light in golden dots,
There sleeps the shade in ebon spots.

.   .   .   .

Floated the yellow butterfly,
A wandering spot of sunshine by.

.   .   .   .

        . . . the buckwheat's scented snow."

He has his prettinesses, too;

                . . . "The holy moon,
A sentinel upon the steeps of heaven.

.   .   .   .

A cluster of low roofs is prest
Against the mountain's leaning breast.

.   .   .   .

One mighty pine, amid the straggling trees,
Lifts its unchanging pyramid to heaven.

.   .   .   .

He marked the rapid whirlwind shoot,
Trampling the pine-tree with its foot.

.   .   .   .

The bee's low hum, the whirr of wings,
And the sweet songs of grass-hid things."

So Vaughan has a hint of this insight:—

"As this loud brook's incessant fall
In streaming rings re-stagnates all,
Which reach by course the bank, and then
Are no more seen.

. . . . . .

Shall my short hour, my inch,
My one poor sand.

. . . . . .

Her art, whose pensive weeping eyes
Were once sin's loose and tempting spies.

. . . .
                                    Heaven
Is a plain watch, and without figures winds
All ages up.

. . . . . .

How shrill are silent tears!"

E. But Vaughan is like the interiors of Fra Angelico.

C. Has this pond an outlet, as methinks it should, when you hold the reflections caught from its waters thus precious?

T. It has: a brook runs from the southerly end, that joins another from Beaver Pond, and, chasing swiftly down fine meadows, amid rocky knolls in Weston, goes to turn water-wheels at Stony Brook.

ROUND HILL IN SUDBURY MEADOWS

C. You judge it is three miles and a half to the point where you propose to take the boat?—

T. Yes: in the rear of the blacksmith's house,—he who calls the bittern "Baked Plum-pudding" and "Cow-poke," and the woodchuck "Squash-belly." A composed, moderate, self-understanding man;—here's the pinnace (as our neighbor names his candle-stick) for a voyage among the lilies. Why look ye so intently at the bottom?

C. I commonly sit, not *in*, but above, the water.

T. Be assured, sir, your feet are not wholly in the Concord. 'T is dry enough in July, outside,—push off; she will not sink more than four feet,—the depth here.

C. Full many a glorious morning have I seen, but not a more superb one than this. How in its glassy folds the dark, wine-colored river lays its unswept carpet across the fragrant meadows! The button-bushes and willows resound with the gleeful chorus of redwings and bobolinks, while the courageous king-bird hovers quivering over his nest. If there is any one thing birds do like, it is to sing in sunshiny mornings. Why, this is the mouth of the Pantry Brook: it comes out of the mysterious interstices of Sudbury, where the mud is up to your middle, and where some of Sam Haynes's folks died. I wish I had a photograph of Sam, the fisherman: as the man did when he was told that Crœsus was the richest man who ever lived: if he beat Sam's stories, he must have been rich. And there is Round Hill,—the river bending, yet not before we anchor in the Port of Lilies (perfumed love-tokens floating in a lapsing dream of turquoise and gold, like Cleopatra's barge); some experiments in rose-tints, too, were tried with that dear creature, the water-lily, and did well.

E. When you thus eulogize Nature, it reminds me how great an advantage he possesses who can turn a verse, over all the

human race. I read in Wood's "Athenæ Oxonienses" a score
of pages of learned nobodies, of whose once odoriferous repu-
tations not a trace remains in the air; and then I come to the
name of some Carew or Herrick, Suckling or Chapman, as
fresh and lustrous as these floating sunlight creams.

C. A Concord poet says:—

> "There are beggars in Iran and Araby,
> Said was hungrier than all;
> Men said he was a fly
> That came to every festival,
> Also he came to the mosque
> In trail of camel and caravan,
> Out from Mecca to Isphahan;—
> Northward he went to the snowy hills,—
> At court he sat in the grave divan.
>
> His music was the south wind's sigh,
> His lamp the maiden's downcast eye,
> And ever the spell of beauty came
> And turned the drowsy world to flame.
> By lake and stream and gleaming hall,
> And modest copse, and the forest tall,
> Where'er he went the magic guide
> Kept its place by the poet's side.
>
> Tell me the world is a talisman,
> To read it must be the art of man;
> Said melted the days in cups like pearl,
> Served high and low, the lord and the churl;
> Loved harebells nodding on a rock,
> A cabin hung with curling smoke,
> And huts and tents, nor loved he less

Stately lords in palaces,
Fenced by form and ceremony."[1]

T. There, on Round Hill, is a true woodman's hut. The hill is low, but from its position enjoys a beautiful outlook upon Sudbury meadows. Yes: this is a good place to fish. Can you keep worms in your mouth, like Indians? Maybe they won't bite.

C. Which,—fish, worms, or Indians? Things that are done it is needless to speak about, or remonstrate against: things that are past are needless to blame.—

THE DOG PETER, OR BOSE[2]

C. I fancied the saying, that man was created a little lower than the angels, should have been, a little lower than the *animals!*

T. Does it not flavor of puerile conceit, that fancy?

C. The conceit of man is dark; but, as we go to Goose-shore swimming-place, on the Assabet, with Peter running before, I feel sorry that Goethe introduced a black dog in "Faust," as the kernel of the elephant. And the wild animals are superior to the tame, just as the Indian treads before the civilized man. Observe Peter capering through bush and briar, plunging into pool or stream, with his smiling tail! and he sweats through his nose. What dull pedants the mirth-provoking creatures consider us! and how more than tame

[1] Verses of Emerson's, first printed by Channing here.
[2] One of Channing's dogs, kept by him in 1853–54.

poor Cowper's three tame hares may have deemed him, in his nightcap, made by Mrs. Unwin! Peter catches no cold, though he wets his feet, and never has the doctor. As the Indians amused the Jesuits in Canada, by sitting all day in a nude manner, frozen to the ice, and fishing complacently through holes in it, as if lolling on feather beds, so I have known Peter take a nap all night on a snow-bank in January.

There, he's at the base of that mud-hole; Lyell was never deeper in geology than he is.

T. [*Journal, August 29, 1851.*] I saw a man by the river, working with a horse in a field, carting dirt, and the horse and man's relations to him struck me as very remarkable. There was the horse, a mere animated machine (though his tail was brushing off the flies), his whole existence subordinated to the man's; with no tradition, perhaps no instinct, in him of a time when he was wild and free,—completely humanized. No compact had been made with him that he should have the Saturday afternoons, or the Sundays, or any holidays; his independence never being recognized, and it being now forgotten both by men and horses that the horse was ever free. For I am not aware that there are any wild horses surely known not to be descended from tame ones. He was assisting that man to pull down that bank and spread it over the meadow; only keeping off the flies with his tail, and stamping and catching a mouthful of grass or leaves from time to time, on his own account,—all the rest for Man. It seemed hardly worth while that he should be *animated* for this. It was plain that the man was not educating the horse; not trying to develop his nature, but merely getting work out of him. That mass of animated matter seemed more completely the servant of man than any inanimate.

For slaves have their holidays; a heaven is conceded to them, but to the horse none; now and for ever he is man's slave. The more I considered, the more the man seemed akin to the horse; only his was the stronger will of the two; for a little further on I saw an Irishman shovelling, who evidently was as much tamed as the horse. He had stipulated that, to a certain extent, his independence be recognized, and yet really he was but little more independent.

I had always regarded the horse as a free people somewhere, living wild; as whatever has not come under the sway of man is wild. In this sense original and independent men are wild,—not tamed and broken by society. Now for my part I have such a respect for the horse's nature as would tempt me to let him alone; not to interfere with him,—his walks, his diet, his loves. But by mankind he is treated simply as an engine which must have rest and is sensible of pain. Suppose that every squirrel was made to turn a coffee-mill; suppose that the gazelles were made to draw milk-carts!

There he was, with his tail cut off because it was in the way, or to suit his master's taste; his mane trimmed and his feet shod with iron, that he might wear longer. What is a horse but an animal that has lost his liberty? what is it but a system of slavery? and do you not by insensible and unimportant degrees come to human slavery? And has man got any more liberty himself for having robbed the horse? Or has he lost just as much of his own, and become more like the horse he has robbed? Is not the other end of the bridle, too, in this case, coiled around his own neck? hence stable-boys, jockeys, and all that class daily transported by fast horses. There he stood, with his oblong, square figure (his tail being cut off) seen against the water, brushing off the flies with his tail, and stamping; braced back while the man was filling the cart.

No doubt man impresses his own character on the beasts which he tames and employs. They are not only humanized, but they acquire his particular human nature. John Hosmer's dog sprang up, ran out and growled at us; and in his eye I seemed to see the eye of his master. How much oxen are like farmers, and cows like farmers' wives, and young steers and heifers like farmers' boys and girls! The farmer acts on the ox, and the ox reacts on the farmer; they do not meet half-way, it is true, but they do meet at a distance from the centre of each, proportionate to each one's intellectual power. The farmer is ox-like in his walk, in his strength, in his trust-worthiness, in his taste.

C. "The ill that's wisely feared is half withstood."

I regard the horse as a human being in a humble state of existence. Virtue is not left to stand alone; he who practises it will have neighbors.

T. [*Journal, September 4, 1851.*] Man conceitedly names the intelligence and industry of animals "instinct," and overlooks their wisdom and fitness of behavior. I saw where the squirrels

had carried off the ears of corn more than twenty rods from
the corn-field, to the woods. A little further on, beyond Hubbard's Brook, I saw a gray squirrel with an ear of yellow
corn, a foot long, sitting on the fence, fifteen rods from the
field. He dropped the corn, but continued to sit on the rail
where I could hardly see him, it being of the same color with
himself, which I have no doubt he was well aware of. He next
went to a red maple, where his policy was to conceal himself
behind the stem, hanging perfectly still there till I passed,
his fur being exactly the color of the bark. When I struck
the tree, and tried to frighten him, he knew better than to
run to the next tree, there being no continuous row by which
he might escape; but he merely fled higher up, and put so
many leaves between us that it was difficult to discover him.
When I threw up a stick to frighten him, he disappeared en-
tirely, though I kept the best watch I could, and stood close
to the foot of the tree.

C. They *are* wonderfully cunning!

T. That is all you can say for *them*. There is something
pathetic to think of in such a life as an average Carlisle *man*
may be supposed to live, drawn out to eighty years; and he
has died, perchance, and there is nothing but the mark of his
cider-mill left. Here was the cider-mill, and there the orchard,
and there the hog-pasture, and so men lived and ate, and
drank, and passed away like vermin. Their long life was mere
duration. As respectable is the life of the woodchuck, which
perpetuates its race in the orchard still. That is the life of
these *select men* spun out. They will be forgotten in a few

years, even by such as themselves, as vermin. They will be known like Kibbe, who is said to have been a large man, who weighed 250, who had five or six heavy daughters who rode to Concord meeting-house on horseback, taking turns; they were so heavy that one could only ride at once. What, then, would redeem such a life? We only know that they ate and drank, and built barns and died, and were buried, and still, perchance, their tombstones cumber the ground,—"time's dead low water." There never has been a girl who learned to bring up a child, that she might afterwards marry.

C. Perhaps you depreciate humanity, and overestimate somewhat else.

E. A whimsical person[1] said once, he should make a prayer to the chance that brought him into the world. He fancied that when the child had escaped out of the womb, he cried, "I thank the bridge that brought me safe over: I would not for ten worlds take the next one's chance!" Will they, one of these days, at Fourierville, make boys and girls to order and pattern? I want, Mr. Christmas-office, a boy between No. 17 and No. 134, half-and-half of both; you might add a trace of 113. I want a pair of little girls like 91, only a tinge more of the Swede, and a tinge of the Moorish.

Men are so careless about their really good side. James Baker does not imagine that he is a rich man, yet he keeps from year to year that lordly park of his, by Fairhaven Pond, lying idly open to all comers, without crop or rent, like another Lord Breadalbane, with its hedges of Arcady, its sump-

---

[1] It was Ellery Channing.

tuous lawns and slopes, its orchard and grape-vines, the mirror at its foot, and the terraces of Hollowell on the opposite bank.

C. Yet I know he would reprove me, as our poet has written:—

> "Said Saadi,—When I stood before
> Hassan the camel-driver's door,
> I scorned the fame of Timour brave,—
> Timour to Hassan was a slave.
> In every glance of Hassan's eye
> I read rich years of victory.
> And I, who cower mean and small
> In the frequent interval,
> When wisdom not with me resides,
> Worship toil's wisdom that abides!
> I shunned his eyes,—the faithful man's,
> I shunned the toiling Hassan's glance."

Work, yes; and good conduct additional. You have been, so I have read, a schoolmaster. I trust you advised your neophytes "to keep company with none but men of learning and reputation; to behave themselves upon the place with candor, caution, and temperance; to avoid compotations; to go to bed in good time, and rise in good time; to let them see you are men that observe hours and discipline; to make much of yourself, and want nothing that is fit for you." The life of Cæsar himself has no greater example for us than our own. We must thrust against a door to know whether it is bolted against us or not. "Where there is no difficulty, there is no praise; and every human excellence must be the product of good fortune, improved by hard work and genius."

THE LATTER YEAR

"Come, sleep! Oh, sleep! the certain knot of peace,
    The baiting-place of wit, the balm of woe,
    The poor man's wealth, the prisoner's release,
    The indifferent judge between the high and low."

SIDNEY.

"You meaner beauties of the night
    That poorly satisfy our eyes,
    More by your number than your light;
    You common people of the skies,
    What are you when the moon shall rise?"

H. WOTTON.

        .   .   .   "in the dust be equal made
    With the poor crooked scythe and spade."

SHIRLEY.

"Astrochiton Heracles, King of fire, Chorus-leader of the world,
Sun, Shepherd of mortal life, who castest long shadows, riding
spirally the whole heaven with burning disk, rolling the twelve-
monthed year, the son of Time, thou performest orbit after orbit."

NONNUS.

"It is not but the tempest that doth show
    The seaman's cunning, but the field that tries
    The captain's courage."

BEN JONSON.

CHAPTER X

THE LATTER YEAR

C. Do you observe how long the cultivated trees hold their leaves, such as apples, cherries, and peaches? As if they said, "We can longer maintain our privileges than yonder uncultured generation." The black willows stand bare along the edges of the river; the balm-of-Gileads and a few triumphant elms yet hang out their dusky banners on the outward walls of the latter year. That Indian summer, too, made its tranquil appearance,—put in leg-bail for the greasy old redskins.

T. After the verdure goes, after the harvest of the year is gathered in, there is a stationary period,—the year travels on a paved road. It is with leaves as with fruits and woods and animals: when they are mature, their different characters appear. That migration of the birds is a cunning get-off. The most peaceful, the sunniest autumn day in New England has a blue background, like some cultivated person at the bottom of whose palaver is ice. I hear the barking of a red squirrel whose clock is set a-going by a little cause in cool weather, when the spring is tense; and a great scolding and ado among the jays. The housewives of Nature wish to see the rooms properly cleaned and swept, before the upholsterer comes and nails down his carpet of snow. The swamp burns along its margin with the scarlet berries of the black alder, or prinos; the leaves of the pitcher-plant (which old Josselyn called

Hollow-leaved Lavender) abound, and are of many colors, from plain green to a rich striped yellow, or deep red.

C. Street says,—

> "The hickory-shell, cracked open by its fall,
> Shows its ripe fruit, an ivory ball, within;
> And the white chestnut-burr displays its sheath
> White glistening with its glossy nuts below.
> Scattered around, the wild rose-bushes hang,
> Their ruby buds tipping their thorny sprays;
> The Everlasting's blossoms seem as cut
> In delicate silver, whitening o'er the slopes;
> The seedy clematis, branched high, is robed
> With woolly tufts; the snowy Indian-pipe
> Is streaked with black decay; the wintergreen
> Offers its berries; and the prince's-pine,
> Scarce seen above the fallen leaves, peers out,
> A firm, green, glossy wreath."

T. Now you allude to it, does not a deception like that of the climate pervade the men? The downright cheer of old England struggling through its brogue, the dazzling stiletto affliction of Italy and France, with us are lacking. Like our climate, and our scale of classes, the sentiment of New England is changeable. It is one of the year's expiring days, one of his death-bed days. The children, playing at the school-house a mile off, the rattle of distant carts, farmers' voices calling to their cattle, cocks crowing in unknown barn-yards, every sound speeds through the attenuated air, as the beat of the death-tick echoes in the funeral chamber! The trees are as bare as my purse. How significant is the effect of these blue smokes, as if they came from some olfactory altar of the Parsees, imploring the protection of yon threadbare luminary! Methinks is something divine in the culinary art, — the silent columns of light-blue vapor rising slowly. Beneath them many a rusty kettle sings.

C. "To intersoar unseen delights the more."
QUARLES.

E. I cannot doubt but the range of the thermometer invades the morals of the people. The puritan element survives in our cultivated conservatism, if there is gilding on the chain. Certain families resolve to divide themselves from the mass by ingenious marriages. And talent tries to keep its head above low-water, yet the agreeable orators, who go to Plymouth and delectate the mass, if you come at them in parlors, are simple creatures; and our great historian, Prescott, took the weight of his waistcoat before he went forth.

C. 'T is well he was not forced to conceal the ravelled sleeve of care by buttoning up his outer garment. A few years past, yonder breezy representative may have been an usher in a school, where, doubtless, filigree was taught.

FROSTY WEATHER

T. Winter is fairly broached. When the year becomes cold, then we know how the pine and cypress are the last to lose their leaves. —

C. I should say he is in such a condition that tapping is impossible: —

[183]

"The moon has set, the Pleiades are gone;
  'T is the mid-noon of night; the hour is by,
  And yet I watch alone,"

says Sappho in Percival.

T. How hollow echoes the frozen road, under the wheels of the teamster's wagon! The muzzles of the patient steers are fringed in ice, and their backs whitened with hoar-frost. For all the singing-birds, the chickadees remain; the sawing and scraping of the jay and the crows do remotely pertain to music. A single night snaps the year in two. In the declaration of Tang, it is said, O sun, when wilt thou expire? We will die with thee. Percival makes Sappho say,—

"Sweet mother! I can weave the web no more,
  So much I love the youth, so much I lingering love."

C. Shadows hang like flocks of ink from the pitch-pines; the winter sunset, the winter twilight, falls slowly down and congeals the helpless valleys; the sky has a base of lustrous apple-green, and then flows softly up to the zenith that tender roseate flush, like a virgin's cheek when she is refusing the youth. Is winter a cheat? "Neighbor," as Margaret says when she finds Faust is, "lend me your smelling-bottle." The weather forms its constitution in our people, and they are equal to it. As we catch a morsel of warmth behind this sunny rock, I'll sing you a song about old King Cole:—

THE LATTER YEAR

TEAMSTERS' SONG

How the wind whistled! how flew the snow!
The teamsters knew not if 't were still or no,
And the trains stood puffing, all kept away back,
And the drifts lay deep o'er the railroad track;
While the snow it flew, and the wind it blew,
And the teamsters bawled, — what a jolly crew!

Their caps are all dressed with the muskrat fur,
But the colder the weather (the truth I aver),
Still less do they turn to the soft, silky lining;
Their ears are of stone, — 't is easy divining, —
And their hearts full of joy, while the snow whirls fast,
And the lash of the North swings abroad on the blast.

And the sky is steel on the white cloud flecked,
And the pines are ghosts in their snow-wreaths decked,
And the stormy surge of the gale is rising
While the teamster enjoys the tempest surprising,
With his lugging-sled and his oxen four;
When the wind roars the hardest, he bawls all the more.

C. Did you never admire the steady, silent, windless fall of
the snow in some lead-colored day, silent save the little tick-
ing of the flakes as they touch the twigs?[1] It is chased silver,
moulded over the pines and oak-leaves. Soft shades hang like
curtains along the closely draped wood-paths. Frozen apples
become little cider-vats. The old, crooked apple-trees, frozen
stiff in the pale shivering sunlight that appears to be dying
of consumption, gleam forth like the heroes of one of Dante's

[1] This was quoted by an English reviewer as one of the best descriptions
of nature by Thoreau. But in fact it was all written by me. w. e. c.

[185]

cold hells; we would not mind a change in the mercury of the dream. The snow crunches under the foot, the chopper's axe rings funereally through the tragic air. At early morn the frost on button-bushes and willows was silvery, and every stem and minutest twig and filamentary weed became a silver thing, while the cottage-smokes came up salmon-colored into that oblique day. At the base of ditches were shooting crystals, like the blades of an ivory-handled pen-knife, and rosettes and favors, fretted of silver, on the flat ice. The little cascades in the brook were ornamented with transparent shields, and long candelabrums, and spermaceti-colored fools' caps, and plaited jellies, and white globes, with the black water whirling along transparently underneath. The sun comes out, and all at a glance rubies, sapphires, diamonds, and emeralds start into intense life on the angles of the snow-crystals.

T. You remember that Dryden says, "common-sense is a rule in everything but matters of faith and revelation."

C. Because he lived in Will's coffee-house. He would have had an *ideal* sense, had he experienced a New England winter. Frost is your safest shoe-leather in the marshes. How red the andromeda-leaves have turned! Snow and ice remind us of architecture. No lathe ever made such handsome scrolls and friezes.

T. And to the arctic man these cold matters make paradise. As Kudlago, the Eskimo, who was going home aboard ship from warmer climes, cried, in his dying moment, "*Teiko-se Ko, teiko-se Ko?*"—Do you see ice, do you see ice?

You once wrote this:—

THE LATTER YEAR

"By fall and fount, by gleaming hill,
And sheltered farmhouse still and gray,
   By broad, wild marsh and wood-set rill,
Dies cold and sere the winter's day.
Oh, icy sunlight, fade away!

"Thou pale magnificence of fate!
Thy arch is but the loitering cloud,
   A tall pine-wood thy palace-gate,
The alder-buds thy painted crowd,
Some far-off road thy future proud,
Much cold security allowed."

C. Art and architecture, I suppose, you consider the same thing. If I visited galleries where pictures are preserved, I would go now, though Hawthorne says he would as soon see a basilisk as one of the old pictures at the Boston Athenæum. I think the fine art of Goethe and company very dubious; and it is doubtful whether all this talk about prints of the old Italian school means anything (Giotto and the rest). It may do very well for idle gentlemen.

E. I reply, there is a fire to every smoke. There were a few Anakim who gave the thing vogue by their realism. If Odin wrought in iron or in ships, these worked as rancorously in paint. Michel Angelo, Ribeira (the man that made the skull and the monk, who is another skull looking at it), and the man who made in marble the old Torso Hercules; the Phidias, man or men, who made the Parthenon friezes, had a drastic style, which a blacksmith or a stone-mason would say was starker than their own. And I adhere to Van Waagen's belief, that there is a pleasure from works of art which nothing else can yield. Yes, we should have a water-color exhibition in Boston; but I should like better to have water-color tried in the art of writing. Let our troubadours have one of these Spanish slopes of the dry ponds or basins which run from Walden to the river at Fairhaven, in their September dress of color, under a glowering sky,—the Walden sierras given as a theme,—and they required to daguerreotype that in good words.

C. I will do my best; but, as we were speaking of architecture, remember that this art consists in the imitation of natural Principles, and not like the other arts in the imitation of natural Forms.

E. I never know the reason why our people have not reached some appropriate style of architecture. In Italy and Switzerland and England, the picturesque seems to spring forth from the soil, in the shapes of buildings, as well seasoned as its trees and flowers themselves. But look at the clapboard farmhouse we are passing! Is there not a needless degree of stiffness and too little ornamentation?

C. Moderate your criticism, my dear Gilpin: utility lies at the bottom of our village architecture; the structure springs out of that. This simple edifice, created out of white pine-boards and painted white; this case of shingles and clapboards appears to its owner—who built it and lives in it—anything but ugly or unpicturesque: so far from it, it fits him like a shell. Our climate has something to answer for with respect to this scarcity of ornament and beauty. The subtle influence of the weather crops out in the very clapboards, as it does also in the garments of the farmer, who gets their benefits: the untamable burning summer, the fatally penetrative winter, with warm places sometimes intercalated, when the honey-bees come forth and the black ploughed fields shine like a horse after he has been rubbed down. Brick and stone are too damp, and the wall-paper will mould and the cellar run with water, even in the dryest wooden house, unless it be warmed throughout, so pungent is the condensing essence of winter. Then, if you put on outside adorning, it will be warred upon to such a degree by the elements as to be scarcely appropriate to the plain fancies of our farmers: the face of the house is only a mirror of the climate. The roof should have sufficient steepness to carry off rain and snow readily, with as few breaks and angles as possible; the windows not too large, — in fact, warmth and coolness must, in one of these New England houses, be consulted at the same time, situated as they are in an excessive climate. On the sea-coast the old houses are usually one story high, thus offering the least surface to the wind. The low cottage, all on one floor, will not keep us cool in summer; and the high Italian style is a comb of ice in February. Then I know that Mr. Gilpin censures the location of the farm-buildings so close upon the road, and that he wishes to set them at the end of an avenue a long distance from the entrance-gate; that he equally detests the position of the barn within a few rods of the house, — privacy, good taste, refinement, as he says, are thus all sacrificed at one blow. Our farmers cut the timber for their mansions in their own woods, shape it themselves, and bring it upon the ground. Utility, economy, comfort, and use,—a dry, warm cellar, a sweet, airy milk-room, a large wood-shed, a barn with its cellars and accommodations, and all in the most solid style,—these matters make the study of the farmer. He desires a house to live in, not to look at. He must have a pump in the kitchen and one in the cow-yard; and the kitchen, indeed, needs to be much considered. It should be warm, airy, well lighted, connected with cellar, shed, yard, road,—and in fact it is a room in use most of the time. The barn and house must be placed with reference to the farm itself: near a village, school, church, store, post-office, station, and the like. All this, it is true, has little to do with the fine art of architecture. Our native democrat, whose brains, boots, and bones are spent in composing a free republic and earning money, is growing up to the fine arts, even if at present utility sways the balance.

T. This creature, whose portrait you have thus fancifully drawn, looks like a mere machine for gravitating to pork and potatoes, an economical syllogism. I say beauty must have an equal place with utility, if not a precedent. Your farmer shirks architecture and landscape-gardening, with one leg in the barn and the other in the kitchen, and the compost-heap in the midst; and whose highest ambition is to have a patent-leather top to his carriage. Go to! you libel my jolly country-man. He is no such thieving rat as this, with a singed tail and his ears snipped off. The duke king of T"se had a thousand teams, each of four horses; but on the day of his death the people did not praise him for a single virtue.

THE LATTER YEAR

C. O brother Gilpin! hearken ere you die. Those inveterate prejudices of yours for Vitruvius and Inigo Jones have left you too little sympathy with the industrious, able yeoman of New England. I have but drawn a few lines of his portrait. The climate is close, the soil difficult, the clapboard edifice not alluring in its aspect. Let this be so: the creator of it, the citizen, stands up like a king in the midst of the local penury. How well he can write and cipher! how intelligent! He receives the news from all lands each day in his paper, and has his monthly journals and lyceum lectures. There is a sweetness, a native pride, in the man, that overtops the rugged necessities of his condition, and shoots its fine branches heavenward. His healthful economic industry, and that practical education derived from a constant use of natural elements, and a life-long struggle against difficulties, renders him incredibly expert and capable of seizing all expedients whereby he can better his conditions. The New England farmer has proved that an independent man, a democratic citizen, on a poor soil and in unfavorable positions, can overcome the outward obstacles. He has solved the problem of democracy, and must give place to some new forms of society, when all the arts shall be employed in the construction of the estate.

E. "Boon nature yields each day a brag which we now first behold,
And trains us on to slight the new as if it were the old;
And blest is he who playing deep, yet haply asks not why,
Too busy with the crowded day to fear to live or die."

WALDEN

C. I believe you take some note of the seasons. Pray, what is this? On our old path to Walden Pond I cannot really decide whether I or the world have had the opiate. Assuredly it must be autumn, if it is not summer. How tacitly the pond sleeps! These pine-stumps, after the pitch is dry, make excellent seats. The semi-clouded sky images itself so truthfully in the slumbering water that sky and water form one piece, and the glancing swallows flying above that invisible surface seem to be playing with their own images reversed. Not with the very utmost scrutiny can I distinguish between the twain. And so you think the superiorities of the Englishman grow out of his insular climate. Shakespeare's beauties were never cradled on the rack of a New English summer. If our landscape stew with heat, the brain becomes another stew-pan. As most of our days are unutterably brilliant, I enjoy the few scattered gray and lowering ones, half-shade and half-shine, the negative days.

> E. In the turbulent beauty
> Of a gusty autumn day,
> Poet on a sunny headland
> Sighed his soul away.
> Farms the sunny landscape dappled,
> Swan-down clouds dappled the farms,
> Cattle lowed in hollow distance
> Where far oaks outstretched their arms.
> Sudden gusts came full of meaning,
> All too much to him they said,

THE LATTER YEAR

South winds have long memories,
Of that be none afraid.
I cannot tell rude listeners
Half the tell-tale south wind said,
'T would bring the blushes of yon maples
To a man and to a maid.

The golden loveliness of autumn, — was that your phrase?
C. Rather fine, methinks, for the like of me!

T. A pretty rustic wreath could be braided of wild berries now, including such as the dark blue magical berries of the red-osier cornel, the maple-leaved viburnum with its small bluish-black berries, and, though so fragile, we might add, for the passing hour, the purple might of the great elderberry clusters. Why not wreathe wild grapes, prinos, and smilax berries together, and the berries of the andromeda? Then the purple-stemmed golden-rod and the blue gentian's flowers should not be omitted from this votive offering to Ceres; and it should be suspended from a white maple whence we could steal a glimpse through the charming Septembrian sunflood, with its sense of fulness and everlasting life, over the quivering river that is blue and sunny, silvery, golden, and azure at once, transparent olives and olive-greens glazed to a complete polish, and bounded by the softest shimmer, not transparent. I have been reading a report on herbaceous plants. The mere names of reeds and grasses, of the milkweeds and the mints, the gentians, the mallows and trefoils, are poems. Erigeron, because it grows old early, is the old man of the spring; *Pyrola umbellata* is called *chimaphila*, lover of winter, since its green leaves look so cheerful in the snow; also called prince's-pine. The plantain (*Plantago major*), which follows man wherever he builds a house, is called by the Indians white-man's foot; and I like well to see a mother or one of her girls stepping outside of the door with a lamp, for its leaf, at night, to dress some slight wound or inflamed hand or foot. My old pet, the *Liatris*, acquires some new interest from being an approved remedy for the bite of serpents, and hence called rattlesnake's-master. Fire-weed, or *Hieracium*, springs up abundantly on burnt land. The aromatic fields of dry *Gnaphalium* with its pearly incorruptible flower, and the sweet-flags with their bayonet-like flash, wave again, thanks to this dull professor, in my memory, on even a cold winter's morning. Even the naming of the localities—ponds, shady woods, wet pastures, and the like—comforts us. But this heavy country professor insults some of my favorites,—the well-beloved *Lespedeza*, for instance; the beautiful *Epigæa*, or Mayflower, —pride of Plymouth hermits. The hills still bear the remembrance of sweet berries; and I suppose the apple or the huckleberry to have this comfortable fitness to the human palate, because they are only the palate inverted: one is man eating, and the other man eatable. The *Mikania scandens*, with its purplish-white flowers, now covers the button-bushes and willows, by the side of streams; and the large-flowered bidens (*chrysanthemoides*), and various-colored polygonums, white and reddish and red, stand high among the bushes and weeds by the river-side; and, in modest seclusion, our scarlet imperialists, the lordly Cardinals.

[194]

C. You have a rare season in your shanty by the pond.

T. I have gained considerable time for study and writing, and proved to my satisfaction that life may be maintained at less cost and labor than by the old social plan. Yet I would not insist upon any one's trying it who has not a pretty good supply of internal sunshine; otherwise he would have, I judge, to spend too much of his time in fighting with his dark humors. To live alone comfortably, we must have that self-comfort which rays out of Nature,—a portion of it at least.

C. I sometimes feel the coldest days
  A beam upon the snow-drift thrown,
As if the sun's declining rays
  Were with his summer comforts sown.

The icy marsh, so cold and gray,
  Hemmed with its alder copses brown,
The ruined walls, the dying day,
  Make in my dream a landscape crown.

And sweet the walnuts in the fall,
  And bright the apples' lavished store;
Thus sweet my winter's pensive call,
  O'er cold, gray marsh, o'er upland hoar.

And happier still that we can roam
  Free and untrammelled o'er the land,
And think the fields and clouds are home,
  Not forced to press some stranger's hand.

MULTUM IN PARVO

> "There's nothing left
> Unto Andrugio but Andrugio: and that
> Not mischief, force, distress, nor hell can take;
> Fortune my fortunes not my mind shall shake."
>
> MARSTON.

> "There, your Majesty, what a glimpse, as into infinite extinct Continents, filled with ponderous, thorny inanities, invincible nasal drawling of didactic Titans, and the awful attempt to spin, on all manner of wheels, road-harness out of split cobwebs: Hoom! Hoom-m-m! Harness not to be had on those terms."
>
> CARLYLE'S FREDERICK.

> "My dears, you are like the heroines of romance, —jewels in abundance, but scarce a rag to your backs."
>
> MADAME DE SÉVIGNÉ.

CHAPTER XI

MULTUM IN PARVO

As already noticed, Thoreau believed that one of the arts of life was to make the most out of it. He loved the *multum in parvo*, or pot-luck; to boil up the little into the big. Thus, he was in the habit of saying,—Give me healthy senses, let me be thoroughly alive, and breathe freely in the very flood-tide of the living world. But this should have availed him little, if he had not been at the same time copiously endowed with the power of recording what he imbibed. His senses truly lived twice.

Many thousands of travellers pass under the telegraph poles, and descry in them only a line of barked chestnuts: to our poet-naturalist they came forth a Dodona's sacred grove, and like the old Grecian landscapes followed the phantasy of our Concord Orpheus, twanging on their road.

(*Thoreau's Journal, September 3, 1851.*) "As I went under the new telegraph wire, I heard it vibrating like a harp high overhead; it was as the sound of a far-off glorious life; a supernal life which came down to us, and vibrated the lattice-work of this life of ours,—an Æolian harp. It reminded me, I say, with a certain pathetic moderation, of what finer and deeper stirrings I was susceptible, which grandly set all argument and dispute aside; a triumphant though transient exhibition of the truth. It told me, by the finest strain that a human ear can hear,—yet conclusively and past all refutation,

[199]

—that there were higher (infinitely higher) planes of life, which it behooved me not to forget. As I was entering the Deep Cut,[1] the wind, which was conveying a message to me from Heaven, dropt it on the wire of the telegraph, which it vibrated as it past. I instantly sat down on a stone at the foot of the telegraph pole, and attended to the communication. It merely said: 'Bear in mind, Child, and never for an instant forget, that there are higher planes, infinitely higher planes of life than this thou art now travelling on. Know that the goal is distant and is upward, and is worthy all your life's efforts to attain to.' And then it ceased; and tho' I sat some minutes longer, I heard nothing more."

(*September 12.*) "There is every variety and degree of inspiration, from mere fulness of life to the most rapt mood. A human soul is played on even as this wire; which now vibrates slowly and gently, so that the passer can hardly hear it; and anon the sound swells and vibrates with such intensity as if it would rend the wire, as far as the elasticity and tension of the wire permits; and now it dies away and is silent; and though the breeze continues to sweep over it, no strain comes from it, and the traveller hearkens in vain. It is no small gain to have this wire stretched through Concord, though there is no office here. I make my own use of the telegraph, without consulting the Directors; like the sparrows, which, I observe, use it extensively for a perch. Shall I not go to this office, to hear if there is any communication for me, as steadily as to the Post-office in the Village?"

[1] Of the Fitchburg Railroad, towards Lincoln.

MULTUM IN PARVO

(*September 22.*) "The stronger winds of autumn have begun
to blow, and the telegraph-harp has sounded loudly. I heard
it especially this afternoon,—the tone varying with the tension of different parts of the wire. The sound proceeds from
near the posts, where the vibration is apparently more rapid.
I put my ear to one post, and it seemed to me as if every pore
of the wood was filled with music. It labored with the strain
as if every fibre was affected, and being seasoned or tuned,—
rearranged according to a new and more harmonious law.
Every swell and change and inflection of tone pervaded and
seemed to proceed from the wood,—a divine tree or wood,—
as if its very substance was transmuted.

"What a recipe for preserving wood,—perchance to preserve it from rotting,—to fill its pores with music! How this
wild tree from the forest, stripped of its bark and set up here,
rejoices to transmit this music! When no music proceeds from
the wire, on applying my ear I hear the hum within the en-
trails of the wood,—the oracular tree acquiring, accumulating
the prophetic fury! The resounding wood! how much the
ancients would have made of it! To have a harp on so great
a scale, girdling the very earth, and played on by the winds
of every latitude and longitude; and that harp (as it were)
the manifest blessing of Heaven on a work of Man's! Shall we
not add a tenth Muse to the immortal Nine, and say that the
invention was divinely honored and distinguished on which
the Muse has condescended to smile? is the magic medium of
communication for mankind? May we read that the ancients
stretched a wire round the earth, attaching it to the trees of

the forest, by which they sent messages by one named Electricity, father of Lightning and Magnetism, swifter far than Mercury,—the stern commands of war and the news of peace, —and that the winds caused this wire to vibrate, so that it emitted an Æolian music in all the lands through which it passed, as if to express the satisfaction of the Gods in this invention? Yet this is fact; and we have yet attributed the invention to no god.

"The Telegraph-harp sounds strongly in the midst of the rain. I put my ear to the tree, and I hear it working terribly within; and anon it swells into a clear tone which seems to concentrate in the core of the tree; for all the sound seems to proceed from the wood. It is as if you had entered some world-famous cathedral, resounding to some vast organ. The fibres of all things have their tension, and are strained like the strings of a lyre. I feel the very ground tremble underneath my feet as I stand near the post. This wire vibrates with great power, as if it would strain and rend the wood. What an awful and fateful music it must be to the worms in the wood! No better vermifuge were needed. As the wood of an old Cremona—its very fibre perchance harmoniously transposed, and educated to resound melody—has brought a great price, so, methinks, these telegraph posts should bear a great price with musical instrument makers. They are prepared to be the material of harps for ages to come; as it were, put a-soak and seasoning in music."

Much more was he, who drew this ravishing noise off a stale

post, a golden wire of communication with the blessed divinities! With poetic insight he married practical perception; avoiding that flying off in space, like the writings of some who pursued the leading of the Rev. Bismiller, where there is the theatrical breadth of a pasteboard sky, with not much life rolling in it,

> "But troops of smoothing people that collaud
>   All that we do."

Or, as he observes, "Not till after several months does an infant find its hands, and it may be seen looking at them with astonishment, holding them up to the light; and so also it finds its toes. How many faculties there are which we have never found! We want the greatest variety within the smallest compass, and yet without glaring diversity, and we have it in the color of the withered oak-leaves." He speaks of fleets of yellow butterflies, and of the gray squirrels on their winding way, on their unweariable legs. Distant thunder is the battle of the air. "A cow looking up at the sky has an almost human or wood-god, faun-like expression, and reminded me of some frontispiece to Virgil's Bucolics. When the red-eye (*Vireo*) ceases, then, I think, is a crisis. The pigeons, with their *quivet*, dashed over the Duganne desert." When the snow-birds flew off, their wave actually broke over him, as if he were a rock. He sees two squirrels answering one to the other, as it were, like a vibrating watchspring,— they withdrew to their airy houses. . . . "When turning my head I looked at the willowy edges of Cyanean meadow, and onward to the sober-colored but fine-grained Clam-shell hills, about which there was no glitter, I was inclined to think that the truest beauty was that which surrounded us, but which we failed to discern; that the forms and colors which adorn our daily life, not seen afar in the horizon, are our fairest jewelry. The beauty of Clam-shell hill near at hand, with its sandy ravines, in which the cricket chirps,—this is an *occidental* city, not less glorious than we dream of in the sunset sky.

"At Clematis Brook I perceive that the pods or follicles of the common milkweed (*Asclepias syriaca*) now point upward. They are already bursting. I release some seeds with the long, fine silk attached: the fine threads fly apart at once (open with a spring), and then ray themselves out into a hemi-spherical form, each thread freeing itself from its neighbor, and all reflecting rainbow or prismatic tints. The seeds beside are furnished with wings, which plainly keep them steady, and prevent their whirling round. I let one go, and it rises slowly and uncertainly at first, now driven this way, then that, by currents which I cannot perceive, and I fear it will shipwreck against the neighboring wood; but no! as it ap-proaches, it surely rises above it, and then, feeling the strong north wind, it is borne off rapidly in the opposite direction, ever rising higher and higher, and tossing and heaved about with every fluctuation of the gale, till at a hundred feet above the earth, and fifty rods off, steering south, I lose sight of it. I watched this milkweed-seed, for the time, with as much interest as his friends did Mr. Lauriat disappearing

in the skies. How many myriads go sailing away at this season,—high over hill and meadow and river, to plant their
race in new localities,—on various tacks, until the wind lulls,
who can tell how many miles! And for this end these silken
streamers have been perfecting all summer, snugly packed in
this light chest, a prophecy not only of the fall, but of future
springs. Who could believe in the prophecies of a Daniel or
of Miller, that the world would end this summer, while one
milkweed with faith matured its seeds? Densely packed in a
little oblong chest, armed with soft, downy prickles, and lined
with a smooth, silky lining, lie some hundreds of seeds, pear-
shaped, or like a steelyard's poise, which have derived their
nutriment through a band of extremely fine, silken threads,
attached by their extremities to the core. At length, when
the seeds are matured and cease to require nourishment from
the parent plant, being weaned, and the pod with dryness
and frost bursts, the extremities of the silken thread detach
themselves from the core, and from being the conduits of
nutriment to the seed become the buoyant balloon which,
like some spiders' webs, bear the seeds to new and distant
fields. They merely serve to buoy up the full-fed seeds, far
finer than the finest thread. Think of the great variety of
balloons which, at this season, are buoyed up by similar
means. I am interested in the fate, or success, of every such
venture which the autumn sends forth."

A well-known writer says he looked at the present moment
as a man does upon a card upon which he has staked a considerable sum, and who seeks to enhance its value as much as

he can without exaggeration. Thoreau had a like practice,—
the great art is judiciously to limit and isolate one's self, and
life is so short we must miss no opportunity of giving pleasure to one another. No doubt our author's daily writing, his
careful observation in his own mind, lay as a mass of gold,
out of which he should coin a good circulating medium for
the benefit of other minds. Nothing which has not sequence
is of any value in life. And he held to an oft-repeated dic-
tum, "Whatever is very good sense must have been common-
sense in all times. I fairly confess I have served myself all I
could by writing: that I made use of the judgment of authors,
dead and living. If I have written well, let it be considered it
is what no man can do without good sense,—a quality that
renders one not only capable of being a good writer, but a
good man. To take more pains and employ more time cannot
fail to produce more complete pieces. The ancients constantly
applied to art, and to that single branch of an art to which
their talent was most powerfully bent; and it was the business of their lives to correct and finish their works for posterity:—

> "Nor Fame I slight, nor for her favors call;
> She comes unlook'd for, if she comes at all.—
> Who pants for glory finds but short repose."

Then thinkers are so varied. The Mahometans taught fate
in religion, and that nothing exists that does not suppose its
contrary. Some believe that cork-trees grow merely that we
may have stoppers to our bottles. St. Augustine, in his "City
of God," mentions a man who could perspire when he pleased.

MULTUM IN PARVO

Napoleon classed the Old and New Testaments, and the Koran, under the head of politics. One says, a fact of our lives is valuable, not according as it is true, but as it is significant. Thoreau would scarcely have upheld this. But he could assert "that no greater evil can happen to any one than to hate reasoning. Man is evidently made for thinking: this is the whole of his dignity, and the whole of his merit. To think as he ought is the whole of his duty."

After our dear lover of Nature had retired from Walden, a rustic rhymer[1] hung up on the walls of his deserted sanctuary some irregular verses, as an interpretation:—

WALDEN HERMITAGE

Who bricked this chimney small
I well do know;
Know who spread the mortar on the wall,
And the shingles nailèd through;
Yes, have seen thee,
Thou small, rain-tinted hermitage!
And spread aside the pitch-pine tree
That shaded the brief edge
Of thy snug roof,—
'T was water-proof!

Have seen thee, Walden lake!
Like burnished glass to take
With thy daguerreotype
Each cloud, each tree,
More firm yet free:

[1] Channing.

THOREAU

Have seen and known, —
Yes, as I hear and know
Some echo's faintest tone.
All, all have fled,
Man, and cloud, and shed.

"What man was this,
Who thus could build,
Of what complexion,
At what learning skilled?
Is 't the lake I see down there,
Like a glass of simmering air?"
So might that stranger say.
To him I might reply, —
"You ask me for the man. Hand yesterday,
Or to-morrow, or a star from the sky:
More mine are they than he;
But that he lived, I tell to thee.

"That man's heart was true,
As the sky in living blue,
And the old contented rocks
That the mountains heap in blocks.
Wilt dare to do as he did,
Dwell alone and bide thy time?
Not with lies be over-rid,
And turn thy griefs to rhyme?
True! do you call him true?
Look upon the eaglet's eye,
Wheeled amid the freezing blue,
In the unfathomable sky,
With cold and blasts and light his speed to try!

MULTUM IN PARVO

"And should I tell thee that this man was good?
Never thought his neighbor harm,
Sweet was it where he stood,
Sunny all, and warm.
Good?
So the rolling star seems good,
That miscalculates not,
Nor sparkles even a jot
Out of its place, —
Period of unlettered space."

Might once more some stranger ask,
I should reply :
"Why this man was high,
And lofty, is not his task,
Nor mine, to tell :
Springs flow from the invisible.
But on this shore he used to play ;
There his boat he hid away,
And where has this man fled to-day?
Mark the small, gray hermitage
Touch yon curved lake's sandy edge ;
The pines are his you firmly see.

"He never goes, —
But thou must come,
As the wind blows ;
He surely sits at home.
In his eye the thing must stand,
In his thought the world command ;
As a clarion shrills the morn,
On his arms the world be borne.

THOREAU

Beat with thy paddle on the boat,
Midway the lake, — the wood repeats
The ordered blow; the echoing note
Has ended in the ear, yet its retreats
Contain more possibilities;
And in this Man the nature lies
Of woods so green,
And lakes so sheen,
And hermitages edged between."

Chatterton, a literary disciple, whose shanty stood on London streets, thus vents *his* history: "I am quite familiar at the Chapter Coffee-house, and know all the geniuses there. A character is now unnecessary: an author carries his character in his pen. Good God, how superior is London to that despicable Bristol! The poverty of authors is a common observation, but not always a true one. No author can be poor who understands the arts of booksellers. No: it is my pride, my damned, native, unconquerable pride, that plunges me into distraction." And another asks, "What could Stephen Duck do? what could Chatterton do? Neither of them had opportunities of enlarging their stock of ideas. No man can coin guineas but in proportion as he has gold." Even that touch upon booksellers' arts did not prevent our brother from starving to death three months after in London.

Thoreau would not have said, with Voltaire, "*Ah, croyez-moi, l'erreur a son mérite,*"—believe me, sin has something worthy in it,—which is the same as Goethe's "Even in God I discover defects"; but he would recognize the specific value

of events. The directions of men are singular. He knew one
in Sudbury who used to fat mud-turtles, having a great appetite for them; another used to eat those imposthumes on wild
rose-bushes, which are made by worms and contain an ounce
of maggots each. But why criticise poor human nature, when
a black snake that has just laid her eggs on a tussock in the
meadow (some were hatching, and some hatched), upon being
alarmed, swallows them all down in a lump for safe keeping,
and no doubt produces them afresh at a convenient time? Nature, as Thoreau said, does have her dawn each day; and her
economical code of laws does not consult taste or high art, as
in the above salvation of so inconvenient a morsel as a snake's
offspring. He sometimes caught sight of the inside of things
by artificial means; and notices that the young mud-turtle is a
hieroglyphic of snappishness a fortnight before it is hatched,
like the virtue of bottled cider. "When the robin ceases, then
I think is an exit, . . . the concert is over." He could see a
revolution in the end of a bird's song, and he used working
abroad, like the artist who painted out-of-doors, and believed
that lights and a room were absurdities, and that a picture
could be painted anywhere. So must a man be moral everywhere, and he must not expect that Nature will take a scrub-
bing-brush and clean her entries for his steps, seeing how
sentimental a fellow is our brother.

The *Bombyx pini*, the pine spider, the most destructive of
all forest insects, is infested, so says Ratzeburg, by thirty-five
parasitical ichneumonidæ. And infirmity that decays the wise
doth ever make the better fool. Wisdom is

THOREAU

"Not to know at large of things remote
From use, obscure and subtle, but to know
That which before us lies in daily use."

The love of our poet-naturalist for the open air, his hy-pæthral character, has been dwelt upon. Such was his enjoyment in that outward world, it seemed as if his very self became a cast of nature, with the outlines of humanity fair and perfect; but that intensity of apprehension did, with certain minds, accuse him of egotism. Not self, but rather that creation of which he was a part, asserted itself there. As it was said:—

"For chiefly here thy worth,—
Greatly in this, that unabated trust,
Amplest reliance on the unceasing truth
That rules and guides the darting sphere about us,—
Truth that drives thoughtful round the unthinking ball,
And buds the ignorant germs on life and time,
Of men and beasts and birds, themselves the sport
Of a clear, healthful prescience, still unspent."

He admired plants and trees: truly, he loved them. Doubt not it was their infinite beauty which first impressed them on him; but then he greatly held that art of science which, taking up the miscellaneous crowd, impaled them in the picket-fences of order, and coined a labelled scientific plan from the phenomenal waste-basket of vulgar observation. A hearty crack in Latin he rejoiced at; not merely because he had digested it early, but as a stencil-tool for the mind. He prized a substantial name for a thing beyond most sublunary joys.

[212]

Name it! name it! he might have cried to the blessed fortune.

"He shall be as a god to me who can rightly define and divide. The subjects on which the master did not talk were,— extraordinary things, feats of strength, disorder, and spiritual beings. What the superior man seeks is in himself: what the mean man seeks is in others. By weighing we know what things are light and what heavy; by measuring we know what things are long and what short. It is of the greatest importance to measure the motions of the mind."

"Mills of the gods do slowly wind,
But they at length to powder grind."

He loved what the Prussian king says to his brother,—"I write this letter with the rough common-sense of a German, who speaks what he thinks, without employing equivocal terms and loose assuagements which disfigure the truth." But it may be feared he would have stopped running, when Fichte thus laid his finger on the destination of man: "My conscious-ness of the object is only a yet unrecognized consciousness of my production of the representation of an object;" although he admired Blake's description,—

"My mother bore me in the southern wild,
And I am black, but, oh! my soul is white,—
White as an angel is the English child,
But I am black as if bereaved of light."

For pure, nonsensical abstractions he had no taste. No work on metaphysics found room on his shelves unless by suffer-ance; there being some Spartan metaphysicians who send you their books,—like the witty lecturer who sent cards of invitation to his lectures, and then you had to come. Neither did he keep moral treatises, though he would not say, "what we call good is nothing else than egoism painted with verbiage," like the Frenchman. "Stick your nose into any gutter, entity, or object, this of Motion or another, with obstinacy, you will easily drown if that be your determination. Time, at its own pleasure, will untie the knot of destiny, if there be one, like a shot of electricity through an elderly, sick household cat." We do not bind ourselves to men by exaggerating those peculiarities in which we happen to differ from them.

(*August 21–27, 1851.*) "I perceive on the blue vervain (*Verbena hastata*) that only one circle of buds, about half a dozen, blossoms at a time; and there are about thirty circles in the space of three inches; while the next circle of buds above at the same time shows the blue. Thus this triumphant blossoming circle travels upward, driving the remaining buds off into space. It is very pleasant to measure the progress of the season by this and similar clocks. So you get not the absolute but the true time of the season.

"I have now found all the Hawkweeds. Singular are these genera of plants,—plants manifestly related, yet distinct. They suggest a history to nature,—a natural history in a new sense. I saw some smilax vines in the swamp, which were connected with trees ten feet above the ground wherein they grew, and four or five feet above the surrounding bushes. Have the trees and shrubs by which they once climbed been cut down? or perchance do the young and flexible shoots blow up in high winds, and fix themselves? Any anomaly in vegetation makes Nature seem more real and present in her working,— as the various yellow and red excrescences on young oaks. I am affected as if it were a different nature that produced them; as if a poet were there who had designs in his head. It is remarkable that animals are often obviously, manifestly, related to plants which they feed upon or live among; as caterpillars, butterflies, tree-toads, partridges, chewinks; I noticed a *yellow* spider on a golden-rod. As if every condition might have its expression in some form of animated being.

"The interregnum in the blossoming of flowers being well over, many small flowers blossom now in the low grounds, having just reached their summer. It is now dry enough, and they feel the heat their tenderness required. Golden-rods, and asters and John's-wort, though they have made demonstrations, have not yet commenced to reign. Tansy is already [*August 24*] getting stale; it is perhaps the first conspicuous yellow flower that passes off the stage. Elderberries are ripe. What a miserable name has the *Gratiola aurea*,—hedge-hyssop! whose hedge does it grow by, pray, in this part of the world?

"We love to see Nature fruitful in whatever kind. I like to see the acorns plenty on the shrub-oaks; aye, and the nightshade berries. It assures us of her vigor, and that she may equally bring forth the fruits we prize. I love to see the potato balls numerous and large, as I go through a plough-field, —the plant thus bearing fruit at both ends; saying, ever and anon, 'Not only these tubers I offer you for the present; but if you will have new varieties (if these do not satisfy you), plant these seeds.' Fruit of the strong soils containing potash, the vintage is come, the olive is ripe. Why not, for my coat of arms, 'for device a cluster of potato-balls in a potato field'? Do they not concern New Englanders a thousand times more than all her grapes? How they take to the virgin soil! *Rubus sempervirens*, the small, low blackberry, is now in fruit; *Medeola Virginica*, the cucumber root, is now in green fruit. The *Polygala cruciata*, cross-leaved polygala, with its handsome calyx and leaves, has a very sweet, but, as it were, intermittent fragrance, as of checkerberry and Mayflower combined."

On such Latin thorns do botanists hang the Lilies of the Vale,—things that can only be crucified into order upon the justification of a splitting-hair microscope. We are assured they have no nerves, sharing the comfort with naturalists.

"The ivy-leaves are turning red; fall dandelions stand thick in the meadows. The leaves on the hardhack are somewhat *appressed*, clothing the stem and showing their downy undersides, like white waving wands. I walk often in drizzly weather, for then the small weeds (especially if they stand on bare ground), covered with raindrops like beads, look more beautiful than ever. They are equally beautiful when covered with dew, fresh and adorned, almost spirited away in a robe of dewdrops. At the Grape Cliffs the few bright red leaves of the tupelo contrast with the polished green ones,—the tupelos with drooping branches. The grape-vines, over-running and bending down the maples, form little arching bowers over the meadow five or six feet in diameter, like parasols held over the ladies of the harem in the East. The rhomboidal joints of the tick trefoil (*Desmodium paniculatum*) adhere to my clothes, and thus disperse themselves. The oak-ball is a dirty drab now. When I got into the Lincoln road, I perceived a singular sweet scent in the air, which I suspected arose from some plant now in a peculiar state owing to the season [*September 11*]; but though I smelled everything around I could not detect it, but the more eagerly I smelled the further I seemed to be from finding it; but when I gave up the search, again it would be wafted to me, the intermitting perfume! It was one of the sweet scents which go to make the autumn air, — which fed my sense of smell rarely, and dilated my nostrils. I felt the better for it. Methinks that I possess the sense of smell in greater perfection than usual, and have the habit of smelling of every plant I pluck. How autumnal now is the scent of ripe grapes by the road-side! The cross-leaved polygala emits its fragrance as if at will. You must not hold it too near, but on all sides and at all distances. How beautiful the sprout-land, a young wood thus springing up! Shall man then despair? Is he not a sprout-land too?

"In Cohosh Swamp the leaves have turned a very deep red, but have not lost their fragrance. I notice wild apples growing luxuriantly in the midst of the swamp, rising red over the colored, painted leaves of the sumac, reminding me that they were colored by the same influences, — some green, some yellow, some red. I fell in with a man whose breath smelled of spirit, which he had drunk. How could I but feel it was his own spirit that I smelt? A sparrow-hawk, hardly so big as a night-hawk, flew over high above my head, — a pretty

little, graceful fellow, too small and delicate to be rapacious.
I found a grove of young sugar-maples. How silently and yet
startlingly the existence of these was revealed to me, which I
had not thought grew in my immediate neighborhood, when
first I perceived the entire edges of its leaves and their ob-
tuse sinuses! Such near hills as Nobscot and Nashoba have
lost all their azure in this clear air, and plainly belong to
earth. Give me clearness, nevertheless, though my heavens be
moved further off to pay for it. It is so cold I am glad to sit
behind the wall; still, the great bidens blooms by the causeway side, beyond the bridge. On Mount Misery were some
very rich yellow leaves (clear yellow) of the *Populus grandi-
dentata*, which still love to wag and tremble in my hands."

This qualification hides the plant celebrated by the en-
tombed novelist, Walter Scott, when he speaks of—

"the shade
By the light quivering aspen made."

It is a poplar whose leaves are soft and tremulous, and some
botanist has smashed his Latinity on the little, trembling,
desponding thing. To Henry these names were a treat, and
possessed a flavor beyond the title of emperor.

The river never failed to act as a Pacific for his afternoon,
and few things gave him so great a delight as a three hours'
voyage on this mitigated form of Amazon.

"Seek then, again, the tranquil river's breast.
July awakes new splendor in the stream,
Yet more than all, the water-lily's pomp,
A star of creamy perfume, born to be

[218]

MULTUM IN PARVO

Consoler to thy solitary voyage;
In vast profusion from the floor of pads,
They floating swim, with their soft beauty decked.
Nor slight the pickerel-weed, whose violet shaft
Controls the tall reed's emerald, and endows
With a contrasted coloring the shore.
No work of human art can faintly show
The unnoticed lustre of these summer plants,
These floating palaces, these anchored orbs,
These spikes of untold richness crowning earth.

The muskrat glides, and perch and pout display
Their arrowy swiftness, while the minnows dart
And fright the filmy silver of the pool;
And the high-colored bream, a ring of gems,
Their circular nests scoop in the yellow sands.
Yet never ask, Why was this beauty wasted
On these banks? nor soon believe that love in vain
Is lavished on the solitude, nor deem
Absence of human life absence of all!
Why is not *here* an answer to thy thought?
   Or mark in August, when the twilight falls,
Like wreaths of timid smoke her curling mist
Poured as from some yet smouldering fire across
The meadows cool; whose modest shadows, thrown
So faintly, seem to fall asleep with day.
Oh, softly pours the thin and curling mist!
Thou twilight hour! abode of peace how deep,
May we not envy him who in thee dwells?
And, like thy soft and gently falling beauty,
His dreams repose on flood-tide of the soul."

CHANNING'S NEAR HOME.

Or let us hear this dear lover of wood and glen, of early morn and deep midnight, sing a strain of the autumnal wind as it goes hurrying about, regardless of the plucked manni-kins freezing amid its polarities:—

"The wind roars amid the pines like the surf. You can hardly hear the crickets for the din, or the cars. Such a blow-ing, stirring, bustling day! what does it mean? All light things decamp, straws and loose leaves change their places. It shows the white and silvery under-sides of the leaves. I perceive that some farmers are busy cutting turf now. You dry and burn the very earth itself. I see the volumes of smoke,—not quite the blaze,—from burning brush, as I suppose, far in the western horizon: the farmers' simple en-terprises! They improve this season,—which is the dryest,— their haying being done and their harvest not begun, to do these jobs: burn brush, build walls, dig ditches, cut turf; also topping corn and digging potatoes. May not the succory, tree-primrose, and other plants, be distributed from Boston on the rays of the railroad? The shorn meadows looked of a living green at eve, even greener than in spring. This re-minded me of the *fenum cordum*, the after-math; *sicilimenta de pratis*, the second mowing of the meadow, in Cato. His remedy for sprains would be as good in some cases as opo-deldoc. You must repeat these words: 'Hauat, hauat, hauat ista pista sista damia bodanna ustra.' And his notion of an auction would have had a fitness in the South: 'If you wish to have an auction, sell off your oil, if it will fetch something, and anything in the wine and corn line left over; sell your old oxen, worthless sheep and cattle, old wool, hides and carts; old tools, old slaves and sick slaves; and if you can scrape up any more trash, sell it along with them.' I now begin to pick wild apples.

"We scared a calf out of the meadows, which ran, like a ship tossed on the waves, over the hills: they run awkwardly, —red, oblong squares, tossing up and down like a vessel in a storm, with great commotion. I observe that the woodchuck has two or more holes, a rod or two apart: one, or the front door, where the excavated sand is heaped up; another, not so easily discovered, which is very small, round, and without sand about it, being that by which he emerged, and smaller directly at the surface than beneath, on the principle by which a well is dug. I saw a very fat woodchuck on a wall, evidently prepared to go into the ground."

> "'Want and woe which torture us,
> Thy sleep makes ridiculous.'"

As the woodchuck dines chiefly on crickets, he will not be at much expense in seats for his winter quarters. Since the anatomical discovery, that the *thyroid* gland, whose use in man is *nihil*, is for the purpose of getting digested during the hibernating jollifications of the woodchuck, we sympathize less at his retreat. Darwin, who hibernates in science, cannot yet have heard of this use of the above gland, or he would have derived the human race to that amount from the *Mus montana*, our woodchuck, instead of landing him flat on the *simiadæ*, or monkeys. We never can remember that our botanist took a walk that gave him a poor turn or disagreed with him. It is native to him to say,—

"It was pleasant walking where the road was shaded by a high hill, as it can be only in the morning; also, looking back, to see a heavy shadow made by some high birches reaching quite across the road. Light and shadow are sufficient contrast and furnish sufficient excitement when we are well. Now we were passing a sunshiny mead, pastured with cattle and sparkling with dew,— the sound of crows and swallows was heard in the air, and leafy-columned elms stood about, shining with moisture. The morning freshness and unworldliness of that domain! When you are starting away, leaving your more familiar fields for a little adventure like a walk, you look at every object with a traveller's, or at least historical, eyes; you pause on the foot-bridge where an ordinary walk hardly commences, and begin to observe and moralize. It is worth the while to see your native village thus, sometimes. The dry grass yields a crisped sound to my feet; the cornstalks, standing in stacks in long rows along the edges of the corn-fields, remind me of stacks of muskets. As soon as berries are gone, grapes come. The flowers of the meadow-beauty are literally little reddish chalices now, though many still have petals,—little cream-pitchers. There was a man in a boat, in the sun, just disappearing in the distance around a bend, lifting high his arms, and dipping his paddles, as if he were a vision bound to the land of the blessed, far off as in a picture. When I see Concord to purpose, I see it as if it were not real, but painted; and what wonder if I do not speak to *thee?*"

MULTUM IN PARVO

There was nothing our poet loved or sang better, albeit in
prose, than the early morning:—

"Alone, despondent? then art thou alone,
On some near hill-top, ere of day the orb
In early summer tints the floating heaven,
While sunk around thy sleeping race o'ershade
With more oblivion their dim village-roofs.

Alone? Oh, listen hushed!
What living hymn awakes such studious air,
A myriad sounds that in one song converge,
Just as the added light lifts the far hamlet
Or distant wood? These are the carols sweet
Of the unnumbered birds that drench the sphere
With their prodigious harmony, prolonged
And ceaseless, so that at no time it dies,—
Vanquishing the expectation with delay.
Still crowding notes from the wild robin's larum
In the walnut's bough, to the veery's flute,
Who, from the inmost shades of the wet wood,
His liquid lay rallies in martial trills.
And mark the molten flecks fast on those skies;
They move not, musing on their rosy heights
In pure, celestial radiance.

Nor these forms,
That chiefly must engross and ask thy praise.
It is a startling theme, this lovely birth,
Each morn, of a new day, so wholly new,
So absolutely penetrated by itself,—
This fresh, this sweet, this ever-living grace,
This tender joy that still unstinted clothes

[223]

An orb of beauty, of all bliss the abode.
Cast off the night, unhinge the dream-clasped brow,
Step freely forth, exulting in thy joy;
Launch off, and sip the dewy twilight time;
Come ere the last great stars have fled, ere dawn
Like a spirit seen, unveils the charm
Of bosky wood, deep dell, or odorous plain;
Ere, blazed with more than gold, some slow-drawn mist
Retreats its distant arm from the cool meads."

As in the song, such a "getting up we never did see,"—our author sallying forth like Don Quixote, ere the stingiest farmer commenced milking his cow-yard cistern. All that he did was done with order due: the late walk came out at two in the morning, and the early one came on at the same crisis.

"His drink the running stream, his cup the bare
Of his palm closed, his bed the hard, cold ground."

Cleanness, punctuality, the observation of the law he truly followed. "Treat with the reverence due to age the elders of your own family, so that the elders in the families of others shall be similarly treated; treat with the kindness due to youth the young in your own family, so that the young in the families of others shall be similarly treated: do this, and the empire may be made to go round in your palm." He might have said, with Victor Hugo, "The finest of all altars is the soul of an unhappy man who is consoled, and thanks God. *Nisi Dominus custodierit domum, in vanum vigilant qui custodiant eam* (Unless God watches over our abode, they watch in vain who are set to keep it). Let us never fear robbers or murderers. They are external and small dangers: let us fear ourselves; prejudices are the true thefts, vices the fatal murders." His notions about the privileges of real property remind us of the park of King Van, which contained seventy square *le;* but the grass-cutters and the fuel-gatherers had the privilege of entrance. He shared it with the people; and was it not with reason they looked on it as small? Of every ten things he knew, he had learned nine in conversation; and he remembered that between friends frequent reproofs lead to distance, and that in serving the neighbor frequent remonstrances lead to disgrace. Nor did he follow that old rule of the nuns,—Believe Secular men little, Religious still less. He was one of those men of education who, without a certain livelihood, are able to maintain a fixed pursuit.

> "Thou art not gone, being gone, where'er thou art:
> Thou leav'st in us thy watchful eyes, in us thy loving heart."

HIS WRITINGS

"The dark-colored ivy and the untrodden grove of God, with its myriad fruits, sunless and without wind in all storms; where always the frenzied Dionysus dwells."

SOPHOCLES.

"When, like the stars, the singing angels shot
To earth."

GILES FLETCHER.

"Patience! why, 't is the soul of peace,
It makes men look like gods! The best of men
That e'er wore earth about him was a Sufferer,
A soft, meek, patient, humble, tranquil spirit;
The first true gentleman that ever breathed."

DECKER.

"Friendship has passed me like a ship at sea."

FESTUS.

CHAPTER XII

HIS WRITINGS

ONE of the objects of our poet-naturalist was to acquire
the art of writing a good English style. So Goethe, that slow
and artful formalist, spent himself in acquiring a good German style. And what Thoreau thought of this matter of writing may be learned from many passages in this sketch, and
from this among the rest: "It is the fault of some excellent
writers, and De Quincey's first impressions on seeing London
suggest it to me, that they express themselves with too great
fulness and detail. They give the most faithful, natural, and
lifelike account of their sensations, mental and physical, but
they lack moderation and sententiousness. They do not affect
us as an ineffectual earnest, and a reserve of meaning, like a
stutterer: they say all they mean. Their sentences are not concentrated and nutty,—sentences which suggest far more than
they say, which have an atmosphere about them, which do not
report an old, but make a new impression; sentences which
suggest on many things, and are as durable as a Roman aque-
duct: to frame these,—that is the *art* of writing. Sentences
which are expressive, towards which so many volumes, so
much life, went; which lie like boulders on the page up and
down, or across; which contain the seed of other sentences,
not mere repetition, but creation; and which a man might
sell his ground or cattle to build. De Quincey's style is nowhere kinked or knotted up into something hard and signifi-

cant, which you could swallow like a diamond, without digesting."

As in the story, "And that 's Peg Woffington's notion of an actress! Better it, Cibber and Bracegirdle, if you can!" This moderation does, *for the most part,* characterize his works, both of prose and verse. They have their stoical merits, their uncomfortableness! It is one result to be lean and sacrificial; yet a balance of comfort and a house of freestone on the sunny side of Beacon Street can be endured, in a manner, by weak nerves. But the fact that our author lived for a while alone in a shanty near a pond or *stagnum,* and named one of his books after the place where it stood, has led some to say he was a barbarian or a misanthrope. It was a writing-case:—

> "This, as an amber drop enwraps a bee,
> Covering discovers your quick soul, that we
> May in your through-shine front your heart's thoughts see."
>
> DONNE.

Here, in this wooden inkstand, he wrote a good part[1] of his famous "Walden"; and this solitary woodland pool was more to his muse than all oceans of the planet, by the force of that faculty on which he was never weary of descanting, —Imagination. Without this, he says, human life, dressed in its Jewish or other gaberdine, would be a kind of lunatic's hospital,—insane with the prose of it, mad with the drouth of society's remainder-biscuits; but add the phantasy, that glorious, that divine gift, and then—

[1] The book was written from his journals—not specially at Walden; but he did write or edit the "Week" there. W. E. C.

HIS WRITINGS

"The earth, the air, and seas I know, and all
The joys and horrors of their peace and wars;
And now will view the gods' state and the stars."

CHAPMAN.

Out of this faculty was his written experience chiefly constructed,—upon this he lived; not upon the cracked wheats
and bread-fruits of an outward platter.° His essays, those
masterful creations, taking up the commonest topics; a sour
apple, an autumn leaf, are features of this wondrous imagination of his; and, as it was his very life-blood, he, least of all,
sets it forth in labored description. He did not bring forward
his means, or unlock the closet of his Maelzel's automaton
chess-player. The reader cares not that the writer of a novel,
with two-lovers in hand, should walk out in the fool's-cap,
and begin balancing some peacock's feather on his nose.

"Begin, murderer,—leave thy damnable faces, and begin!"

He loved antithesis in verse. It could pass for paradox,—
something subtractive and unsatisfactory, as the four her-
rings provided by Caleb Balderstone for Ravenswood's dinner:
come, he says, let us see how miserably uncomfortable we can
feel. Hawthorne, too, enjoyed a grave, and a pocket full of
miseries to nibble upon.

There was a lurking humor in almost all that he said,—
a dry wit, often expressed. He used to laugh heartily and
many times in all the interviews I had, when anything in
that direction was needed. Certainly he has left some exqui-
sitely humorous pieces, showing his nice discernment; and he

[231]

has narrated an encounter truly curious and wonderful,—
the story of a snapping-turtle swallowing a horn-pout. In the
latest pieces on which he worked he showed an anxiety to
correct them by leaving out the few innuendoes, sallies, or
puns, that formerly luxuriated amid the serious pages. No
one more quickly entertained the apprehension of a jest;
and his replies often came with a startling promptness, as
well as perfection,—as if premeditated. This offhand talent
lay in his habit of deep thought and mature reflection; in
the great treasury of his wit he had weapons ready furnished
for nearly all occasions.

Of his own works, the "Week" was at his death for the
most part still in the sheets, unbound; a small edition of
"Walden" was sold in some seven years after its publishing.
His dealings with publishers (who dealt with him in the
most mean and niggardly style) affected him with a shyness
of that class. It was with the utmost difficulty he was paid
for what he wrote by the persons who bought his wares; for
one of his printed articles the note of the publishers was put
by him in the bank for collection. Of the non-sale of the
"Week" he said, "I believe that this result is more inspiring
and better for me than if a thousand had bought my wares.
It affects my privacy less, and leaves me freer." Some cultivated minds place "Walden" in the front rank; but both his
books are so good they will stand on their own merits. His
latest-written work (the "Excursions"—a collection of lectures, mainly) is a great favorite with his friends. His works
are household words to those who have long known them;

and the larger circle he is sure, with time, to address will follow in our footsteps. Such a treasure as the "Week,"—so filled with images from nature,—such a faithful record of the scenery and the people on the banks,—could not fail to make a deep impression. Its literary merit is also great; as a treasury of citations from other authors, it gives a favorable view of his widely extended reading. Few books in this respect can be found to surpass it.

In his discourse of Friendship, Thoreau starts with the idea of "*underpropping* his love by such pure hate, that it would *end* in sympathy," like sweet butter from sour cream. And in this:—

> "Two solitary stars,—
> Unmeasured systems far
> Between us roll;"

getting off into the agonies of space, where everything freezes, yet he adds as inducement,—

> "But by our conscious light we are
> Determined to one pole."

In other words, there was a pole apiece. He continues the antithesis, and says there is "no more use in friendship than in the tints of flowers" (the chief use in them); "pathless the gulf of feeling yawns," and the reader yawns, too, at the idea of tumbling into it. And so he packs up in his mind "all the clothes which outward nature wears," like a young lady's trunk going to Mount Desert.

We must not expect literature, in such case, to run its

hands round the dial-plate of style with cuckoo repetition: the snarls he criticises De Quincey for *not* getting into are the places where *his* bundles of sweetmeats untie. As in the Vendidad, "Hail to thee, O man! who art come from the transitory place to the imperishable":—

"In Nature's nothing, be not nature's toy."

This feature in his style is by no means so much bestowed upon his prose as his poetry. In his verse he more than once attained to beauty, more often to quaintness. He did not court admiration, though he admired fame; and he might have said to his reader,—

"Whoe'er thou beest who read'st this sullen writ,
Which just so much courts thee as thou dost it."

He had an excellent turn of illustration. Speaking of the *débris* of Carnac, he says:—

"Erect ourselves, and let those columns lie;
If Carnac's columns still stand on the plain,
To enjoy our opportunities they remain."

The little Yankee squatting on Walden Pond was not deceived by an Egyptian stone post, or sand heap. In another verse:—

"When life contracts into a vulgar span,
And human nature tires to be a man,—
Greece! who am I that should remember thee?"

And he let Greece slide. At times he hangs up old authors, in the blaze of a New England noon.

"Plutarch was good, and so was Homer too,
  Our Shakespeare's life was rich to live again;
  What Plutarch read, that was not good nor true,
  Nor Shakespeare's books, unless his books were men."

"Tell Shakespeare to attend some leisure hour,
  For now I've business with this drop of dew."

He could drop Shakespeare; and it were well if both he and Dante were prescribed, rather than poured out of bath-tubs. Every one must, however, admire the essay of Mr. Brown on the Bard of Avon, and the translation of Dante by Mr. Black: neatness is the elegance of poverty.

The following verses are pretty, the last line from Milton's "Penseroso," with the change of a syllable. He did not fear to *collect* a good line any more than a good flower:—

RUMORS FROM AN ÆOLIAN HARP

"There is a vale which none hath seen,
  Where foot of man has never been,
  Such as here lives with toil and strife,
  An anxious and a sinful life.

There every virtue has its birth,
  Ere it descends upon the earth,
  And thither every deed returns,
  Which in the generous bosom burns.

There love is warm, and youth is young,
  And poetry is yet unsung;
  For Virtue still adventures there,
  And freely breathes her native air.

And ever, if you hearken well,
You still may hear its vesper bell,
And tread of high-souled men go by,
Their thoughts conversing with the sky."

He has no killing single shots,—*his* thoughts flowed.

"Be not the fowler's net,
    Which stays my flight,
And craftily is set
    T' allure my sight.

But be the favoring gale
    That bears me on,
And still doth fill my sail
    When thou art gone."

"Some tender buds were left upon my stem
    In mimicry of life.

.   .   .   .

Some tumultuous little rill,
    Purling round its storied pebble.

.   .   .   .

Conscience is instinct bred in the house.

.   .   .   .

Experienced river!
    Hast thou flowed for ever?"

As an instance of his humor in verse:—

"I make ye an offer,
    Ye gods, hear the scoffer!
The scheme will not hurt you,
If ye will find goodness, I will find virtue.
I have pride still unbended,

And blood undescended;
I cannot toil blindly,
Though ye behave kindly,
And I swear by the rood
I 'll be slave to no god."

He early gave us his creed:—

"Nature doth have her dawn each day,
But mine are far between;
Content, I cry, for sooth to say,
Mine brightest are, I ween.

For when my sun doth deign to rise,
Though it be her noontide,
Her fairest field in shadow lies,
Nor can my light abide.

Through his discourse I climb and see,
As from some eastern hill,
A brighter morrow rise to me
Than lieth in her skill.

As 't were two summer days in one,
Two Sundays come together,
Our rays united make one sun,
With fairest summer weather."

July 25, 1839.

This date is for those who, unlike Alfieri, are by nature *not* almost destitute of curiosity; and the subject, Friendship, is for the like:—

"For things that pass are past, and in this field
The indeficient spring no winter flaws."

FLETCHER.

[237]

What subtlety and what greatness in those quatrains! then
how truly original, how vague! His Pandora's box of a head
carried all manner of sweets. No one would *guess* the theme,
Yankee though he be. He has that richness which

> "Looks as it is with some true April day,
>   Whose various weather strews the world with flowers."

As he well affirms (if it be applied antithetically), a man
cannot wheedle nor overawe his genius. Nothing was ever
so unfamiliar and startling to a man as his own thoughts.
To the rarest genius it is the most expensive to succumb and
conform to the ways of the world. It is the worst of lumber
if the poet wants to float upon the breeze of popularity. The
bird of paradise is obliged constantly to fly against the wind.
The poet is no tender slip of fairy stock, but the toughest son
of earth and of heaven. He will prevail to be popular in spite
of his faults, and in spite of his beauties too. He makes us
free of his hearth and heart, which is greater than to offer
us the freedom of a city. Orpheus does not hear the strains
which issue from his lyre, but only those which are breathed
into it. The poet will write for his peers alone. He never
whispers in a private ear. The true poem is not that which
the public read. His true work will not stand in any prince's
gallery.

> "My life has been the poem I would have writ,
>   But I could not both live and utter it."

> "I hearing get, who had but ears,
>   And sight, who had but eyes before.

I moments live, who lived but years,
And truth discern, who knew but learning's lore."

He has this bit of modesty:—

THE POET'S DELAY

"In vain I see the morning rise,
  In vain observe the western blaze,
Who idly look to other skies,
  Expecting life by other ways.

Amidst such boundless wealth without,
  I only still am poor within,
The birds have sung their summer out,
  But still my spring does not begin.

Shall I then wait the autumn wind,
  Compelled to seek a milder day,
And leave no curious nest behind,
  No woods still echoing to my lay?"

Again he asks, "Shall I not have words as fresh as my
thought? Shall I use any other man's word? A genuine
thought or feeling would find expression for itself, if it had
to invent hieroglyphics. I perceive that Shakespeare and Milton did not foresee into what company they were to fall. To
say that God has given a man many and great talents, fre-
quently means that he has brought his heavens down within
reach of his hands." He sometimes twanged a tune of true
prose on the strings of his theorbo, as where, instead of Cowper's church-going bell, he flatly says:—

"Dong sounds the brass in the east,"

which will pass for impudence with our United Brethren. It is difficult to comprehend his aloofness from these affectionate old symbols, drawling out from the sunshiny past, and without which our New England paradise is but a "howling wilderness"; although he loves the *echo* of the meeting-house brass. It is his species of paradoxical quintessence. He draws a village: "it has a meeting-house and horse-sheds, a tavern and a blacksmith's shop for centre, and a good deal of wood to cut and cord yet."

> "A man that looks on glass,
>   On it may stay his eye;
> Or, if he pleaseth, through it pass,
>   And the heavens espy."

Of architecture Thoreau thought that, as he had no wines nor olives in his cellar, why need build arches to cover what he had not? Towards humanity in the lump, I think no one ever felt a more philanthropic quiet; he looked not to the Past, or the men of the Past, as having so special a value for him as our present doings. It was for others to do this,—to toddle about after the nomadic ghosts of wit and sense,—and, no doubt, they pass profitable lives (for them); but it was not Thoreau who aided or abetted them. I have tried often, in conversing with him, to fathom the secret of these and similar opinions,—having myself the due respect for all formality and tradition,—but he loved not argument in discourse, had his own opinions (wherever they came from) and his company could accept them or not,—he had not time nor inclination to spend effort in dusting them or shaking them out, like carpets. But no man was a more careful and punctilious citizen, or more faithfully respected the callings and professions of his fellow-men.

This taste for novelty and freedom, and distaste for forms and fetters, came practically to the surface in his violent hatred of American slavery. Nothing so vile in all history forced itself on his mind. For Garrison, Phillips, and Parker Pillsbury he had the proper admiration; for Captain John Brown, from the first he had undivided respect and esteem; nor had that devoted man a sincerer mourner at his death. We took our usual walk after the affecting funeral ceremony in Concord, and the cool twilight cast its reproach over that fearful slaughter; as on later events that followed the tragedy at Charlestown, fell a twilight of terror, succeeded by a resurrection of peaceful and serene freedom. Thoreau ranks in the front of the storming-party against the old Golgotha of slavery. He never faltered, but from first to last lived and worked a faithful friend to the American slave. Not one slave only has he housed and placed "aboard the cars" on his way to Canada, — Concord being on the direct route to that free country.

His notions of institutions were like his views of sepulchres. Another has said, "It is my business to rot dead leaves," symbolizing a character working like water. "A man might well pray that he may not taboo or curse any portion of nature by being buried in it. It is, therefore, much to the credit of Little John, the famous follower of Robin Hood, that his grave was 'long celebrous for the yielding of excellent whetstones.' Nothing but great antiquity can make grave-yards interesting to me. I have no friends there. The farmer who has skimmed his farm might perchance leave his body to Nature to be ploughed in. 'And the king seide, What is the biriel which I se? And the citeseynes of that cite answeride to him, It is the sepulchre of the man of God that cam fro Juda.'"

He makes us a photograph of style, which touches some of his chief strength. "There is a sort of homely truth and naturalness in some books which is very rare to find, and yet looks cheap enough. Homeliness is almost as great a merit in a book as in a house, if the reader would abide there. It is next to beauty, and a very high art. Some have this merit only. Very few men can speak of Nature, for instance, with any truth. They overstep her modesty, somehow or other, and confer no favor. They do not speak a good word for her. The ırliness with which the wood-chopper speaks of his woods, ɹandling them as indifferently as his axe, is better than the ɛaly-mouthed enthusiasm of the lover of nature." So Philina cried, "Oh! that I might never hear more of nature and scenes of nature! When the day is bright you go to walk, and to dance when you hear a tune played. But who would think a moment on the music or the weather? It is the dancer that interests us, and not the violin; and to look upon a pair of bright black eyes is the life of a pair of blue ones. But what on earth have we to do with wells and brooks and old rotten lindens?"

THE HARPER'S SONG [1]

"'I sing but as the linnet sings,
   That on the green bough dwelleth;
A rich reward his music brings,
   As from his throat it swelleth:
Yet might I ask, I'd ask of thine
One sparkling draught of purest wine,
   To drink it here before you.'

He viewed the wine, he quaffed it up:
   'Oh! draught of sweetest savor!
Oh! happy house, where such a cup
   Is thought a little favor!
If well you fare, remember me,
And thank kind Heaven, from envy free,
   As now for this I thank you.'"

Goethe, who wrote this, never signed the temperance-pledge: no more did Thoreau, but drank the kind of wine "which never grew in the belly of the grape," nor in that of the corn. He was made more dry by drinking. These affections were a kind of *résumé*, or infant thanatopsis, sharp on both edges. Yet, in spite of this abundant moderation, he says, "I trust that you realize what an exaggerator I am,—that I lay myself out to exaggerate whenever I have an opportunity,— pile Pelion upon Ossa, to reach heaven so. Expect no trivial truth from me, unless I am on the witness stand. I will come as near to lying as you will drive a coach-and-four. If it isn't thus and so with *me*, it is with something." As for writing

---

[1] In "Wilhelm Meister."

letters, he mounts above prose. "Methinks I will write to you. Methinks you will be glad to hear. We will stand on solid foundations to one another,—I am a column planted on this shore, you on that. We meet the same sun in his rising. We were built slowly, and have come to our bearing. We will not mutually fall over that we may meet, but will grandly and eternally guard the straits."

> "My life is like a stroll upon the beach, —
> I have but few companions by the shore."
>
> .   .   .   .
>
> "Go where he will, the wise man is at home;
> His hearth the earth, his hall the azure dome;
> Where his clear spirit leads him, there's his road."
>
> EMERSON.

This well-known speech to his large and respectable circle of acquaintance beyond the mountains is a pretty night-piece: "Greeting: My most serene and irresponsible neighbors, let us see that we have the whole advantage of each other. We will be useful, at least, if not admirable to one another. I know that the mountains which separate us are high, and covered with perpetual snow; but despair not. Improve the serene weather to scale them. If need be, soften the rocks with vinegar. For here lies the verdant plain of Italy ready to receive you. Nor shall I be slow on my side to penetrate to your Provence. Strike then boldly at head or heart, or any vital part. Depend upon it the timber is well seasoned and tough, and will bear rough usage; and if it should crack, there is plenty more where it came from. I am no piece of crockery, that cannot be jostled against my neighbor without being in danger of being broken by the collision, and must needs ring false and jarringly to the end of my days when once I am cracked; but rather one of the old-fashioned wooden trenchers, which one while stands at the head of the table, and at another is a milking-stool, and at another a seat for children; and, finally, goes down to its grave not unadorned with honorable scars, and does not die till it is worn out. Nothing can shock a brave man but dulness. Think how many rebuffs every man has experienced in his day,—perhaps has fallen into a horse-pond, eaten fresh-water clams, or worn one shirt for a week without washing. Indeed, you cannot receive a shock, unless you have an electric affinity for that which shocks you. Use me, then; for I am useful in my way, and stand as one of many petitioners,—from toadstool and henbane up to dahlia and violet,—supplicating to be put to any use, if by any means you may find me serviceable: whether for a medicated drink or bath, as balm and lavender; or for fragrance, as verbena and geranium; or for sight, as cactus; or for thoughts, as pansy. These humbler, at least, if not those higher uses."

So good a writer should

"live
Upon the alms of his superfluous praise."

He was choice in his words. "All these sounds," says he, "the crowing of cocks, the baying of dogs, and the hum of insects at noon, are the evidence of nature's health or *sound* state."

For so learned a man he spared his erudition; neither did
he, as one who was no mean poet, use lines like these to cele-
brate his clearness:—

> "Who dares upbraid these open rhymes of mine
>   With blindfold Aquines, or darke Venusine?
>   Or rough-hewn Teretisius, writ in th' antique vain
>   Like an old satire, and new Flaccian?
>   Which who reads thrice, and rubs his ragged brow,
>   And deep indenteth every doubtful row,
>   Scoring the margent with his blazing stars,
>   And hundredth crooked interlinears
>   (Like to a merchant's debt-roll new defaced,
>   When some crack'd Manour cross'd his book at last),
>   Should all in rage the curse-beat page out-rive,
>   And in each dust-heap bury me alive."
>
> HALL'S SATIRES.

There are so few obscurities in Thoreau's writing, that the
uneasy malevolence of ephemeral critics has not discovered
enough to cite, and his style has that ease and moderateness
which appeal to taste.

He had the sense of humor, and in one place indulges
himself in some Latin fun, where he names the wild apples,
creatures of his fancy. "There is, first of all, the wood-apple,
Malus sylvatica; the blue-jay apple; the apple which grows
in dells in the woods, *sylvestrivallis;* also in hollows in pastures, *campestrivallis;* the apple that grows in an old cellar-
hole, *Malus cellaris;* the meadow-apple; the partridge-apple;
the truants' apple, *cessatoris;* the saunterer's apple,—you
must lose yourself before you can find the way to that; the

beauty of the air, *decus aeris;* December-eating; the frozen-thawed, *gelato-soluta;* the brindled apple; wine of New England; the chickadee apple; the green apple,—this has many synonymes; in its perfect state it is the *Cholera morbifera aut dysenterifera, puerulis dilectissima;* the hedge-apple, *Malus sepium;* the slug apple, *limacea;* the apple whose fruit we tasted in our youth; our particular apple, not to be found in any catalogue, *pedestrium solatium,*" and many others. His love of this sour vegetable is characteristic: it is the wild flavor, the acidity, the difficulty of eating it, which pleased. The lover of gravy, the justice lined with capon, apoplectic professors in purple skulls, who reckon water a nuisance, never loved his pen that praised poverty: "Quid est paupertas? odibile bonum, sanitatis mater, curarum remotio, absque sollicitudine semita, sapientiæ reparatrix, negotium sine damno, intractabilis substantia, possessio absque calumnia, incerta fortuna, sine sollicitudine felicitas." [1]

Or in what he names complemental verses from Wither:—

> "Thou dost presume too much, poor needy wretch,
>   To claim a station in the firmament,
>   Because thy humble cottage, or thy tub,
>   Nurses some lazy or pedantic virtue,
>   With roots and pot-herbs. We, more high, advance
>   Such virtues only as admit excess,—
>   Brave, bounteous acts, regal magnificence,

[1] A free rendition: "What is poverty? Kerosene lamps, taking tea out, Dalley's pain-killer, horse-cars, scolding help, bookseller's accounts, modern rubber boots, what nobody discounts, the next tax-bill, sitting in your minister's pew." (The original is in Secundus. F. B. S.)

All-seeing prudence, magnanimity
That knows no bound, and that heroic virtue
For which antiquity hath left no name,
But patterns only, such as Hercules,
Achilles, Theseus; — back to thy loath'd cell!"

He neglected no culture, left nothing undone that could
aid him in his works; and a paragraph he left for guidance
in such pursuits may be cited: "Whatever wit has been
produced on the spur of the moment will bear to be reconsidered and re-formed with phlegm. The arrow had best not
be loosely shot. The most transient and passing remark must
be reconsidered by the writer, made sure and warranted, as if
the earth had rested on its axle to back it, and all the natural forces lay behind it. The writer must direct his sentences
as carefully and leisurely as the marksman his rifle, — who
shoots sitting, and with a rest, with patent sights, and conical
balls beside. If you foresee that a part of your essay will
topple down after the lapse of time, throw it down yourself."
This advice may be pressed on all writers, and this on all
livers: "I cannot stay to be congratulated; I would leave
the world behind me." No labor was too great, no expense
too costly, if only laid out in the right direction; and the
series of extracts he has left on the history of the Indians is
a proof of this. These books, forming a little library of themselves, consist of such extracts from all the writers on the
Indians, all the world over, as would have value and advantage for him. He read the long and painful series of Jesuit
Relations, by the Canadian originals, — the early works in

American history at Harvard College; collected, compared, and copied the early maps, early figures of the Indians (such as those of De Bry); read all travels which he could procure, and carefully excerpted all facts bearing on the subject of Indians, yet this vast labor and expense and toil,—far more than most literary men willingly undergo in their lives,— were but the pursuit of a collateral topic.

He had that pleasant art of convertibility, by which he could render the homely strains of Nature into homely verse and prose, holding yet the flavor of their immortal origins; while meagre and barren writers upon science do perhaps intend to describe that quick being of which they prose, yet never loose a word of happiness or humor. The art of describing realities, and imparting to them a touch of human nature, is something comfortable. A few bits of such natural history as this follow:—

(*October, 1851.*) "A hornets'-nest I discovered in a rather tall huckleberry-bush, the stem projecting through it, the leaves spreading over it. How these fellows avail themselves of these vegetables! They kept arriving, the great fellows (with white abdomens), but I never saw whence they came, but only heard the buzz just at the entrance. At length, after I had stood before the nest for five minutes, during which time they had taken no notice of me, two seemed to be consulting at the entrance, and then made a threatening dash at me, and returned to the nest. I took the hint and retired. They spoke as plainly as man could have done. I examined this nest again: I found no hornets buzzing about; the en-

trance seemed to have been enlarged, so I concluded it had
been deserted, but looking nearer I discovered two or three
dead hornets, men-of-war, in the entry-way. Cutting off the
bushes which sustained it, I proceeded to open it with my
knife. It was an inverted cone, eight or nine inches by seven
or eight. First, there were half a dozen layers of waved,
brownish paper resting loosely over one another, occupying
nearly an inch in thickness, for a covering. Within were the
six-sided cells, in three stories, suspended from the roof and
from one another by one or two suspension-rods only; the
lower story much smaller than the rest. And in what may
be called the attic or garret of the structure were two live
hornets partially benumbed with cold. It was like a deserted
castle of the Mohawks, a few dead ones at the entrance to
the fortress."

"The prinos berries (*Prinos verticillatus*) are quite red; the
dogwood has lost every leaf, its bunches of dry, greenish
berries hanging straight down from the bare stout twigs,
as if their peduncles were broken. It has assumed its winter
aspect,—a Mithridatic look. The black birch (*Betula lenta*) is
straw-colored, the witch-hazel (*Hamamelis Virginica*) is now
in bloom. I perceive the fragrance of ripe grapes in the air.
The little conical burrs of the agrimony stick to my clothes;
the pale lobelia still blooms freshly, and the rough hawk-
weed holds up its globes of yellowish fuzzy seeds, as well as
the panicled. The declining sun falling on the willows and on
the water produces a rare, soft light I do not often see,—a
greenish-yellow."

"Thus, perchance, the Indian hunter,
   Many a lagging year agone,
Gliding o'er thy rippling waters,
   Lowly hummed a natural song.

"Now the sun's behind the willows,
   Now he gleams along the waves,
Faintly o'er the wearied billows
   Come the spirits of the braves.

"The reach of the river between Bedford and Carlisle, seen from a distance, has a strangely ethereal, celestial, or elysian look. It is of a light sky-blue, alternating with smoother white streaks, where the surface reflects the light differently, like a milk-pan full of the milk of Valhalla partially skimmed, more gloriously and heavenly fair and pure than the sky itself. We have names for the rivers of hell, but none for the rivers of heaven, unless the Milky Way may be one. It is such a smooth and shining blue, like a panoply of sky-blue plates,—

   "'Sug'ring all dangers with success.'

"Fairhaven Pond, seen from the Cliffs in the moonlight, is a sheeny lake of apparently a boundless primitive forest, untrodden by man; the windy surf sounding freshly and wildly in the single pine behind you, the silence of hushed wolves in the wilderness, and, as you fancy, moose looking off from the shores of the lake; the stars of poetry and history and unexplored nature looking down on the scene. This light and this hour take the civilization all out of the landscape. Even at this time in the evening (8 P.M.) the crickets chirp and the small birds peep, the wind roars in the wood, as if it were just before dawn. The landscape is flattened into mere light and shade, from the least elevation. A field of ripening corn, now at night, that has been topped, with the stalks stacked up, has an inexpressibly dry, sweet, rich ripening scent: I feel as I were an ear of ripening corn myself. Is not the whole air a compound of such odors indistinguishable? Drying cornstalks in a field, what an herb garden! What if one moon has come and gone with its world of poetry, so divine a creature freighted with its hints for me, and I not use them!"

He loved the πολυφλοίσβον θαλάσσην, the noisy sea, and has left a pleasant sketch of his walks along the beach; but he never attempted the ocean passage. The shore at Truro, on Cape Cod, which he at one time frequented, has been thus in part described.[1]

> A little Hamlet hid away from men,
> Spoil for no painter's eye, no poet's pen,
> Modest as some brief flower, concealed, obscure,
> It nestles on the high and echoing shore;
> Yet here I found I was a welcome guest,
> At generous Nature's hospitable feast.
> The barren moors no fences girdled high,
> The endless beaches planting could defy,
> And the blue sea admitted all the air,
> A cordial draught, so sparkling and so rare.
>
> The aged widow in her cottage lone,
> Of solitude and musing patient grown,
> Could let me wander o'er her scanty fields,
> And pick the flower that contemplation yields.

[1] By Channing, —the whole is in "Poems of Sixty-five Years."

This vision past, and all the rest was mine, —
The gliding vessel on the ocean's line,
That left the world wherein my senses strayed,
Yet long enough her soft good-by delayed
To let my eye engross her beauty rare,
Kissed by the seas, an infant of the air.
Thou, too, wert mine, the green and curling wave,
Child of the sand, a playful child and brave;
Urged on the gale, the crashing surges fall;
The zephyr breathes, how softly dances all!

Dread ocean-wave! some eyes look out o'er thee
And fill with tears, and ask, Could such things be?
Why slept the All-seeing Heart when death was near?
Be hushed each doubt, assuage thy throbbing fear!
Think One who made the sea and made the wind
Might also feel for our lost human kind;
And they who sleep amid the surges tall
Summoned great Nature to their funeral,
And she obeyed. We fall not far from shore;
The sea-bird's wail, the surf, our loss deplore;
The melancholy main goes sounding on
His world-old anthem o'er our horizon.

As Turner was in the habit of adding what *he* thought explanatory verses to his landscapes, so it may be said of some books, besides the special subject treated they are *diversified* with quotations. Thoreau adhered closely to his topic, yet in his "Week" as many as a hundred authors are quoted, and there are more than three hundred passages either cited or touched upon. In fact, there are some works that have rather a peculiar value for literary gentry, like Pliny, Montaigne, and Burton's "Anatomy of Melancholy," upon which last work Lord Byron thought many authors had constructed a reputation.

Thoreau's style is one of the best English styles that I am acquainted with; not tumultuous or exaggerated, nor dry and pointed, it has the mellowness of the older English,—sometimes almost its quaintness,—but usually expresses admirably the intent of his mind. It was no small practice which fulfilled his motto,—"Improve every opportunity to express yourself in writing as if it were your last." His facility was truly marvellous; he seemed made for holding a pen between his fingers and getting excellent sentences, where other writers hobble and correct. Yet he used the file very often,—nowhere more, I fancy, than in some of his "Maine Woods" papers, which indeed were not easy to write. Think of the fertility of such a mind—not wielding the pen for taskwork, but pleasure—pouring forth this admirable portrait-painting of fish, bird, or insect, the season or the hour of the day; never wearied, never worn, but always exhilarate and full of cheer. Few objects impressed him more than the form of birds, and his few felicitous touches are well worth citing. He speaks of "a gull pure white, a wave of foam in the air,—all wing, like a birch-scale." He mistook two white ducks for "the foaming crest of a wave" and sees a small duck that is "all neck and wings, —a winged roll-pin." Snow-buntings he calls "winged snow-balls." The flight of the peetweet reminds him of an impression we all have had,—but who has described it? "Their wings appear double as they fly by you."

HIS WRITINGS

A list follows of the writings of Thoreau, as they appeared chronologically. These have been since printed in separate volumes, if they did not so appear at first (with few exceptions), under the titles of "Excursions, 1863," "The Maine Woods, 1864," "A Yankee in Canada, 1866," "Cape Cod, 1865," and in addition a volume of letters, 1865.[1]

A WALK TO WACHUSETT. — In the "Boston Miscellany."

IN THE DIAL. — 1340–1844: —

Vol. I. — Sympathy. Aulus Persius Flaccus. Nature doth have her dawn each day.

Vol. II. — Sic Vita. Friendship.

Vol. III. — Natural History of Massachusetts. In "Prayers," the passage beginning "Great God." The Black Knight. The Inward Morning. Free Love. The Poet's Delay. Rumors from an Æolian Harp. The Moon. To the Maiden in the East. The Summer Rain. The Laws of Menu. Prometheus Bound. Anacreon. To a Stray Fowl. Orphics. Dark Ages.

Vol. IV. — A Winter Walk. Homer, Ossian, Chaucer. Pindar. Fragments of Pindar. Herald of Freedom.

IN THE DEMOCRATIC REVIEW, 1843. — The Landlord. Paradise (to be) Regained.

IN GRAHAM'S MAGAZINE, 1847. — Thomas Carlyle and his Works.

IN THE UNION MAGAZINE. — Ktaadn and the Maine Woods.

IN ÆSTHETIC PAPERS. — Resistance to Civil Government.

A WEEK ON THE CONCORD AND MERRIMAC RIVERS. Boston: James Monroe and Company, 1849.

IN PUTNAM'S MAGAZINE. — Excursion to Canada (in part). Cape Cod (in part).

WALDEN. Boston: Ticknor and Company, 1854.

[1] *Since then (1894) the letters have been reprinted with many additions, and there are now a dozen volumes of Thoreau's works.*

THOREAU

IN THE LIBERATOR. —Speech at Framingham, July 4, 1854. Reminiscences of John Brown (read at North Elba, July 4, 1860).

IN "ECHOES FROM HARPER'S FERRY." —1860. Lecture on John Brown, and Remarks at Concord on the day of his execution.

IN THE ATLANTIC MONTHLY, 1859. — Chesuncook, 1862. Walking. Autumnal Tints. Wild Apples.

IN THE NEW YORK TRIBUNE. — The Succession of Forest Trees (also printed in the Middlesex Agricultural Transactions). 1860.

"Nil mihi rescribas, attamen ipse veni."

PERSONALITIES

"If great men wrong me, I will spare myself;
If mean, I will spare them."

DONNE.

"As soon as generals are dismembered and distributed into parts, they become so much attenuated as in a manner to disappear; wherefore the terms by which they are expressed undergo the same attenuation, and seem to vanish and fail."

SWEDENBORG.

"The art of overturning states is to discredit established customs, by looking into their origin, and pointing out that it was defective in authority and justice."

PASCAL.

"Adspice murorum moles, præruptaque saxa,
Obrutaque horrenti vasta theatra situ,
Hæc sunt Roma. Viden' velut ipsa cadavera tantæ
Urbis adhuc spirent imperiosa minas."

JANUS VITALIS.

CHAPTER XIII

PERSONALITIES

OUR author's life can be divided in three parts: first, to the year 1837, when he left college; next, to the publishing of his "Week," in 1849 (ten years after his first excursion up the Merrimac River, of which that work treats); and the remainder of his doings makes the third. It was after he had graduated that he began to embalm his thoughts in a diary, and not till many years' practice did they assume a systematic shape. This same year (1837) brought him into relation with a literary man (Emerson), by which his mind may have been first soberly impregnated with that love of letters that after accompanied him, but of whom he was no servile copyist. He had so wisely been nourished at the collegiate fount as to come forth undissipated; not digging his grave in tobacco and coffee, — those two perfect causes of paralysis. "I have a faint recollection of pleasure derived from smoking dried lily-stems before I was a man. I have never smoked anything more noxious." His school-keeping was a nominal occupancy of his time for a couple of years; and he soon began to serve the mistress to whom he was afterward bound, and to sing the immunity of Pan. Some long-anticipated excursion set the date upon the year, and furnished its materials for the journal. And at length, in 1842, he printed in a fabulous quarterly, "The Dial," a paper; and again, in 1843, came out "The Walk to Wachusett," a bracing revival of exhilarat-

[259]

ing thoughts caught from the mountain atmosphere. In the "Dial" came the poems before commented upon; it afforded him sufficient space to record his pious hopes and sing the glories of the world he habitually admired. With the actual publication of the "Week," at his own expense, and which cost him his labor for several years to defray, begins a new era,—he is introduced to a larger circle and launches forth his paper nautilus, well pleased to eye its thin and many-colored ribs shining in the watery sunshine. His early friends and readers never failed, and others increased; thus was he rising in literary fame,—

"That like a wounded snake drags its slow length along."

Then came the log-book of his woodland cruise at Walden, his critical articles upon Thomas Carlyle and others; and he began to appear as a lecturer, with a theory, as near as he could have one. He was not to try to suit his audience, but consult the prompting of his genius and suit himself. If a demand was made for a lecture, he would gratify it so far as in him lay, but he could not descend from the poetry of insight to the incubation of prose. Lecture committees at times failed to see the prophetic god, and also the statute-putty. "Walden" increased his repute as a writer, if some great men thought him bean-dieted, with an owl for his minister, and who milked creation, not the cow. It is in vain for the angels to contend against stupidity.

He began to take more part in affairs (the Anti-slavery crisis coming to the boil) in 1857. Captain John Brown, after of Harper's Ferry, was in Concord that year, and had talk with Thoreau, who knew nothing of his revolutionary plans. He shot off plenty of coruscating abolition rockets at Framingham and elsewhere, and took his chance in preaching at those animated free-churches which pushed from the rotting compost of the Southern hot-bed. At Worcester he is said to have read a damaging-institution lecture upon "Beans," that has never got to print. He carried more guns than they, at those irritable reform meetings, which served as a discharge-pipe for the virus of all the regular scolds; for he did not spatter by the job. At the time of Sims's rendition he offered to his townsmen that the revolutionary monument should be thickly coated with black paint as a symbol of that dismal treason. He, too, had the glory of speaking the first public good word for Captain John Brown, after his attack upon the beast run for the American plate,—that Moloch entered by Jeff. Davis and backers. In three years more the United States, that killed instead of protecting bold Osawatomie, was enlisting North Carolina slaves to fight against Virginia slaveholders.

It must be considered the superior and divine event of his human experience when that famed hero of liberty forced the serpent of slavery from its death-grasp on the American Constitution. John Brown "expected to endure hardness"; and this was the expectation and fruition of Thoreau, naturally and by his culture. His was a more sour and saturnine hatred of injustice, his life was more passive, and he lost the glory of action which fell to the lot of Brown. He had naught in his thoughts of which a plot could spin; neither did he believe in civil government, or that form of police against the Catiline or Cæsar, who has ready a *coup d'état*, such as the speckled Napoleonic egg, now addled, that was laid in Paris. Thoreau worshipped a hero in a mortal disguise, under the shape of that homely son of justice: his pulses thrilled and his hands involuntarily clenched together at the mention of Captain Brown, at whose funeral in Concord he said a few words, and prepared a version of Tacitus upon Agricola, some lines of which are:—

"You, Agricola, are fortunate, not only because your life was glorious, but because your death was timely. As they tell us who heard your last words, unchanged and willing you accepted your fate. . . . Let us honor you by our admiration, rather than by short-lived praises; and, if Nature aid us, by our emulation of you." He had before said: "When I now look over my common-place book of poetry, I find that the best of it is oftenest applicable, in part or wholly, to the case of Captain Brown. The sense of grand poetry, read by the light of this event, is brought out distinctly like an invisible writing held to the fire. As Marvell wrote:—

> "'When the sword glitters o'er the judge's head,
> And fear has coward churchmen silenced,
> Then is the poet's time; 't is then he draws,
> And single fights forsaken virtue's cause:
> Sings still of ancient rights and better times,
> Seeks suffering good, arraigns successful crimes.'

"And George Chapman:—

PERSONALITIES

> "'There is no danger to a man who knows
>   What life and death is; there's not any law
>   Exceeds his knowledge.'

"And Wotton:—

> "'Who hath his life from rumors freed,
>   Of hope to rise or fear to fall;
>   Lord of himself, though not of lands,
>   And having nothing, yet hath all.'"

The foundation of his well-chosen attainment in Modern and Classic authors dates from the origin of his literary life. In college he studied only what was best, and made it the rule. He could say to young students: "*Begin with the best!* start with what is so; never deviate." That part of American history he studied was pre-pilgrim: the Jesuit Relations, early New England authors, Wood, Smith, or Josselyn, afforded him cordial entertainment. Henry's Travels, Lewis and Clark, and such books, he knew remarkably well, and thought no one had written better accounts of things or made them more living than Goethe in his letters from Italy.

Alpine and sea-side plants he admired, besides those of his own village: of the latter, he mostly attended willows, goldenrods, asters, polygonums, sedges, and grasses; fungi and lichens he somewhat affected. He was accustomed to date the day of the month by the appearance of certain flowers, and thus visited special plants for a series of years, in order to form an average; as his white-thorn by Tarbell's Spring, "good for to-morrow, if not for to-day." The bigness of noted trees, the number of their rings, the degree of branching by which their

age may be drawn; the larger forests, such as that princely
"Inches Oak-wood" in West Acton, or Wetherbee's patch, he
paid attentions to. Here he made his cards, and left more
than a pack; his friends were surely disengaged, unless they
had been cut off. He could sink down in the specific history
of a woodland by learning what trees now occupied the soil. In
some seasons he bored a variety of forest trees, when the sap
was amiable, and made his black-birch and other light wines.
He tucked plants away in his soft hat in place of a botany-
box. His study (a place in the garret) held its dry miscellany
of botanical specimens; its corner of canes, its cases of eggs
and lichens, and a weight of Indian arrow-heads and hatchets,
besides a store of nuts, of which he was as fond as squirrels.
"Man comes out of his winter quarters in March as lean as a
woodchuck," he said.

In the varieties of tracks he was a philologist; he read that
primeval language, and studied the snow for them, as well as
for its wonderful blue and pink colors, and its floccular deposits
as it melts. He saw that hunter's track who always steps *before*
you come. Ice in all its lines and polish he peculiarly admired.
From Billerica Falls to Saxonville ox-bow, thirty miles or more,
he sounded the deeps and shallows of the Concord River, and
put down in his tablets that he had such a feeling. Gossamer
was a shifting problem, beautifully vague. Street says:—

> "A ceaseless glimmering, near the ground, betrays
> The gossamer, its tiny thread is waving past,
> Borne on the wind's faint breath, and to yon branch,
> Tangled and trembling, clings like snowy silk."

PERSONALITIES

Insects were fascinating, from the first gray little moth, the *perla*, born in February's deceitful glare, and the "fuzzy gnats" that people the gay sunbeams, to the last luxuriating *Vanessa antiope*, that gorgeous purple-velvet butterfly somewhat wrecked amid November's champaign breakers. He sought for and had honey-bees in the close spathe of the marsh-cabbage, when the eye could detect no opening of the same; water-bugs, skaters, carrion beetles, devil's-needles ("the French call them *demoiselles*, the artist loves to paint them, and paint must be cheap"); the sap-green, glittering, iridescent cicindelas, those lively darlings of Newbury sandbanks and Professor Peck,[1] he lingered over as heaven's never-to-be repainted Golconda. Hornets, wasps, bees, and spiders, and their several nests, he carefully attended. The worms and caterpillars, washed in the spring-freshets from the meadow-grass, filled his soul with hope at the profuse vermicular expansion of Nature. The somersaults of the caracoling stream were his vital pursuit, which, slow as it appears, now and then jumps up three feet in the sacred ash-barrel of the peaceful cellar. Hawks, ducks, sparrows, thrushes, and migrating warblers, in all their variety, he carefully perused with his field-glass, — an instrument purchased with toilsome discretion, and carried in its own strong case and pocket. Thoreau named all the birds without a gun, a weapon he never used in mature years. He neither killed nor imprisoned any animal, unless driven by acute needs. He brought home a flying squirrel, to study its mode of flight, but quickly carried it back to the wood.

[1] An entomologist of seventy years ago, who "collected" near Curzon's Mill.

He possessed true instincts of topography, and could conceal choice things in the brush and find them again; unlike Gall, who commonly lost his locality and himself, as he tells us, when in the wood, master as he was in playing on the organ. If he needed a box on his walk, he would strip a piece of birch-bark off the tree, fold it when cut straightly together, and put his tender lichen or brittle creature therein. In those irritable thunderclaps which come, he says, "with tender, graceful violence," he sometimes erected a transitory house by means of his pocket-knife; where he sat, pleased with "the minute drops from off the eaves," not questioning the love of electricity for trees. If out on the river, haul up your boat, turn it upside-down, and yourself under it. Once he was thus doubled up, when Jove let drop a pattern thunderbolt in the river in front of his boat, while he whistled a lively air as accompaniment. This is noted, as he was much distressed by storms when young, and used to go whining to his father's room, and say, "I don't feel well," and then take shelter in the paternal arms, where his health improved.

> "His little son into his bosom creeps,
> The lively image of his father's face."

While walking in the woods, he delighted to give the falling leaves as much noise and rustle as he could, all the while singing some cheerful stave; thus celebrating the pedestrian's service to Pan as well as to the nymphs and dryads, who never live in a dumb asylum.

PERSONALITIES

"The squirrel chatters merrily,
   The nut falls ripe and brown,
And, gem-like, from the jewelled tree
   The leaf comes fluttering down;
And, restless in his plumage gay,
From bush to bush loud screams the jay."

STREET.

Nothing pleased him better than our native vintage days, when the border of our meadows becomes a rich plantation, whose gathering has been thus described:—

WILD GRAPES[1]

"Bring me some grapes," she cried, "some clusters bring,
Herbert! with large flat leaves, the purple founts."
Then answering he, — "Ellen, if in the days
When on the river's bank hang ripely o'er
The tempting bunches red, and fragrance fills
The clear September air, if then" — "Ah! then,"
Broke in the girl, — "then" —

                September coming,
Herbert, the day of all those sun-spoiled days
Quite petted by him most, wishing to choose,
Alone set off for the familiar bank
Of the blue river, nor to Ellen spake;
That thing of moods long since forgetting all
Request or promise floating o'er the year.
On his right arm a white ash basket swung,
Its depth a promise of its coming stores;
While the fair boy, o'ertaking in his thought

[1] By Channing.

THOREAU

Those tinted bubbles, the best lover's game,
Sped joyous on through the clear mellowing day.
At length he passed Fairhaven's cliff, whose front
Shuts in a curve of shore, and soon he sees
The harvest-laden vine.

                Large hopes were his,
And with a bounding step he leaped along
O'er the close cranberry-beds, his trusty foot
Oft lighting on the high elastic tufts
Of the promiscuous sedge. Alas, for hope!
For some deliberate hand those vines had picked
By most subtracting rule! yet on the youth
More eager sprang, dreaming of prizes rare.
To the blue river's floor fell the green marsh,
And a white mountain cloud-range slowly touched
The infinite zenith of September's heaven.
"I have you now!" cried Herbert, tearing through
The envious thorny thicket to the vines,
Crushing the alder sticks, where rustling leaves
Conceal the rolling stones and wild-rose stems,
And always in the cynic cat-briar pricked.
"I have you now!"

              And rarely on the scope
Of bold adventurer, British or Spaniard,
Loomed Indian coasts, till then a poet's dream,
More glad to them than this Etruscan vase
On his rash eyes, reward of hope deferred.
There swum before him in the magic veil
Of that soft shimmering autumn afternoon,
On the black speckled alders, on the ground,
On leaf and pebble flat or round, the light

PERSONALITIES

Of purple grapes, purple or faintly bloomed,
And a few saintly bunches Muscat-white!
Nor Herbert paused, nor looked at half his wealth,
As in his wild delight he grasped a bunch,
And till his fingers burst still grasped a bunch,
Heaping the great ash basket till its cave
No further globe could hold. And then he stopped,
And from a shrivelled stub picked off three grapes,
Those which he ate.

        'T is right he wreathe about
This heaped and purple spoil that he has robbed
Those fresh unfrosted leaves, green in the shade,
And then he weighs upon his hand the prize,
And springs,—the Atlas on his nervous arm.
Now buried 'neath the basket Herbert sunk,
Or seemed, and showers of drops tickled his cheeks,
Yet with inhuman nerve he struggles on.
At times the boy, half fainting in his march,
Saw twirl in coils the river at his feet,
Reflecting madly the still woods and hills,
The quiet cattle painted on the pool
In far-off pastures, and the musing clouds
That scarcely sailed, or seemed to sail, at all.
Till the strong shadows soothed the ruby trees
To one autumnal black, how hot the toil,—
With glowing cheeks coursed by the exacted tide,
Aching, yet eager, resolute to win,
Nor leave a berry though his shoulder snap.

Within the well-known door his tribute placed,
A fragrance of Italian vineyards leagued
The dear New English farmhouse with sweet shores

In spicy archipelagoes of gold,
Where the sun cannot set, but fades to moonlight,
And tall maids support amphoras on their brows.

And Ellen ran, all Hebe, down the stair
Almost at one long step, while the youth still stood,
And wonder-stricken how he reached that door,
She cried, "Dear mother, fly and see this world of grapes."
Then Herbert puffed two seconds, and went in.

Much fresh enjoyment Thoreau would have felt in the observing wisdom of that admirably endowed flower-writer, Annie S. Downs,[1] a child of Concord (the naturalist's heaven), full of useful knowledge, and with an out-of-doors heart like his; a constant friend to flowers, ferns, and mosses, with an affectionate sympathy, and a taste fine and unerring, reflected by the exquisite beings she justly celebrates. Must she not possess a portion of the snowdrop's prophecy herself as to her writings and this world's winter? when she says:—

"The tender Snowdrop, erect and brave,
    Gayly sprang from her snow-strewn bed.
She doubted not there was sunshine warm
    To welcome her shrinking head;
The graceful curves of her slender stem,
    The sheen of her petals white,
As looking across the bank of snow
    She shone like a gleam of light."

Annie Downs and Alfred B. Street were *native American* writers in the original packages, not extended by the critics,

---

[1] She died in 1901, a few months earlier than Channing.

—writers, under the providence of God, to be a blessing to those who love His works, like Thoreau!

Thoreau's view of a future world and its rewards and punishments was peculiar to himself, and was seldom very clearly expressed; yet he did not bite at a clergyman's skilfully baited hook of immortality, of which, he said, could be *no* doubt. He spoke of the reserved meaning in the insect metamorphosis of the moth, painted like the summer sunrise, that makes its escape from a loathsome worm, and cheats the wintry shroud, its chrysalis. One sweet hour of spring, gazing into a grassy-bottomed pool, where the insect youth were disporting, the *gyrinæ* (boat flies) darting, and tadpoles beginning, like magazine writers, to drop their tails, he said: "Yes, I feel positive beyond a doubt, I *must* pass through *all* these conditions, one day and another; I must go the whole round of life, and come full circle."

If he had reason to borrow an axe or plane, his habit was to return it more sharply. In a walk, his companion, a citizen, said, "I do not see where you find your Indian arrowheads." Stooping to the ground, Henry picked one up, and presented it to him, crying, "Here is one." After reading and dreaming, on the Truro shore, about the deeds of Captain Kidd and wrecks of old pirate ships, he walked out after dinner on the beach, and found a five-franc piece of old France, saying, "I thought it was a button, it was so black; but it is *cob-money*" (the name given there to stolen treasure). He said of early New English writers, like old Josselyn, "They give you one piece of nature, at any rate, and that is themselves,

smacking their lips like a coach-whip,—none of those emas-
culated modern histories, such as Prescott's, cursed with a
style."

> "As dead low earth eclipses and controls
>   The quick high moon, so doth the body souls."

His titles, if given by himself, are descriptive enough. His
"Week," with its chapters of days, is agglutinative, and chains
the whole agreeably in one,—

> "Much like the corals which thy wrist enfold,
>   Laced up together in congruity."

"Autumnal Tints" and "Wild Apples" are fair country
invitations to a hospitable house: the platter adapts itself to
its red-cheeked shining fruit. In his volume called (without
his sensitiveness) "Excursions," the contents look like essays,
but are really descriptions drawn from his journals. Thoreau,
unlike some of his neighbors, could not *mosaic* an essay; but
he loved to tell a good story. He lacked the starch and buck-
ram that vamps the Addison and Johnson mimes. His letters
—of which most have now been printed—are abominably
didactic, fitted to deepen the heroic drain. He wasted none
of those precious jewels, his moments, upon epistles to Rosa
Matilda invalids, some of whom, like leeches, fastened upon
his horny cuticle, but did not draw. Of this gilt vermoulu,
the sugar-gingerbread of Sympathy, Hawthorne had as much.
There was a blank simper, an insufficient sort of affliction, at
your petted sorrow, in the story-teller,—more consoling than
the boiled maccaroni of pathos. Hawthorne—swallowed up

in the wretchedness of life, in that sardonic puritan element that drips from the elms of his birthplace—thought it inexpressibly ridiculous that any one should notice man's miseries, these being his staple product. Thoreau looked upon it as equally nonsense, because men had no miseries at all except those of indigestion and laziness, manufactured to their own order. The writer of fiction could not read the naturalist, probably; and Thoreau had no more love or sympathy for fiction in books than in character. "Robinson Crusoe" and "Sandford and Merton," it is to be feared, were lost on him, such was his abhorrence of lies. Yet in the stoical *fond* of their characters they were alike; and it is believed that Hawthorne truly admired Thoreau. A vein of humor had they both; and when they laughed, like Shelley, the operation was sufficient to split a pitcher. Hawthorne could have said: "People live as long in Pepper Alley as on Salisbury Plain; and they live so much happier that an inhabitant of the first would, if he turned cottager, starve his understanding for want of conversation, and perish in a state of mental inferiority." Henry would never believe it.

As the important consequence from his graduation at Harvard, he urged upon that fading luminary, Jared Sparks, the need he had of books in the library; and by badgering got them out. His persistence became traditional. His incarceration for one night in Concord jail, because he refused the payment of his poll-tax, is described in his tract, "Civil Disobedience," in the volume, "A Yankee in Canada." In this is his signing-off: "I, H. D. T., have signed off, and do not hold

myself responsible to your multifarious, uncivil chaos, named
Civil Government." He seldom went to or voted at a town
meeting,—the instrument for operating upon a New England village,—nor to "meeting" or *church;* nor often did
things he could not understand. In these respects Hawthorne
mimicked him. The Concord novelist was a handsome, bulky
character, with a soft rolling gait. A wit[1] said he seemed like
a *boned pirate.* Shy and awkward, he dreaded the stranger in
his gates; while, as customs-inspector, he was employed to
swear the oaths *versus* English colliers. When surveyor, finding the rum sent to the African coast was watered, he vowed
he would not ship another gill if it was anything but pure
proof spirit. Such was his justice to the oppressed. One of
the things he most dreaded was to be looked at after he was
dead. Being at a friend's demise,[2] of whose extinction he had
the care, he enjoyed—as if it had been a scene in some old
Spanish novel—his success in keeping the waiters from steal-
ing the costly wines sent in for the sick. Careless of heat and
cold indoors, he lived in an Æolian-harp house, that could
not be warmed: that he entered it by a trap-door from a rope-
ladder is false. Lovely, amiable, and charming, his absent-
mindedness passed for unsocial when he was hatching a new
tragedy. As a writer, he loved the morbid and the lame. The
"Gentle Boy" and "Scarlet Letter" eloped with the girls'
boarding-schools. His reputation is master of his literary
taste. His characters are not drawn from life; his plots and
thoughts are often dreary, as he was himself in some lights.

[1] T. G. Appleton.   [2] W. D. Ticknor, in Philadelphia.

His favorite writers were "the English novelists," Boccaccio, Horace, and Johnson.

A few lines have been given from some of Thoreau's accepted authors: he loved Homer for his nature; Virgil for his finish; Chaucer for his health; the Robin Hood Ballads for their out-door blooming life; Ossian for his grandeur; Persius for his crabbed philosophy; Milton for his neatness and swing. He never loved, nor did, anything but what was good, yet he sometimes got no bargain in buying books, as in "Wright's Provincial Dictionary"; but he prized "Loudon's Arboretum," of which, after thinking of its purchase and saving up the money for years, he became master. It was an affair with him to dispense his hardly earned pistareen. He lacked the suspicious generosity, the disguise of egoism: on him peeling or appealing was wasted; he was as close to his aim as the bark on a tree. "Virtue is its own reward," "A fool and his money are soon parted." His property was packed like seeds in a sunflower. There was not much of it, but *that* remained. He had not the "mirage of sympathies," such as Gortchakoff describes as wasted upon bare Poles. He squeezed the sandbanks of the Marlboro' road with the soles of his feet to obtain relief for his head, but did not throw away upon unskilled idleness his wage of living. No one was freer of his means in what he thought a good cause. "His principal and primary business was to be a poet: he was a natural man without design, who spoke what he thought, and just as he thought it." Antiquities, Montfaucon, or Grose, trifles instead of value, dead men's shoes or fancies, he laid not up. At Walden he

[275]

flung out of the window his only ornament, — a paper weight, — because it needed dusting. At a city eating-house his usual order was "boiled apple" (a manual of alum with shortening), seduced by its title. He could spoil an hour and the shopman's patience in his search after a knife, never buying till he got the short, stout blade with the like handle. He tied his shoes in a hard lover's-knot, and was intensely nice in his personal, —

> "Life without thee is loose and spills."

He faintly piqued his curiosity with pithy *bon-mots*, such as: "Cows in the pasture are good milkers. You cannot travel four roads at one time. If you wish the meat, crack the nut. If it does not happen soon, it will late. Take time as it comes, people for what they are worth, and money for what it buys. As the bill, so goes the song; as the bird, such the nest. Time runs before men. A good dog never finds good bones. Cherries taste sour to single birds. No black milk, no white crows. Foul weather and false women are always expected. Occasion wears front-hair. No fish, fresh nor salt, when a fool holds the line. A poor man's cow — a rich man's child — dies. Sleep is half a dinner. A wit sleeps in the middle of a narrow bed. Good heart, weak head. Cocks crow as fortune brightens. A fool is always starting. At a small spring you can drink at your ease. Fire is like an old maid, the best company. Long talk and little time. Better days, a bankrupt's purchase. What men do, not what they promise."

> "The poor man's childe invited was to dine,
> With flesh of oxen, sheep, and fatted swine,

(Far better cheer than he at home could finde,)
And yet this childe to stay had little minde.
You have, quoth he, no apple, froise, nor pie,
Stew'd pears, with bread and milk and walnuts by."

HALL.

As the early morning represented to him the spring of the
day, so did March and April and May ever renew in him his
never-changing, undying faith in a new life for all things.
"You must take the first glass of the day's nectar," he says,
"if you would get all the spirit of it, before its fixed air begins to stir and escape." Thus he rejoiced greatly in the
spring-song of birds,—the songs of our familiar blackbird,

"*That comes before the swallow dares,*"

and picks the alder catkins and the drift along the river-shore.
The birds cheered him, too, in the solitudes of winter, when
the deep snows line the woods, and one needs not only warm
boots, but a warm heart to tread rejoicingly their congealed
vicissitudes. These little things—these (to some) trivial experiences—were to him lofty and ennobling,—raised by his elevation of thought and subtlety of spirit into intellectual glory.
Really, his life and its surroundings were one grand whole.
If he carefully noted what came in the seasons, he no less
loved the seasons themselves in their full quartette. He was
of too catholic a temperament not to love them all for what
they brought. November was the month which impressed him
as the hardest to front; or, as he phrased it,—"In November
a man will eat his heart, if in any month." His seriousness
and his fortitude were native,—and he paddled his boat up

[277]

and down the river into December, when the drops froze on the blade; singing some cheery song, rejoicing with the musk-rats, and listening to the icicles as they jarred against the stems of the button-bushes. Yet certainly this inward cheer, which surpassed the elements, grew out of no insensibility.

Originalities in the individual bear the impress of egotism, because they differ from the action of the mass; but we must distinguish a true and worthy egotism from that captious vanity which sets itself above all other values, merely because really worthless. Our genius once said, "It is as sweet a mystery to me as ever what this world is." Such is not the utterance of the egotist, but of a free and healthy man, living and looking for social and natural responses. If he passed over some things that others insist on, it was because his time and means were fully occupied with other matters,—his capital invested elsewhere. To one (Cholmondeley) who wished to get his opinion upon some theories connected with original sin and future punishment, he replied, "Those voluntaries I did not take," —a term for certain studies at the pleasure of the student in Harvard College. (What are since called "electives.") To use his words elsewhere, "Life is not long enough for one man."

The result of his plan of life, whether conscious or not, was joy,—the joy of the universe,—and kindness and industry. As he declares of the strawberry,— "It is natural that the first fruit which the earth bears should emit (and be, as it were, an embodiment of) that vernal fragrance with which the air has teemed,"—so he represented the purity and sweetness of youth, which in him never grew old.

FIELD SPORTS

"At length I hailed him, seeing that his hat
  Was moist with water-drops, as if the brim[1]
  Had newly scooped a running stream."

WORDSWORTH.

"I, to my soft still walk."

DONNE.

"Scire est nescire, nisi id me scire alius scierit."

LUCILIUS.

"Unus homo, nullus homo."

THEMISTIUS.

"What beauty would have lovely styled;
  What manners pretty, nature mild,
  What wonder perfect, all were fil'd
  Upon record in this blest child."

BEN JONSON.

[1] *One of Bewick's vignettes pictures him drinking from his hat's brim. W. E. C.*

CHAPTER XIV

FIELD SPORTS

As an honorary member, Thoreau appertained to the Boston Society of Natural History, adding to its reports, besides comparing notes with the care-takers or curators of the *mise en scène*. To this body he left his collections of plants, Indian tools, and the like. His latest traffic with it refers to the number of bars or fins upon a pike, which had more or less than was decent. He sat upon his eggs with theirs. His city visit was to their books, and there he made his call, not upon the swift ladies of Spruce Street; and more than once he entered by the window before the janitor had digested his omelet,—

> "How kind is Heaven to men!" VAUGHAN.

When he found a wonder, he sent it, as in the case of the *ne plus ultra* balls from Flint's Pond, in Lincoln, made of grass, reeds, and leaves, triturated by washing upon the sandy beach, and rolled into polished reddish globes, about the bigness of an orange. A new species of mouse, three Blanding cistudas, and several box-turtles (rare here) were among his prizes. Of the *Cistuda Blandingii*, the herpetologist Holbrook says that its *sole* locality is the Illinois and Wisconsin prairies, and the one he saw came from the Fox *River*.

> "Striving to save the whole, by parcells die."

On the Andromeda Ponds, between Walden and Fairhaven, he found the red snow; for things tropic or polar can be found

[281]

if looked for. "There is no power to see in the eye itself, any more than in any other jelly: we cannot see anything till we are possessed with the idea of it. The sportsman had the meadow-hens half-way into his bag when he started, and has only to shove them down. First, the idea or image of a plant occupies my thoughts, and at length I surely see it, though it may seem as foreign to this locality as Hudson's Bay is." His docility was great, and as the newest botanies changed the name of Andromeda to Cassandra, he accepted it, and became an accomplice to this tragic deed. Macbeth and Catiline are spared for the roses. His annual interest was paid, his banks did not fail; the lampreys' nests on the river yet survive, built of small stones and sometimes two feet high. It is of this *petromyzon* our fishermen have the funereal idea (as they are never seen coming back after going up stream) that they all die. The dead suckers seen floating in the river each spring inspired his muse. He admired the otters' tracks, the remains of their scaly dinners, and the places on the river where they amused themselves sliding like boys. He had chased and caught woodchucks, but failed in this experiment on a fox; and caught, instead of him, a bronchial cold that did him great harm. He was in the habit of examining the squirrels' nests in the trees: the gray makes his of leaves; the red, of grass and fibres of bark. He climbed successively four pines after hawks' nests, and was "much stuck up"; and once he gathered the brilliant flowers of the white-pine from the very tops of the tallest pines, when he was pitched on the highest scale. Being strained, by such imprudent exertion, and by that of wheeling heavy loads of driftwood, he impaired his health, always doing ideal work. Fishes' nests and spawn—more especially of the horn-pout and bream—he often studied; and he carried to the entomologist Harris the first lively snow-flea he enjoyed.

> "In earth's wide thoroughfare below,
> Two only men contented go,—
> Who knows what's right and what's forbid,
> And he from whom is knowledge hid."
>
> EMERSON.

Turtles were his pride and consolation. He piloted a snapping-turtle, *Emysaurus serpentina*, to his house from the river, that could easily carry him on his back; and would sometimes hatch a brood of these Herculean monsters in his yard. They waited for information, or listened to their instinct, before setting off for the water. "If Iliads are not composed in our day, the snapping-turtle is hatched and arrives at maturity. It already thrusts forth its tremendous head for the first time in this sphere, and slowly moves from side to side, opening its small glistening eyes for the first time to the light, expressive of dull rage, as if it had endured the trials of this world for a century. They not only live after they are dead, but begin to live before they are alive. When I behold this monster thus steadily advancing to maturity, all nature abetting, I am convinced that there must be an irresistible necessity for mud-turtles. With what unshaking tenacity Nature sticks to one idea! These eggs, not warm to the touch, buried in the ground, so slow to hatch, are like the seeds of vegetable life. I am affected by the thought that the earth nurses these eggs. They are planted in the earth, and the earth takes care of them; she is genial to them, and does not kill them. This mother is not merely inanimate and inorganic. Though the immediate mother-turtle abandons her offspring, the earth and sun are kind to them. The old turtle, on which the earth rests, takes care of them, while the other waddles off. Earth was not made poisonous and deadly to them. The earth has some virtue in it: when seeds are put into it, they germinate; when turtles' eggs, they hatch in due time. Though the mother-turtle re-mained and boarded them, it would still be the universal World-turtle which, through her, cared for them as now. Thus the earth is the maker of all creatures. Talk of Hercules, —his feats in the cradle! what kind of nursery has this one had?"

"Life lock't in death, heav'n in a shell."

The wood-tortoise, *Emys insculpta*, was another annual favorite. It is heard in early spring, after the mud from the freshets has dried on the fallen leaves in swamps that border the stream, slowly rustling the leaves in its cautious advances, and then mysteriously tumbling down the steep bank into the river,—a slightly startling operation. He patiently specu-lates upon its shingled, pectinately engraved roof or back, and its perennial secrets in indelible hierogram. The mud-turtle, he thought, only gained its peculiar odors after spring had come, like other flowers; and he alludes to the high-backed, elliptical shell of the stink-pot covered with leeches. Of the trim painted tortoise he asks: "He who painted the tortoise thus, what were his designs?" "The gold-bead turtle glides anxiously amid the spreading calla-leaves near the warm depths of the black brook. I have seen signs of spring: I have seen a frog swiftly sinking in a pool, or where he dimpled the surface as he leapt in; I have seen the brilliant spots of the tortoises stirring at the bottom of ditches; I have seen the clear sap trickling from the red maple. The first pleasant days of spring come out like a squirrel, and go in again. I do not know at first what charms me."

THE COMING OF SPRING [1]

With the red leaves its floor was carpeted,—
Floor of that Forest-brook across whose weeds
A trembling tree was thrown,—those leaves so red
Shed from the grassy bank when Autumn bleeds
In all the maples; here the Spring first feeds
Her pulsing heart with the specked turtle's gold,
Half-seen emerging from the last year's reeds,—
Spring that is joyous and grows never old,
Soft in aerial hope, sweet, and yet well controlled.

Gently the bluebird warbled his sad song,
Shrill came the robin's whistle from the hill,
The sparrows twittering all the hedge along,
While darting trout clouded the reed-born rill,
And generous elm-trees budded o'er the mill,
Weaving a flower-wreath on the fragrant air;
And the soft-moving skies seemed never still,
And all was calm with peace and void from care,
Both heaven and earth, and life and all things there.

[1] By Channing.

[285]

The early willows launched their catkins forth
To catch the first kind glances of the sun,
Their larger brethren smiled with golden mirth,
And alder tassels dropt, and birches spun
Their glittering rings, and maple buds begun
To cloud again their rubies down the glen,
And diving ducks shook sparkling in the run,
While in the old year's leaves the tiny wren
Peeped at the tiny titmouse, come to life again.

Frogs held his contrite admiration. "The same starry geometry looks down on their active and their torpid state." The little peeping hyla winds his shrill, mellow, miniature flageolet in the warm overflowed pools, and suggests to him this stupendous image: "It was like the light reflected from the mountain ridges, within the shaded portion of the moon, forerunner and herald of the spring." He made a regular business of studying frogs,—waded for them with freezing calves in the early freshet, caught them, and carried them home to hear their sage songs. "I paddle up the river to see the moonlight and hear the bull-frog." He loved to be present at the instant when the springing grass at the bottoms of ditches lifts its spear above the surface and bathes in the spring air. "The grass-green tufts at the spring were like a green fire. Then the willow-catkins looked like small pearl buttons on a waistcoat. The bluebird is like a speck of clear blue sky seen near the end of a storm, reminding us of an ethereal region and a heaven which we had forgotten. With his warble he drills the ice, and his little rill of melody flows a short way down the concave of the sky. The sharp whistle of the blackbird, too, is heard, like single sparks; or a shower of them, shot up from the swamp, and seen against the dark winter in the rear. Here, again, in the flight of the goldfinch, in its ricochet motion, is that undulation observed in so many materials, as in the mackerel-sky." He doubts if the season will be long enough for such oriental and luxurious slowness as the croaking of the first wood-frog implies. Ah, how weatherwise he must be! Now he loses sight completely of those November days, in which you must hold on to life by your teeth. About May 22, he hears the willowy music of frogs, and notices the pads on the river, with often a scolloped edge like those tin platters on which country people bake "turnovers." The earth is all fragrant as one flower, and life perfectly fresh and uncankered. He says of the wood-frog, *Rana sylvatica:* "It had four or five dusky bars, which matched exactly when the legs were folded, showing that the painter applied his brush to the animal when in that position." The leopard-frog, the marsh-frog, the bull-frog, and that best of all earthly singers, the toad, he never could do enough for. It was, he says, a great discovery, when first he found the ineffable trilling concerto of early summer, after sunset, was arranged by the toads,—when the very earth seems to steam with the sound. He makes up his mind reluctantly, as if somebody had blundered about that time. "It would seem then that snakes undertake to swallow toads that are too big for them. I saw a snake by the roadside, and touched him with my foot to see if he were dead. He had a toad in his jaws which he was preparing to swallow, with the latter distended to three times his width; but he relinquished his prey, and fled. And I thought, as the toad jumped leisurely away, with his slime-covered hind-quarters glistening in the sun (as if I, his deliverer, wished to interrupt his meditations), without a shriek or fainting,—I thought, 'What a healthy indifference is manifested!' 'Is not this the broad earth still?' he said." He thinks the yellow, swelling throat of the bull-frog comes with the water-lilies. It is of this faultless singer the good young English lord courteously asked, on hearing it warble in the Concord marsh one day, "What Birds are those?"

> "Dear, harmless age! the short, swift span,
> When weeping virtue parts with man."

In Thoreau's view, the squirrel has the key to the pitch-pine cone, that conical and spiry nest of many apartments; and he is so pleased with the flat top of the muskrat's head in swimming, and his back even with it, and the ludicrous way he shows his curved tail when he dives, that he cannot fail to draw them on the page. Many an hour he spent in watching the evolutions of the minnows, and the turtle laying its eggs, running his own patience against that of the shell; and at last concludes the stink-pot laid its eggs in the dark, having watched it as long as he could see without their appearance. "As soon as these reptile eggs are laid, the skunk comes and gobbles up the nest." Such is a provision of Nature, who keeps that universal eating-house where guest, table, and keeper are on the bill.

His near relation to flowers, their importance in his landscape and his sensibility to their colors, have been joyfully reiterated. He criticised his floral children: "Nature made ferns for pure leaves, to show what she could do in that line. The oaks are in the gray, or a little more; and the deciduous trees invest the woods like a permanent mist. What a glorious crimson fire as you look up to the sunlight through the thin edge of the scales of the black spruce! the *cones* so intensely glowing in their cool green buds, while the purplish sterile blossoms shed pollen upon you. . . . It seemed like a fairy fruit as I sat looking towards the sun, and saw the red maple-keys, made all transparent and glowing by the sun, between me and the body of the squirrel." The excessively minute thread-like stigmas of the hazel, seen against the light, pleased him with their ruby glow, and were almost as brilliant as the jewels of an ice-glaze. It is like a crimson star first detected in the twilight. These facts and similar ones, observed afresh each year, verify his criticism, that he observes with the risk of endless iteration; he milks the sky and the earth. He alludes to a bayberry bush without fruit, probably a male one,—"it made me realize that this was only a more distant and elevated sea-beach, and that we were within the reach of marine influences," —and he sees "banks sugared with the aster Tradescanti. I am detained by the very bright red blackberry-leaves strewn along the sod, the vine being inconspicuous,—how they spot it! I can see the anthers plainly on the great, rusty, fusty globular buds of the slippery elm. The leaves in July are the dark eyelash of summer; in May the houstonias are like a sugaring of snow. These little timid wayfaring flowers were dried and eaten by the Indians,—a delicate meal,—

THOREAU

"Speechless and calm as infant's sleep.

"The most interesting domes I behold are not those of oriental temples and palaces, but of the toadstools. On this knoll in the swamp they are little pyramids of Cheops or Cholula (which also stand on the plain), very delicately shaded off. They have burst their brown tunics as they expanded, leaving only a clear brown apex; and on every side these swelling roofs or domes are patched and shingled with the fragments, delicately shaded off thus into every tint of brown to the edge, as if this creation of a night would thus emulate the weather-stains of centuries; toads' temples,—so charming is gradation. I hear the steady (not intermittent) shrilling of apparently the alder-cricket,—hear it but see it not,—clear and autumnal, a season round. It reminds me of past autumns and the lapse of time, suggests a pleasing, thoughtful melancholy, like the sound of the flail. Such preparations, such an outfit has our life, and so little brought to pass. Having found the *Calla palustris* in one place, I soon found it in another." He notes the dark-blue domes of the soap-wort gentian. "The beech-trunks impress you as full of health and vigor, so that the bark can hardly contain their spirits, but lies in folds or wrinkles about their ankles like a sock, with the *embonpoint* of infancy,—a wrinkle of fat. The fever-bush is betrayed by its little spherical buds, in January. Yellow is the color of spring; red, that of midsummer: through pale golden and green we arrive at the yellow of the buttercup; through scarlet to the fiery July red, the red lily." He finds treasures in the golden basins of the cistus. The water-target leaves in mid-June at Walden are scored

[290]

as by some literal characters. Some dewy cobwebs arrange themselves before his happy eyes, like little napkins of the fairies spread on the grass. The scent of the partridge-berry is between that of the rum-cherry and the Mayflower, or like peach-stone meats.

"How hard a man must work in order to acquire his language,—words by which to express himself. I have known a particular rush by sight for the past twenty years, but have been prevented from describing some of its peculiarities, because I did not know its name. With the knowledge of the name comes a distincter knowledge of the thing. That shore is now describable, and poetic even. My knowledge was cramped and confused before, and grew rusty because not used: it becomes communicable, and grows by communication. I can now learn what *others* know about the same thing. In earliest spring you may explore,—go looking for radical leaves. What a dim and shadowy existence have now to our memories the fair flowers whose localities they mark! How hard to find any trace of the stem now after it has been flatted under the snow of the winter! I go feeling with wet and freezing fingers amid the withered grass and the snow for their prostrate stems, that I may reconstruct the plant:—

"'Who hath the upright heart, the single eye,
The clean, pure hand?'

"It is as sweet a mystery to me as ever what this world is. The hickories are putting out young, fresh, yellowish leaves, and the oaks light-grayish ones, while the oven-bird thrums his sawyer-like strains, and the chewink rustles through the dry leaves, or repeats his jingle on a tree-top, and the wood-thrush, the genius of the wood, whistles for the first time his clear and thrilling strain. It sounds as it did the first time I heard it. I see the strong-colored pines, the grass of trees, in the midst of which other trees are but as weeds or flowers, a little exotic. The variously colored blossoms of the shrub-oaks, now in May hang gracefully like ear-drops; the frequent causeways and the hedge-rows, jutting out into the meadows, and the islands, have an appearance full of life and light. There is a sweet, wild world which lies along the strain of the wood-thrush, rich intervales which border the stream of its song, more thoroughly genial to my nature than any other."

> I heard the Spring tap at the door of Winter;
> Silently she drew herself within his house;
> Softly she with the sun undraped its lights,
> And made her cottage gay. With buds, with flowers,
> With her frail flowers, she painted the soft floors
> Of the romantic woods, and then the trees
> She broke into their clouds of foliage.
> The humming flies came forth, the turtles' gold
> Shone o'er the red-floored brook, the thrasher sang
> His singular song near by.
>
>   O Thou! the life
> That flames in all the maples, and whose hand
> Touches the chords of the mute fields until
> They sing a colored chorus, thou, my God,
> Let mortals kneel until thou callest them!

The neottia and the rattle-snake plantain are little things which make one pause in the wood,—take captive the eye.

The morning-glory by Hubbard's bridge is a goblet full of purest morning air, and sparkling with dew, showing the dew-point. He scents the perfume of the penny-royal which his feet have bruised; the *Clethra alnifolia* is the sweet-smelling queen of the swamp. The white waxen berries of the white-berried or panicled cornel are beautiful, both when full of fruit and when its cymes are naked,—delicate red cymes or stems of berries, spreading their little fairy fingers to the skies, their little palms; *fairy palms* they may be called. "I saw a delicate flower had grown up two feet high between the horses' path and the wheel-track. An inch more to right or left had sealed its fate, or an inch higher; and yet it lived to flourish as much as if it had a thousand acres of untrodden space around it, and never knew the danger it incurred. It did not borrow trouble, nor invite an evil fate by apprehending it."

"I think of what times there are, such as when they begin to drive cows to pasture, May 20, and when the boys go after the cows in July. There is that time about the first of June, the beginning of summer, when the buttercups blossom in the now luxuriant grass, and I am first reminded of mowing and the daisy; when the lady's slipper and the wild-pink have come out on the hill-sides amid the goodly company of the blue lupines. Then has its summer-hour fairly struck upon the clock of the seasons. In distant groves the partridge is sitting on her eggs. When the fresh grass waves rank, and the toads dream, and the buttercups toss their heads, and the heat disposes us to bathe in the ponds and streams, then is the summer begun. I saw how he fed his fish, they, swimming in the dark nether atmosphere of the river, rose easily to swallow such swimmers (June-bugs) of the light upper atmosphere, and sank to its bottom." He noticed the *Datura stramonium* (thorn-apple) as he was crossing the beach of Hull, and felt as if he was on the highway of the world at the sight of this veteran and cosmopolite traveller. Nature in July seems like a hen with open mouth panting in the grass. He hears then, as it were, the mellow sounds of distant horns in the hollow mansions of the upper air, and he thinks more than the road-full. "While I am abroad the ovipositors plant their seeds in me; I am fly-blown with thoughts, and go home to hatch and brood over them. It is now the royal month of August. When I hear the sound of the cricket, I am as dry as the rye which is everywhere cut and housed, though I am drunk with the season's pain. The swallow goes over with a watery twitter-ing. The farmer has driven in his cows, and is cutting an armful of green corn-fodder for them. The loads of meadow-hay pass, which the oxen draw indifferently. The creak of the cricket and the sight of the prunella and the autumnal dande-lion say: 'Work while it is day, for the night cometh in which no man can work.'"

"Both the common largest and the smallest hypericums and the pin-weeds were very rich browns at a little distance (in the middle of March), coloring whole fields, and also withered and falling ferns reeking wet. It was a prospect to excite a reindeer: these tints of brown were as softly and richly fair and sufficing as the most brilliant autumnal tints. There are now respectable billows on our vernal seas; the water is very

high, and smooth as ever it is. It is very warm; I wear but
one coat. On the water, the town and the land it is built on
seem to rise but little above the flood. I realize how water
predominates on the surface of the globe; I am surprised to
see new and unexpected water-lines drawn by the level edge
of the flood about knolls in the meadows and in the woods,
—waving lines which mark the boundary of a possible or
probable freshet any spring. In September we see the ferns
after the frost, like so many brown fires they light up the
meadows. In March, when the browns culminated, the sun
being concealed, I was drawn toward and worshipped the
brownish light in the sod and the withered grass on barren
hills; I felt as if I could eat the very crust of the earth,—I
never felt so terrene, never sympathized so with the surface
of the earth. At the same date comes the arrow-head crop,
humanity patent to my eyes as soon as the snow goes off. Not
hidden away in some crypt or grave, or under a pyramid, no
disgusting mummery, but a clean stone; the best symbol that
could have been, transmitted to me, the Red Man, his mark.
They are not fossil bones, but, as it were, fossil thoughts.
When I see these signs, I know that the maker is not far off,
into whatever form transmuted. This arrow-headed character
promises to outlast all others. Myriads of arrow-points lie
sleeping in the skin of the revolving earth while meteors revolve in space. The footprint, the mind-print of the oldest
men,—for they have camped on the plains of Mesopotamia
and Marathon too. . . . I heard lately the voice of a hound
hunting by itself. What an awful sound to the denizens of the

[295]

wood, that relentless, voracious, demonic cry, like the voice of a fiend! at the hearing of which the fox, hare, and marmot tremble for their young and themselves, imagining the worst. This, however, is the sound which the lords of creation love, and accompany with their bugles and *mellow* horns, conveying a singular dread to the hearer, instead of whispering peace to the hare's palpitating breast."

> "And their sun does never shine,
> And their fields are bleak and bare,
> And their ways are filled with thorns:
> It is eternal winter there."
>
> W. BLAKE.

"As the pine-tree bends and waves like a feather in the gale, I see it alternately dark and light, as the sides of the needles which reflect the cool sheen are alternately withdrawn from and restored to the proper angle. I feel something like the young Astyanax at the sight of his father's flashing crest. A peculiarity of these days (the last week of May) is the first hearing the cricket's creak, suggesting philosophy and thought. No greater event transpires now. It is the most interesting piece of news to be communicated, yet it is not in any newspaper. I went by Temple's,—for rural interest give me the houses of the poor. The creak of the mole cricket has a very afternoon sound. The heron uses these shallows on the river, as I cannot,—I give them up to him. I saw a goldfinch eating the seeds of the coarse barnyard grass, perched on it: it then goes off with a cool twitter. No tarts that I ever tasted at any table possess such a refreshing, cheering, encouraging

[296]

acid that literally put the heart in you and an edge for this world's experiences, bracing the spirit, as the cranberries I have plucked in the meadows in the spring. They cut the winter's phlegm, and now I can swallow another year of this world without other sauce. These are the warm, west-wind, dream-toad, leafing-out, willowy, haze days [*May 9*]. No instrumental music should be heard in the streets more youthful and innocent than willow whistles. Children are digging dandelions by the roadside with a pan and a case knife." This recalls that paradisiacal condition,—

COUNTRY-LIVING [1]

Our reputation is not great,
Come! we can omit the date;
And the sermon,—truce to it;
Of the judge buy not a writ,
But collect the grains of wit,
And sound knowledge sure to hit.
Living in the country then,
Half remote from towns and men,
With a modest income, not
More than amputates the scot;
Lacking vestures rich and rare,
Those we have the worse for wear,
Economic of the hat,
And in fulness like the rat,
Let us just conclude we *are*,
Monarchs of a rolling star!
Fortune is to live on little,

[1] By Channing.

Happily the chip to whittle,
He who can consume his ills,
Daintily his platter fills.
   What's the good of hoarding gold?
Virtue is not bought and sold.
He who has his peace of mind
Fears no tempest, seas, nor wind:
He may let the world boil on,
Dumpling that is quickly done,
And can drain *his* cup so pleasing,
Not the ear of Saturn teasing;
Thus defended in his state,
Pass its laws without debate,
And, not wasting friends or fortune,
Yet no distant stars importune.

He thus describes the last moments of an unfortunate minister: "Then this musky lagune had put forth in the erection of his ventral fins, expanding suddenly under the influence of a more than vernal heat, and his tender white belly where he kept no sight, and the minister squeaked his last! Oh, what an eye was there, my countrymen,—buried in mud up to the lids, meditating on what? Sleepless at the bottom of the pool, at the top of the bottom, directed heavenward, in no danger from motes! Pouts expect not snapping-turtles from below. Suddenly a mud volcano swallowed him up,—seized his midriff. He fell into those relentless jaws which relax not even in death.

"I saw the cat studying ornithology between the corn-rows. She is full of sparrows, and wants no more breakfast this morning, unless it be a saucer of milk,—the dear beast! No tree has so fair a bole and so handsome an instep as the beech. The botanists have a phrase, *mantissa*, an additional matter about something, that is convenient." He uses "crichicroches, zigzagging, brattling, tussucky, trembles, flavid, z-ing"; and says of a farmer, that he keeps twenty-eight cows, which are milked at four and a half o'clock A.M.; but he gives his hired men none of the milk with their coffee. "Frogs still sound round Callitriche Pool, where the tin is cast; no doubt the Romans and Ninevites had such places: to what a perfect system this world is reduced! I see some of those little cells, perhaps of a wasp or bee, made of clay: it suggests that these insects were the first potters. They look somewhat like small stone jugs. Evergreens would be a good title for my things, or Gill-go-over-the-ground, or Winter Green, or Checkerberry, or Usnea lichens. Methinks the scent is a more oracular and trustworthy inquisition than the eye. When I criticise my own writing, I go to the scent, as it were. It reveals, of course, what is concealed from the other senses; by it, I detect earthiness. How did these beautiful rainbow tints get into the shell of the fresh-water clam, buried in the mud at the bottom of our dark river?

"When my eyes first rested on Walden, the striped bream rested on it though I did not see it, and when Tahatawan paddled his canoe there. How wild it makes the pond and the township to find a new fish in it! America renews her youth here. The bream *appreciated* floats in the pond as the centre of the system, a new image of God. Its life no man can explain

more than he can his own. I want you to perceive the mystery
of the bream: I have a contemporary in Walden. How was it
when the youth first discovered fishes? was it the number of
the fin-rays or their arrangement? No! but the faint recognition of a living and new acquaintance, a friend among the
fishes, a provoking mystery.

"I see some feathers of a blue jay scattered along a wood-
path, and at length come to the body of the bird. What a
neat and delicately ornamented creature! finer than any work
of art in a lady's boudoir, with its soft, light purplish-blue
crest, and its dark blue or purplish secondaries (the narrow
half) finely barred with dusky. It is the more glorious to live
in Concord because the jay is so splendidly painted. . . . In
vain were the brown spotted eggs laid [of a hen-hawk killed],
in vain were ye cradled in the loftiest pine of the swamp!
Where are your father and mother? will they hear of your
early death, before ye had acquired your full plumage? They
who nursed and defended ye so faithfully!" "It is already
fall [*August 4*] in low swampy woods where the cinnamon-fern
prevails. So do the seasons revolve, and every chink is filled.
While the waves toss this bright day, the ducks asleep are drifting before it across the ponds; snow-buntings are only winged
snow-balls (where do they pass the night?). This [*April 3*]
might be called the Day of the Snoring Frogs, or the Awak-
ening of the Meadows; and toad-spawn is like *sun-squawl*,
relating our marshes to Provincetown Beach. We love to wade
through the shallows to the Bedford shore; it is delicious to
let our legs drink air. The *palustris* frog has a hard, dry, un-

musical, fine, watchman's-rattle-like stertoration; he knows no winter. . . . Nature works by contraries: that which in summer was most fluid and unresting is now, in February, most solid and motionless. Such is the cold skill of the artist, he carves a statue out of a material which is as fluid as water to the ordinary workman,—his sentiments are a quarry with which he works. I see great bubbles under the ice (as I settle it down), three or four feet wide, go waddling or wabbling away, like a scared lady impeded by her train. So Nature condenses her matter: she is a thousand thick."

"Some circumstantial evidence is very strong, as when you find a trout in the milk. 'Says I to Myself,'—should be the motto to my journal. . . . They think they love God! It is truly his old clothes of which they make scarecrows for the children. When will they come nearer to God than in those very children? Hard are the times when the infants' shoes are second-foot,—truncated at the toes. There is one side of Abner's house painted as if with the pumpkin pies left over after Thanksgiving, it is so singular a yellow:—

> "And foul records
> Which thaw my kind eyes still."

"I saw the seal of evening on the river. After bathing, even at noonday, a man realizes a morning or evening life,—a condition for perceiving beauty. How ample and generous was Nature! My inheritance is not narrow. The water, indeed, reflects heaven because my mind does. The trivialness of the day is past; the greater stillness, the serenity of the air, its coolness and transparency, are favorable to thought (the pensive

[301]

eve). The shadow of evening comes to condense the haze of noon, the outlines of objects are firm and distinct (chaste eve). The sun's rays fell at right angles on the pads and willow-stems, I sitting on the old brown geologic rocks, their feet submerged and covered with weedy moss. There was a quiet beauty in the landscape at that hour which my senses were prepared to appreciate. I am made more vigorous by my bath, more continent of thought. Every sound is music now in view of the sunset and the rising stars, as if there were two persons whose pulses beat together."

CHARACTERS

"Without misfortunes, what calamity!
And what hostility without a foe?"

YOUNG.

"O thou quick heart, which pantest to possess
All that anticipation feigneth fair!
Thou vainly curious mind 'which wouldest guess
Whence thou didst come, and whither thou mayst go,
And that which never yet was known would know."

SHELLEY.

"How seldom, Friend! a good great man inherits
Honor or wealth, with all his worth and pains?
Greatness and goodness are not means, but ends, —
Hath he not always treasures, always friends,
The great good man? three treasures, love and light
And calm thoughts, regular as infant's breath."

COLERIDGE.

"The very dust of his writings is gold."

BENTLEY OF BISHOP PEARSON.

CHAPTER XV

CHARACTERS

RECOURSE can once more be had to the note-books of Thoreau's conversations, as giving his opinions in a familiar sort as well as to afford in some measure a shelter from the blasts of fate. "Here is news for a poor man, in the raw of a September morning, by way of breakfast to him."

SOCIETY

E. The house looks shut up.

C. Oh, yes! the owner is gone; he is absolutely out.

E. We can then explore the grounds, certain not to interrupt the studies of a philosopher famed for his hospitality.

C. Now just hop over with your eyes to yonder garden, which realizes Goldsmith's description, "The rusty beds, unconscious of a poke,"—or is it Cowper; the rusty nail over the latch of the gate; the peach-trees are rusty, the arbors rusty, and I think the proprietor, if there be one, is buried under that heap of old iron.

E. But look across the fence into Captain Hardy's [1] land: there's a musician for you, who knows how to make men dance for him in all weathers,—all sorts of men, Paddies, felons, farmers, carpenters, painters,—yes! and trees and grapes, and ice and stone, hot days, cold days. Beat that true Orpheus

[1] This was Captain Abel Moore, whose farm lay between Emerson's and Alcott's.

lyre if you can. He knows how to make men sow, dig, mow, and lay stone-wall, and make trees bear fruit God never gave them: and foreign grapes yield the juices of France and Spain on his south side. He saves every drop of sap, as if it were his blood. His trees are full of brandy. See his cows, his horses, his swine. And he, the piper that plays the jig which they all must dance, biped and quadruped and centipede, is the plainest, stupidest harlequin in a coat of no colors. His are the woods, the waters, hills, and meadows. With one blast of his pipe, he danced a thousand tons of gravel from yonder blowing sand-heap to the bog-meadow, where the English grass is waving over thirty acres; with another, he winded away sixty head of cattle in the spring, to the pastures of Peterboro', in the hills.

C. And the other's ruins ask, with Henry Vaughan: —

> "Why lies this hair despised now,
>   Which once thy care and art did show?
>   Who then did dress the much-loved toy,
>   In spires, globes, angry curls and coy,
>   Which with skill'd negligence seemed shed
>   About thy curious, wild young head?
>   Why is this rich, this pistic nard
>   Spilt, and the box quite broke and marred?"

How like you the aspect of the place now we have passed the gate?

E. It seems well designed, albeit the fences are dropping away, the arbors getting ready for a decent fall, and the bolts and pins lacking in the machinery of the gardens. I think mostly of the owner, whom you, however, know so much better than I can.

C. I know him as I know old fables and Grecian mythologies. Further from all this modern life, this juggling activity, this superfluous and untamable mediocrity, seems he to remove with each season. Dear Eidolon [1] dwelleth in the rainbow vistas in skies of his own creating. No man in history reminds me of him, nor has there been a portrait left us of so majestic a creature, who certainly hath more a fabled and half-divine aspect than most of those so liberally worshipped by the populace. Born in the palmy days of old Greece, and under the auspices of Plato, he would have founded a school of his own, and his fame had then descended to posterity by his wise sayings, his lovely manners, his beautiful person, and the pure austerities of a blameless and temperate life. Gladly had the more eminent sculptors of the Athenian metropolis chiselled in stone his mild and serene countenance, his venerable locks; and in the free and majestic garb of those picturesque eras he would have appeared as the most graceful and noble of all their popular figures. He would have founded their best institutions, especially chosen by the youth of both sexes, and all who loved purity, sanctity, and the culture of the moral sentiment had flocked about this convenient and natural leader. Nor should his posthumous writings have been left inedited; for the worthiest of his scholars, seizing upon these happy proofs of his indefatigable industry, and such evidences of his uninterrupted communications with higher

[1] Bronson Alcott in 1853.

natures, would have made it the most chosen pleasure of his life to have prepared them in an orderly and beautiful design for coming ages. I know not but he had been worshipped formally, in some peculiar temple set apart for his particular religion, for there inevitably springs out of him a perfect *cultus*, which a wise and imaginative age could have shaped into its practical advantage. Born upon a platform of sordid and mechanical aims, he has somewhat eclipsed and atrophied, and, if detected critically, blurred with scorn or ridicule, so that perchance he had been more pleasantly omitted from all observation.

T. Thou hast drawn, O Musophilus! the portrait of a null imaginary paragon. I have not seen the Phœnix of whom thou hast been discoursing.

E. No: there is not much of the worshipping kind in thee, though thou shouldst pass well for being worshipped. Thou art, I fear, among the scoffers. Be certain that the truth is so; that our ancient Eidolon does represent those aspects of the worthier ages, and yet shall his memory be respected for these properties.

C. I admire not thy notices and puffs of a better age, of a happier time: Don Quixote's oration to the goat-herds should have despatched that figment. I like better Jarno's opinion, —"our America is here or nowhere." Beneath our eyes grow the flowers of love, religion, sentiment, and valor. To-day is of all days the one to be admired. Alas for the sentimental tenderness of Jean Paul, that amusing madman with a remnant of brains! he has flung up his Indian ocean with the peacock-circle of its illuminated waves before our island; and Thomas Carlyle with his bilious howls and bankrupt draughts on hope distracts us. Give this class of unhappy people a little more room and less gloom. What canker has crept into so many kind-hearted creatures to deride our respectable times? I believe, too, in the value of Eidolon, but it is as good company. There are no milestones, no guide-posts, set up in that great listener's waste. His ears are open spaces, abysses of air into which you may pour all day your wisest and best, your moonshine and your dreams, and still he stands like one ready to hear. All other men seem to me obstructive. Their minds are full of their own thoughts,—things of Egypt, as Mr. Borrow's gypsy Antonio calls them,—but Eidolon has reached this planet for no purpose but to hear patiently, smoothly, and *in toto* the doings of your muse; and if he replies, it is in a soft, sweet, and floating fashion, in a sea of soap-bubbles that sets your dull phlegmatism going, loosens the rusty anchor of your cupidity, and away sails your sloop.

T. What we so loosely name a community should have been the appropriate sphere for this excellent genius. Even in these flatulent attempts they demand what they call a practical man, a desperate experimenter, sure to run the communal bank under the water. A few gravelly acres, some dry cows and pea-hens to saw up the sunny noons, with our good Eidolon at the head, behold a possible community. In his pocket lies the practical man's notions of communing,—I mean his purse.

E. I have fancied Cervantes shadows in his novel the history of our socialists.

C. Not of the whole: ere long the community must be the idea and the practice of American society. Each year more clearly sets forth the difficulties under which we labor to conduct the simplest social operations, like mere household service. Such a rough grindstone is your Christian American family to the hard-worked Irish girl, and wild is the reaction of the strong-tempered blade on the whirling stone. To make coffee and bake bread,—not to do the thing for yourself constitutes the person who does it at once the possessor of your moneys, goods, and estate; and, from the lack of sympathy and equality in the contract, Bridget slides out of your kitchen the victor in this unequal contest, when you have made her by your lessons valuable to others. And what better is your relation with the gentleman you send to Washington by means of your votes and good wishes, having his eye bent on the main chance. Cities are malignant with crime; paupers are classed and studied like shrimps; the railroad massacres its hundreds at a smash; steamboats go down, and blow up; and these evils are increasing steadily, till the social crisis comes. Nothing for all these cases but the community, no more selfish agents, no corporations fighting each other, no irresponsible actors,—all must be bound as one for the good of each, labor organized for the whole equally.

E. We have sat too long in this crazy arbor: it is contagious. Let us walk amid last year's stalks. "Little joy has he who has no garden," says Saadi. "He who sees my garden sees my heart," said the prince to Bettine. I prefer the names

of pears to those of most men and women. Our little gentleman, with his gaseous inflamed soul, can never be satisfied
with that little which he needs and not for long. Satisfied!
No, Faintheart, you are as unsatisfied as the toper without
his glass, the maid without her lover, or the student without
his book.

T. I can allow thee, mortal as I am, but six minutes to
tell thy story. What needest thou, then, added to that thou
hast? Community, indeed! a mere artifice of the do-nothings
to profit by the labors of industry. There thou art, with thy
five feet eight in thy shoes, and a certain degree of bodily
vigor and constitution. I have not heard thee complain of the
headache or the gout; thou hast never St. Anthony's fire; thy
corns, if thou hast, are limited; and thou canst, on occasion,
plod thy dozen of miles and not expire. Let us agree that
middle-age has come, and one half the vital candle has been
burnt and snuffed away. Some kind of shed, with a moderate
appurtenance of shingle, belongs to your covering, on the out-
skirts of yonder village; some little table-linen, not damask
I grant; maybe a cup of coffee to your breakfast, and some
crust of haddock, or soured residuum of starch, called bread,
to thy meal. Of clothing thou hast not cloth of gold,—we
are plain country people and decline it. A few friends remain,
as many or more than thou hast deserved. Having all this,
some liberty and hope of Marston's[1] immortality (that depends
on personal value), I seriously demand, what more could you
have? Can nothing appease the ever disorderly cravings of

[1] Marston Watson of Plymouth.

that adamantine contradiction, thy imbecile soul? Buy him up or flatter him into quiet; or could you not give him away or sell him into splendid exile? at least, expunge him!

C. Whichever way we choose in the fields, or down the loco-motive spine that bands with yellow the else green meadow, you will observe the haymaker. Now is the high holiday and the festival of that gramineous sect; now are the cattle kneeled to by humanity; and all these long baking days there they toil and drudge, collating the winter hay-mow of cow and ox, determined by some secret fate to labor for an inferior race.

E. They are so serious in such matters, one might suppose they never speculate on the final cause of pitching hay.

C. Just as seriously this excellent society contemplates the butcher, the grocer, or the clergyman. As if, given time and the human race, at once follows absurd consequence. Spring to your pitch, jolly haymakers! you fancy you are putting time to good advantage in chopping away so many innocent spires of grass, drying them, and laying them industriously in the mow. In spite of that official serenity which nothing can disturb, if you would forego the cow and horse from your contemplations you might leave the grass unmown for ever and a day. Organize an idea among the brethren of spending their hours after a certain fashion, and then woe be to the lunatics who discern its imperfections. In history, haymaking may figure as an amazing bit of the antique, and pitchforks be exhibited in museums for curiosities.

E. I understand your jest: it is your old notion to abbreviate human work. You would fain introduce the study of botany or metaphysics for these vigorous games of our sun-burnt swains, and convert them into sedentary pedants, to be fed on huckleberries and mast. In the sweat of thy face shalt thou earn thy bread. Labor comes out of human exist-ence, like the butterfly out of the caterpillar.

C. How tremendously that vigorous Hibernian pokes aloft his vast pitchfork of blue timothy! May I never be seated on the prong! And his brogue is as thick as his hay-mow. No law ever made such a police as labor. "Early to bed and early to rise" grows by farming. Tire him, says Destiny; wear him out, arms, legs, and back; secure his mischievous wild energy; get him under, the dangerous cartridge he is, of exploding unli-censed sense; and whether it be good for cow or horse, what-ever the means, the end is delightful. Nature must have made the human race, like most of her things, when she had the chance, and without consideration of the next step. She drove along the business, and so invented mankind as rapidly as pos-sible; and observing the redskin, cousin to the alligator,— living on the mud of rivers, the sap of trees, with a bit of flat stone for his hatchet, and a bit of pointed stone for his cannon, —Redskin, a wild fellow, savage and to the manner born,— leaving the woods and fields, the flowers, insects, and minerals untouched, she was thus far content. This imperfect redskin was surely some improvement upon the woodchuck and the musquash. But after coming to the age of bronze, the Danish Kitchen-möddings, and the Swiss lake-dwellings, some million centuries, and a certain development, the aboriginal began to develop a new series of faculties that Nature in eliminating him never thought nor dreamed of; for we must carefully confess Nature misses imagination. Our redskin had fenced himself from bears and deer with their own skins, lit a perennial fire (was it not hard, yet to be expected in the Greeks, that they had never a temple of Prometheus?), dug out some stones and melted them, burnt the trunks of trees into boats, at length built houses, and all the while with his arts, fine or coarse, grew up his passions. Our whiteskin—for now the color of him, by shelter and clothing, had turned white— became a cultivated savage, and, still luxuriating in his old cannibal propensities, hacked and hewed, fought and killed his kind, much to the surprise of his sleepy mother; and not after the honest primeval fashions that she liked well enough, being of her own invention, but after every excruciating device of artist-demonism. Now what could she do for him, how keep him in place, circumvent his trucidating mania, and make him somewhat helpless? It was the work of a moment (Nature's moments being rather extended), an accident. She not only taught whiteskin how to work, but he came to be just a mere laboring machine; the savage had his *insouciance*, the civilizee has his competitive industry,—"Dearest, choose between the two!"

T. This new toy is the true Danaïdes sieve, the rock of Tantalus, which is christened industry, economy, or money. Like the boy's toad in the well, whose position his master set him to make out as a task,—the toad jumping one step up and falling two steps back, how long would it require for him to get to the top? The boy ciphered a long time and filled his slate, went through "recess," and noon and afternoon: at last his instructor asked him, after keeping him at it all day, as to his progress and how far he had got the toad. "What?" said the boy,—"that toad, that nasty little toad? Why, to be sure, he's half-way down into —— by this time." That is where the great mother, blessings on her comfort, has located our brother-man, with his pitchfork, plough-tail, and savings-bank.

C. It is the consequence of a quandary, this *boasted civilization*, as Fourier terms it, when Nature, having hurried her poor plucked creature into existence (even if Darwin thinks he rubbed off his wool, climbing bread-fruit trees and flinging down cocoa-nuts to his offspring), was compelled for safety to set up this golden calf, this lovely mermaid-civilization, with a woman's head and a fish's tail, clipper-ships, and daily papers. Expediency is Nature's mucilage, her styptic. Never shall we see the terminus of this hastily built railroad, no station. But there must be a race that will; when the mind shall be considered before the belly, and when raising food for cows, other things being possible, may not be to every human being just an inscrutable penalty. Cows may get postponed, after a time, for mere men and women; but even milking a beast is a better course of policy than cutting holes in your brother's skull with a bushwhack. Our mythology hath in it a great counterpoise of ethics and compensation. The Greeks hung aloft their theoretical people, where at least they could do no harm if they did not any benefit; while some of our goodies to-day seem to be, like the spider, spinning an immortal coil of ear-wax.

T. I strive to be courtesy itself, yet I may not accept thy fact nor thy conclusion. That redskin was nearer nature, was truer than this pale-face; his religion of the winds, the waters, and the skies, was clearer and fresher than your dry and desiccated theologies, dug out of Egyptian tombs and Numidian sandbanks. He properly worshipped the devil, the evil spirit, wisely agreeing that if the good spirit was of that ilk he was harmless, like the Latins, whom I look upon as the best type of Indians that ever lived. As Tiberius says, who made his Latin rhyme (no doubt they had as much rhyme as they wanted), "*deorum injuriæ, dis curæ*,"—"the gods may cut their own corns for all me." Or what old Ennius thinks:—

"Ego deum genus dixi et dicam cœlitum,
    Sed eos non curare, opinor, quid agat humanum genus;
    Nam, si curent, bene bonis sit, male malis, quod nunc abest."

In other words, "I know all about your race of gods, but little they trouble their heads about your folks; if they cared a snap, they would see the good well off and the bad punished, which is just the opposite to the fact." Is not that good Indian? Or what Lucan says in his "Pharsalia" (vii. 447):—

"Mentimur regnare Jovem . . . mortalia nulli
    Sunt curata Deo."

"Every fool knows it's a lie that Jove reigns,—the gods don't busy their brains about such nobodies as men." I try to give you the ideas of these solemn Latin savages, who had

[316]

neither hats to their heads, shirts to their bodies, nor shoes to their feet. Why might not some learned professor derive us from the Romans? I believe a return to the savage state would be a good thing, interpolating what is really worthy in our arts and sciences and thousand appliances,—

"That the wind blows,
Is all that anybody knows."

C. I believe in having things as they are not! Ay, down to the dust with them, slaves as they *are!* Down with your towns, governments, tricks and trades, that seem like the boy who was building the model of a church in dirt as the minister was passing! "Why, my little lad," said he, "why! making a meeting-house of that stuff? Why, why!" "Yes," answered the youth, "yes, I am; and I expect to have enough left over to make a Methodist minister besides."

T. There is always some new fatality attending our civility. Here is our town, six miles square, with so many dogs and cats, so many men and women upon it, a town library and a bar-room, taxes, prisons, churches, railroads,—and always more and more to come. And I must be taxed as well as the others; as if I am ripe for chains or the gibbet, because the drunkard, poisoned with his own rum while selling it for the good of his neighbors, dies of cerebral congestion or a pistol. Society has no definitions, and of course no distinctions; accepts no honesties, believes too much in going to the bad.

C. You are over-critical. The true art of life consists in accepting things as they are, and not endeavoring vainly to

[317]

better them. It is but a drawing of lots. I am melted when I see how finely things come out, and pin-pricks decide grave affairs. A certain man (I will not name him here, as personalities must be avoided) determined to keep house on a better plan: no flies, no bills,—even the cry of offspring at night cancelled. This was enough evil for that day: the next all the doors were open, flies abounded, children cried in swarms, cash for bills was needed. Our friend began again with it all, put his reforms in practice, and serenity came from his efforts for the time being; but there is another relapse as soon as his hand leaves the crank of the household. So he consults Mrs. Trip,—she has experience as a housekeeper,—details his wretchedness: life is at such a pass, expense vast, little to be had for it and nothing to defray it; a ream of German fly-paper has produced double the number of flies that it kills; as for his babies, there seems to have been a combination among them to blow their lungs out with squalls. Mrs. Trip heard the social horrors, and said, "Mr. Twichett, excuse me, there is a little matter." "Yes, mum, I know it," says our gentleman, supposing it the latest infant or the bill for salt-fish. "It appears, Mr. Twichett, that you keep your eyes open. Yes, sir! you keep your eyes open."

CHRYSOSTOM[1]

C. I lately paid a visit upon an ingenious gentleman, and found him mopping up a topic which had a singular importance in his eyes, and that was New England. "Indeed," I

[1] This was Alcott in another aspect.

thought, "a fine subject for the dead of winter!" You must know, sir, that friend Chrysostom presents the aspect of man talking, as dear Eidolon thinking. And, as the honey-lipped philosopher is about to embark on a voyage to the provinces, he is resolved to enlighten them there on this his favorite problem. "Indeed," I thought to myself, "this man, like Curtius, is also a hero in his way: he is a man of parts; and, next to beating carpets on the Common, I must say he chooses delightful subjects." I fell upon him with my modern flail, to see what grain I could find amid his glittering straws.

T. And how did you prosper? Was there much sediment in the husk?

C. Chrysostom is too learned a master of his weapon to abandon all his treasure to the unreserved gaze of each incredulous worldling. He has, however, attained proximately to something that might be termed a criticism of New England. Good, bad, or indifferent, 't is not a pure vacuity that one finds in this pitiful corner of a continent, with Cape Cod for a seacoast and Wachusett for a mountain. Chrysostom has picked his men as specimens of the mass; his persons on which he so much insists, the merchant, the scholar, the reformer, the proser, and what not,—along the dusty high-roads of life, but you may not greatly expand the list. A few serenities stand sentinel on the watch-towers of thought, not as stars to the mass, but as burnt-out tar barrels. Materialism carves turkeys and cuts tunnels. Be bright, my dear talker, shine and go along; as Dante says, "Hurry on your words." I deemed not so much of his topics as of the man himself,

greater far than all his topics, the ultimate product of all the
philosophies, with an Academe of Types. He has caught the
universe on his thumbnail, and cracked it; he has been at
the banquet of the gods, and borrowed the spoons. Most other
men have some superstitious drawback to them, some want of
confidence in their universal wholes. But our great friend, with
his muscular habit of thought, grasps hold of infinity and
breaks it across his arm, as Gustavus Adolphus, that hero of
Captain Dalgetty's, a horse-shoe. "Never," said he, "can you
get a good brain until all the people of the earth are poured
into one, and when the swarthy Asiatic thinks in the same
skull with the ghostly Swede. And soon I see that this railroad speed of the age shall transmigrate into the brain. Then
shall we make the swiftness of the locomotive into the swiftness of the thought; and the great abolition society shall come,
not of slavery alone,— in dress and diet, in social relations
and religion. It may not prevail for a pair of hermits to go
out together and make a community; for so shall they be the
more solitary. You think the men are too near that I should
draw their portraits truly; but you know not that I am living
as one dead, and that my age is like one walking far off in a
dream to me. That golden steed, the Pegasus, on which I am
mounted, has shot with me far beyond the thoughts and the
men of to-day." As he said this, I looked up at the window,
certainly expecting to see some sort of strange apparition in
the air, some descent of a sign from heaven upon this glorious
expansion beyond time; but all I could see was a fat serving-
maid, in a back casement, arranging some furniture with a

vacillating rag. Types of the ideal and the real, I thought to myself.

"Man should never for an instant blame the animals," he continued, "for showing their apparent inferiorities: they do simply formalize our sins; and Agorax should beware of pork, or he is feasting upon his ancestry. The tail of the dog is the type of the affections." No matter how dry the topic, it seems as if Chrysostom had plunged down into the cellar of the gods, and moistened his intellectual clay at every golden cider-bung. "Nature is a fine setting for man; and when I speak of the New English, how can I forget the departure from their old abbeys, green fields, and populated wheat-lands for this sour fish-skin? Three degrees of elevation towards the pole overturn all jurisprudence, and virtue faints in the city of the Pilgrims. The handsome youth fires the tragic pistol, the handsome girl seeks her swift revenge on prose in her opium. And in these architectures cold, still, and locked, in these flat, red-brick surfaces, and the plate-glass windows that try to flatten your nose when you think to look in,—do you not behold something typical? This prismatic nucleus of trade, deducting its tolls from the country through its roads, is drawing Vermont and New Hampshire and floating them away o'er yon glittering blue sea between those icy islands! Some smaller German orchestra leads off the musical ear, and the shops are cracking with French pictures that would not be sold in Paris. The merchant has his villa, his park, and his *calèche:* it is the recoil of the passions; it is fate, and no star of heaven is visible. The oak in the flower-pot might serve as a symbol; or, as Jugurtha said, when he was thrust into his prison, 'Heavens, how cold is this bath of yours!' If the All-Father had said to our metaphysical Northman, to this Brain-berserkir: Come and sit thee beneath the fluttering palms, and listen to the flow of lordly rivers; thee will I feed on orient pearls of dew, thy bed shall be of sun-flowers, thy dress of the gossamer twilight!"

TO ALCOTT

Light from the spirit-land,
Fire from a burning brand,
If in this cold sepulchral clime,
Chained to an unmelodious rhyme,
   Thou slowly moulderest, —
Yet cheer that great and humble heart,
Prophetic eye and sovereign part,
And be thy future greatly blest,
And by some richer gods impressed,
   And a sublimer art.

Strike on! nor still the golden lyre,
That sparkles with Olympian fire,
And be thy words the soul's desire
   Of this dark savage land;
Nor shall thy sea of glory fail
Whereon thou sweepest, — spread thy sail,
And blow and fill the heaviest gale,
   It shall not swerve thy hand.

Born for a fate whose secrets none
Shall gaze upon beneath earth's sun,

CHARACTERS

Child of the high, the only One,
   Thy glories sleep secure;
Yet on the coast of heaven thy wave
Shall dash beyond an unknown grave,
And cast its spray to light and save
   Some other barks that moor!

MORAL

"Exactissima norma Romanæ frugalitatis."
Said of Mannius Curius.

"Laborers that have no land
  To lyve on but hire handes."
                                    PIERS PLOWMAN.

"Les gros bataillons [1] ont toujours raison."
                                    JOMINI.

"The day that dawns in fire will die in storms,
  Even though the noon be calm."
                                    SHELLEY.

"When thou dost shine, darkness looks white and fair,
Frowns turn to music, clouds to smiles and air."
                                    VAUGHAN.

"Dum in Prœlio non procul hinc
  Inclinatam suorum aciem
  Mente manu voce et exemplo
  Restituebat
  Pugnans ut heroas decet
  Occubuit."   MARSHAL KEITH'S EPITAPH.

---

1 *Frederick the Great has the same saying with the word "regiments" for "bataillons."*

CHAPTER XVI

MORAL

WHAT a life is the soldier's,—like other men's! what a master is the world! Heaven help those who have no destiny to fulfil, balked of every chance or change, of all save the certainty of death! Thoreau had a manifest reason for living. He used to say, "I do not know how to entertain those who can't take long walks. A night and a forenoon is as much confinement to those wards (the house) as I can stand." And although the rich and domestic could "beat him in frames," like that Edinburgh artist whom Turner thus complimented, he was their match in the open. Men affected him more naturally. "How earthy old people become,—mouldy as the grave. Their wisdom smacks of the earth: there is no foretaste of immortality in it. They remind one of earth-worms and mole-crickets." Seeing the negro barber sailing alone up the river on a very cold Sunday, he thinks he must have experienced religion; a man bathing from a boat in Fairhaven Pond suggests: "Who knows but he is a poet in his yet obscure and golden youth?" And he loved to go unmolested. He would not be followed by a dog nor cane. He said the last was too much company. When asked whether he knew a young miss, celebrated for her beauty, he inquired, "Is she the one with the goggles?" He thought he never noticed any one in the street; yet his contemporaries may have known as much of him while living as of Shakespeare when dead. His mental

appearance at times almost betrayed irritability; his words
were like quills on "the fretful porcupine" (a libel on the creature, which is patience *ab ovo*). One of his friends complained
of him: "He is so pugnacious I can love, but I can never like
him." And he had a strong aversion to the Scribes and Phari-
sees. Those cracked potsherds, traditionary institutions, served
him as butts, against whose sides he discharged the arrows of
his wit, echoing against their massive hollowness. Yet, truly,
the worship of beauty, of the fine things in nature, of all
good and friendly pursuits, was his staple; he enjoyed common people; he relished strong, acrid characters. In Boston
he used to visit the end of Long Wharf, having no other business than with the libraries and that brief sight of the sea,
so fascinating to a landsman. (This made our friend [Calvin]
Green [1] say, who happened to have spent forty out of forty-

[1] Calvin H. Green, a mechanic of Rochester, Michigan, admiring Thoreau,
made for Ellery Channing a long cane from the wood of the Californian
manzanilla (an evergreen shrub, bearing a bright red apple), selecting as
a motto for its silver head, —
> "Love equals swift and slow,
> And high and low."

This was intended for Thoreau himself; but he dying before it was ready,
Mr. Green gave it to Mr. Channing, with the additional inscription,
"Thoreau-Channing—Friendship." (This cane E. C. has given to F. B. S.)
Mr. Green came to Concord, September 1, 1863, and stayed a week, visiting Channing, Emerson, the Thoreau family, and myself; he walked with
Channing to Walden, the Cliffs, and the Estabrook country—passing, on
the way to the latter, Thoreau's cabin, on Clarke's farm, where it stood
till it fell in pieces, about June, 1868. It lasted twenty-three years, and
might have stood a century, with care, being well built, but poorly roofed.
Another lover of Thoreau, named Harrington, came from Indiana in September, 1866, who told Channing that Thoreau's death had caused him

five years in a back country [Rochester, Michigan], that he "had taken a boat-ride on the Atlantic.")

When with temperaments radically opposed to his, he drew in the head of his pugnacity like that portion of one of his beloved turtles, and could hiss and snap with any ancient of them all. The measured, conservative class, dried-up Puritan families, who fancy the Almighty Giver of all good things has fitted their exquisite brain precisely to his evangelic night-cap; prosers with their universe of meanness and conceit to change square with you against gold and diamonds; folks of easy manners, polished and oiled to run sharply on the track of lies and compliments,—of *such* he was no great admirer. Neither did he go with Goethe, that other people are wig-blocks on which we must fit our own false heads of hair to fetch them out. Like a cat he would curl up his spine and spit at a fop or monkey, and despised those who were running well down hill to damnation. His advice to a drunkard as the wisest plan for him to reform, "You had better cut your throat,"—that was his idea of moral suasion, and corresponded with his pleasure at John Brown's remark of a border ruffian he had despatched, rapidly paring away his words,—"He had a perfect right to be hung." To this his question points,—"If it were not for virtuous, brave, gen-

more sorrow than that of any person he had ever known. He had never seen him. Channing went with him to Walden.

Thoreau quoted to Alcott, as having come to him in a dream, the old line of Storer:—

"His short parenthesis of life was sweet,"
which may have had reference to John Thoreau.

erous natures, would there be any sweet fragrance? Genius rises above nature; in spite of heat, in spite of cold, works and lives." Persons with whom he had no sympathy were to him more removed than stocks and stones:—

"Looking at the latter, I feel comparatively as if I were with my kindred. Men may talk about measures till all is blue and smells of brimstone, and then go home and expect their measures to do their duty for them: the only measure is integrity and manhood. We seem to have used up all our inherited freedom like the young bird the albumen in the shell. Ah, how I have thriven on solitude and poverty! I cannot overstate this advantage, I am perhaps more wilful than others. Common life is hasty, coarse, and trivial, as if you were a spindle in a factory. No exercise implies more manhood and vigor than joining thought to thought. How few men can tell what they have thought! I hardly know half a dozen who are not too lazy for this. You conquer fate by thought. If you think the fatal thought of men and institutions, you need never pull the trigger. The consequences of thinking inevitably follow. There is no more Herculean task than to think a thought about this life, and then get it expressed. There are those who never do or say anything, whose life merely excites expectation. Their excellence reaches no further than a gesture or mode of carrying themselves; they are a sash dangling from the waist, or a sculptured war-club over the shoulder. They are like fine-edged tools gradually becoming rusty in a shop-window. I like as well, if not better, to see a piece of iron or steel out of which such tools will be made, or the bushwhack in a man's hand. . . .

"'The watchmaker finds the oil from the porpoise's jaw the best thing for oiling his watches. Man has a million eyes, and the race knows infinitely more than the individual. Consent to be wise through your race. We are never prepared to believe that our ancestors lifted large stones or built thick walls. . . . There is always some accident in the best things, whether thoughts, or expressions, or deeds. The memorable thought, the happy expression, the admirable deed are only partly ours. The thought came to us because we were in a fit mood; also we were unconscious and did not know that we had said or done a good thing. We must walk consciously only part way toward our goal, and then leap in the dark to our success. What we do best or most perfectly is what we most thoroughly learned by the longest practice, and at length it fell from us without our notice as a leaf from a tree. It is the *last* time we shall do it,—our unconscious leavings:—

> "'Man is a summer's day, whose youth and fire
> Cool to a glorious evening and expire.'   (*Vaughan.*)

"It is remarkable how little we attend to what is constantly passing before us, unless our genius directs our attention that way. In the course of ages the rivers wriggle in their bed until it feels comfortable under them. Time is cheap and rather insignificant. It matters not whether it is a river which changes from side to side in a geological period, or an eel that wriggles past in an instant. A man's body must be rasped down exactly to a shaving. The mass of men are very

unpoetic, yet that Adam that names things is always a poet.
No man is rich enough to keep a poet in his pay, yet what
a significant comment on our life is the least strain of music.
This poor, timid, unenlightened, thick-skinned creature, what
can it believe? When I hear music, I fear no danger; I am
invulnerable; I see no foe; I am related to the earliest times,
and to the latest. I hear music below; it washes the dust off
my life and everything I look at. The field of my life becomes a boundless plain, glorious to tread, with no death or
disappointment at the end of it. In the light of this strain
there is no Thou nor I. How inspiring and elysian it is to
hear when the traveller or the laborer, from a call to his horse
or the murmur of ordinary conversation, rises into song! It
paints the landscape suddenly; it is at once another land,—
the abode of poetry. Why do we make so little ado about
echoes? they are almost the only kind of kindred voices that
we hear:—

> "'Scattering the myrrhe and incense of thy prayer.'"

A coxcomb was railed at for his conceit: he said, "It is so
common every one has it; why notice it specially in him?"
He gets up a water-color sketch of an acquaintance.[1] "He
is the moodiest person perhaps I ever saw. As naturally whimsical as a cow is brindled, both in his tenderness and in his
roughness he belies himself. He can be incredibly selfish and
unexpectedly generous. He is conceited, and yet there is in
him far more than usual to ground conceit upon. He will not

[1] It was Channing himself.

[332]

stoop to rise. He wants something for which he will not pay the going price. He will only learn slowly by failure, not a noble but a disgraceful failure, and writes poetry in a sublime slip-shod style." But despite his *caveats*, his acceptance was large, he took nearly every bill. The no-money men, butter-egg folks; women who are talking-machines and work the threads of scandal; paupers, walkers, drunk or dry, poor-house poets, no matter, the saying of Terence abided,—"I am a man, and nothing human but what can go down with me." Of such a one he says, "His face expressed no more curiosity or relationship to me than a custard pudding." Of such is the kingdom of poor relations.

No man had a better unfinished life. His anticipations were vastly rich: more reading was to be done over Shakespeare and the Bible; more choice apple-trees to be set in uncounted springs,—for his chief principle was faith in all things, thoughts, and times, and he expected, as he said, "to live for forty years." He loved hard manual work, and did not mean to move every year, like certain literary brethren. In his business of surveying he was measurably diligent, and having entered on a plan would grind his vest away over the desk to have done with it. He laid out every molecule of fidelity upon his employer's interests, and in setting a pine-lot for one says, "*I set every tree with my own hands.*" Yet like moralists, though he tried to "pay every debt as if God wrote the bill," as Emerson says, he takes himself to task: "I remember with a pang the past spring and summer thus far. I have not been an early riser: society seems to have invaded and overrun me."

Thus intensely he endeavored to live, but living is not all. He had now more than attained the middle age, his health sound to all appearance, his plans growing more complete, more cherished; new lists of birds and flowers projected, new details to be gathered upon trees and plants. Now, embarking more closely in the details of this human enterprise which had been something miscellaneous, the time had fairly come to take an account of stock, and to know how he really stood on *terra firma*. Here was a great beginning, in a condition of matchless incompleteness,—to be adjusted by no one but the owner. In December, 1860, he took a severe cold by exposing himself while counting the rings on trees and when there was snow on the ground. This brought on a bronchial affection, which he much increased by lecturing at Waterbury; and although he used prudence after this, and indeed went a-journeying with his friend, Horace Mann, Jr., into Minnesota, this trouble with the bronchiæ continued.

Early in his illness Thoreau began a letter to Ricketson (March 19, 1861), for which he substituted a very different one three days later,—using only the first few lines of this, and substituting an account of his own sickness for that of the Minotts. This first draft runs thus:—

"*Friend R.*

Your letter reached me in due time, but I had already heard the blue-birds. They were here on the 26 of Feb. at least,—but not yet do the larks sing or the flickers call, with us. The blue birds come again, as does the same spring, but it does not find

MORAL

*the same mortals here to greet it. You remember Minott's cottage
on the hillside,—well, it finds some change there, for instance.
The little gray, hip-roofed cottage was occupied at the beginning
of February, this year, by George Minott and his sister Mary,
respectively 78 and 80 years old,—and Miss Potter, 74. These
had been its permanent occupants for many years. Minott had
been on his last legs for some time,—at last off his legs, expecting weekly to take his departure,—a burden to himself and
friends,—yet dry and natural as ever. His sister took care of
him, and supported herself and family with her needle, as usual.
He lately willed his little property to her, as a slight compensation for her care. Feb. 13, their sister, 86 or 87, who lived across
the way, died. Miss Minott had taken cold in visiting her, and
was so sick that she could not go to her funeral. She herself
died of lung fever on the 18th, (which was said to be the same
disease that her sister had),—having just willed her property
back to George, and added her own mite to it. Miss Potter, too,
had now become ill,—too ill to attend the funeral,—and she
died of the same disease on the 23rd. All departed as gently as
the sun goes down, leaving George alone.*

*I called to see him the other day,—the 27th of February,—
a remarkably pleasant spring day,—and as I was climbing the
sunny slope to his strangely deserted house, I heard the first
blue birds upon the elm that hangs over it. They had come as
usual, though some who used to hear them were gone. Even
Minott had not heard them, though the door was open,—for he
was thinking of other things. Perhaps there will be a time when
the blue birds themselves will not return any more.*

[335]

I hear that George, sitting on the side of his bed, a few days after this, called out to his niece, who had come to take care of him, and was in the next room,—to know if she did not feel lonely? 'Yes, I do' said she. 'So do I' added he. He said he was like an old oak, all shattered and decaying. 'I am sure, Uncle,' said his niece, 'you are not much like an oak.' 'I mean' said he, 'that I am like an oak or any other tree, inasmuch as I cannot stir from where I am.'"

Here the draft ends; and when Thoreau took up the subject again, March 22, he gave the date of his "severe cold," from which he never recovered, as December 3, 1860.

With an unfaltering trust in God's mercies and never deserted by his good genius, he most bravely and unsparingly passed down the inclined plane of a terrible malady, pulmonary consumption, working steadily at the completing of his papers to his last hours, or so long as he could hold the pencil in his trembling fingers. Yet, if he did get a little sleep to comfort him in this year's campaign of sleepless affliction, he was sure to interest those about him with his singular dreams, more than usually fantastic: he said once that, having got a few moments of repose, "sleep seemed to hang round my bed in festoons." The last sentence he incompletely spoke contained but two distinct words, "moose" and "Indians," showing how fixed in his mind was that relation. Then the world he had so long sung and delighted in faded tranquilly away from his eyes and hearing, till on that beautiful spring morning of May 6, 1862, it closed on him. He had written long before:—

MORAL

"In this roadstead I have ridden,
   In this covert I have hidden,
   Friendly thoughts were cliffs to me,
   And I hid beneath their lea.

This true people took the stranger,
   And warm-hearted housed the ranger;
   They received their roving guest,
   And have fed him with the best;

Whatsoe'er the land afforded
   To the stranger's wish accorded,
   Shook the olive, stripped the vine,
   And expressed the strengthening wine.

And by night they did spread o'er him
   What by day they spread before him,
   That good-will which was repast
   Was his covering at last."

His state of mind during this, his only decided illness, deserves notice as in part an idiosyncrasy. He accepted it heroically, but in no wise after the traditional manner. He experienced that form of living death when the very body refuses sleep, such is its deplorable dependence on the lungs now slowly consumed by atoms; in its utmost terrors refusing aid from any opiate in causing slumber, and declaring uniformly that he preferred to endure with a clear mind the worst penalties of suffering, rather than be plunged in a turbid dream by narcotics. He retired into his inner mind, into that unknown, unconscious, profound world of existence where he excelled; there he held inscrutable converse with just men made perfect, or what else, absorbed in himself. "The night of time far surpasses the day; and who knows when was the equinox? Every hour adds unto the current arithmetic, which scarce stands one moment. And since death must be the Lucina of life; since our longest sun sets on right declensions, and makes but winter arches, therefore it cannot be long before we lie down in darkness and have our light in ashes. Sense endureth no extremities, and sorrows destroy us or themselves: our delivered senses not relapsing into cutting remembrances, our sorrows are not kept raw by the edge of repetitions." An ineffable reserve shrouded this to him unforeseen fatality: he had never reason to believe in what he could not appreciate, nor accepted formulas of mere opinions; the special vitalization of all his beliefs, self-consciously, lying in the marrow of his theology.

As noticed, he had that forecast of life which by no means fulfils its prediction deliberately; else why are these mortal roads on which we so predictively travel strewn with the ashes of the young and fair, — this Appian Way devised in its tombs, — from the confidence of the forty years to come? "*Quisque suos patimur manes*, — we have all our infirmities first or last, more or less. There will be, peradventure, in an age, or one of a thousand, a Pollio Romulus, that can preserve himself with wine and oil; a man as healthy as Otto Hervardus, a senator of Augsburg in Germany, whom Leovitius, the astrologer, brings in for an example and instance of certainty in his art; who, because he had the significators in his geniture fortunate, and free from the hostile aspects of

Saturn and Mars, — being a very cold man, — could not remember that ever he was sick." The wasting away of his body,
the going forth and exit of his lungs, which, like a steady
lamp, give heat to the frame, was to Henry an inexplicably
foreign event, the labors of another party in which he had no
hand; though he still credited the fact to a lofty inspiration.
He would often say that we could look on ourselves as a third
person, and that he could perceive at times that he was out
of his mind. Words could no longer express these inexplicable
conditions of his existence, this sickness which reminded him
of nothing that went before: such as that dream he had of
being a railroad cut, where they were digging through and
laying down the rails, — the place being in his lungs.

His habit of engrossing his thoughts in a journal, which
had lasted for a quarter of a century; his out-of-door life, of
which he used to say, if he omitted that, all his living ceased,
— all this now became so incontrovertibly a thing of the past
that he said to me once, standing at the window, "I cannot
see on the outside at all. We thought ourselves great philosophers in those wet days, when we used to go out and sit down
by the wall-sides." This was absolutely all he was ever heard
to say of that outward world during his illness; neither could
a stranger in the least infer that he had ever a friend in field
or wood. Meanwhile, what was the consciousness in him, —
what came to the surface? Nothing save duty, duty, work,
work! As Goethe said at the loss of his son, "It is now alone
the idea of duty that must sustain us," Thoreau now concentrated all his force, caught the shreds of his fleeting physical

strength the moment when the destinies accorded to him a
long breath, to complete his stories of the Maine Woods,
then in press; endeavoring vainly to finish his lists of Birds
and Flowers, and arrange his papers on Night and Moonlight.
Never at any time at all communicative as to his own physical condition (having caught that Indian trick of superlative
reticence), he calmly bore the fatal torture, this dying at the
stake, and was torn limb from limb in silence:—

> "When all this frame
> Is but one dramme, and what thou now descriest
> In sev'rall parts shall want a name."

His patience was unfailing: assuredly he knew not aught
save resignation; he did mightily cheer and console those whose
strength was less. His every instant now, his least thought
and work, sacredly belonged to them, dearer than his rapidly
perishing life, whom he should so quickly leave behind. As
long as he could possibly sit up, he insisted on his chair at
the family-table, and said, "It would not be social to take my
meals alone." And on hearing an organ in the streets, playing
some old tune of his childhood he should never hear again,
the tears fell from his eyes, and he said, "Give him some
money! give him some money!"

> "He was retired as noontide dew,
>   Or fountain in a noon-day grove;
>   And you must love him, ere to you
>   He would seem worthy of your love.
>
> The outward shows of sky and earth,
>   Of hill and valley, he has viewed;

MORAL

And impulses of deeper birth
Have come to him in solitude."

His mortal ashes are laid in the Concord burying-ground. A lady[1] on seeing this tranquil spot, and the humble stone under the pitch-pine tree, replied to one who wished for him a star y-pointing monument, "This village is his monument, covered with suitable inscriptions by himself."

Truth, audacity, force, were among Thoreau's mental characteristics, devoted to humble uses. His thoughts burned like flame, so earnest was his conviction. He was transported infinitely beyond the regions of self when pursuing his objects, single-hearted, doing one thing at a time and doing that in the best way! Self-reliance shall serve for his motto,—

"His cold eye truth and conduct scanned."

His love of wildness was real. Whatever sport it was of Nature, this child of an old civilization, this Norman boy with the blue eyes and brown hair, held the Indian's creed, and believed in the essential worth and integrity of plant and animal. This was a religion to him; to us, mythical. He spoke from a deeper conviction than ordinary, which enforced on him that sphere and rule of life he kept. So far an anchorite, a recluse, as never to seek popular ends, he was yet gifted with the ability and courage to be a captain of men. Heroism he possessed in its highest sense,—the will to use his means to his ends, and these the best. Inexplicable he was, if spontaneous action and free genius are not transparent: as they cannot be to those who put aside the principles of being, as

[1] Elizabeth Hoar.

understood by himself, and adopt an estimate that confines all men to one spiteful code,—their own.

As to his results,—possibly the future may determine that our village life, unknown and unnoticed, without name and influence in the present, was essential and vital, as were the realities he affected, the immutable truths he taught,—learned in the school of Nature. Endowed with unusual power and sagacity, if he did not shine in public councils, or lead the State, he yet defended the right, and was not the idle spectator of wrong and oppression. He showed that the private man can be a church and state and law unto himself. In a possible New England he may stand for the type of coming men, who shall invent new forms and truer modes of mortal society. His moral and critical estimates appear in his published writings; here I have united a few memorabilia of his general life, with passages not before published from his pen.

His work was laid out for a long life; since the business he employed himself about required duration, before all others. To see him giving up all without a murmur,—so utterly resigned to the wish of Heaven, even to die, if it must be so, rather than there should be any struggle in his existence against those beautiful laws he had so long worshipped and obeyed (whether consciously or not),—was enough to be described, if pen had the power to do it. For the most he did not realize his illness,—that is, did not make it real; but seemed to look on it as something apart from himself, in which he had no concern. "I have no wish to live, except for my mother and sister," was one of his conclusions. He wrote for the press till his strength was no longer sufficient even to move a pencil; nevertheless he did not relax, but had the papers still laid before him. I am not aware that anywhere in literature there beams a greater heroism; the motive, too, was sacred,—for he was doing these things that his family might reap the advantage.

One of his noblest and ablest associates was a philosopher, whose heart is like a land flowing with milk and honey;[1] and it was affecting to see this venerable man kissing his brow, when the damps and sweat of death lay upon it, even if Henry knew it not. It seemed to me an extreme unction, in which a friend was the best priest.

[1] Alcott.

MEMORIAL VERSES

ILLUSTRATING CHIEFLY SCENES OF THOREAU'S LIFE

MEMORIAL VERSES

I

TO HENRY

Hear'st thou the sobbing breeze complain
　How faint the sunbeams light the shore? —
Thy heart, more fixed than earth or main,
　Henry! thy faithful heart is o'er.

Oh, weep not thou thus vast a soul,
　Oh, do not mourn this lordly man,
As long as Walden's waters roll,
　And Concord river fills a span.

For thoughtful minds in Henry's page
　Large welcome find, and bless his verse,
Drawn from the poet's heritage,
　From wells of right and nature's source.

Fountains of hope and faith! inspire
　Most stricken hearts to lift this cross;
His perfect trust shall keep the fire,
　His glorious peace disarm the loss!

II

WHITE POND

Gem of the wood and playmate of the sky,
How glad on thee we rest a weary eye,
When the late ploughman from the field goes home,
And leaves us free thy solitudes to roam!

[347]

THOREAU

Thy sand the naiad gracefully had pressed,
Thy proud majestic grove the nymph caressed,
Who with cold Dian roamed thy virgin shade,
And, clothed in chastity, the chase delayed,
To the close ambush hastening at high noon,
When the hot locust spins his Zendic rune.

Here might Apollo touch the soothing lyre,
As through the darkening pines the day's low fire
Sadly burns out; or Venus nigh delay
With young Adonis, while the moon's still ray
Mellows the fading foliage, as the sky
Throws her blue veil of twilight mystery.

No Greece to-day; no dryad haunts the road
Where sun-burned farmers their poor cattle goad;
The black crow caws above yon steadfast pine,
And soft Mitchella's odorous blooms entwine
These mossy rocks, where piteous catbirds scream,
And Redskins flicker through the white man's dream.
Who haunts thy wood-path?—ne'er in summer pressed
Save by the rabbit's foot; its winding best
Kept a sure secret, till the tracks, in snow
Dressed for their sleds, the lumbering woodmen plough.

How soft yon sunbeam paints the hoary trunk,
How fine the glimmering leaves to shadow sunk!
Then streams across our grassy road the line
Drawn firmly on the sward by the straight pine;
And curving swells in front our feet allure,
While far behind the curving swells endure;
Silent, if half pervaded by the hum
Of the contented cricket. Nature's sum
Is infinite devotion. Days nor time
She emulates,—nurse of a perfect prime.

MEMORIAL VERSES

Herself the spell, free to all hearts; the spring
Of multiplied contentment, if the ring
With which we 're darkly bound.

                    The pleasant road
Winds as if Beauty here familiar trode;
Her touch the devious curve persuasive laid,
Her tranquil forethought each bright primrose stayed
In its right nook. And where the glorious sky
Shines in, and bathes the verdant canopy,
The prospect smiles delighted, while the day
Contemns the village street and white highway.

Creature all beauteous! In thy future state
Let beauteous Thought a just contrivance date;
Let altars glance along thy lonely shore,
Relumed; and on thy leafy forest floor
Tributes be strewn to some divinity
Of cheerful mien and rural sanctity.
Pilgrims might dancing troop their souls to heal;
Cordials, that now the shady coves conceal,
Reft from thy crystal shelves, we should behold,
And by their uses be thy charms controlled.

Naught save the sallow herdsboy tempts the shore,
His charge neglecting, while his feet explore
Thy shallow margins, when the August flame
Burns on thy edge and makes existence tame;
Naught save the blue king-fisher rattling past,
Or leaping fry that breaks his lengthened fast;
Naught save the falling hues when Autumn's sigh
Beguiles the maple to a sad reply;
Or some peculiar air a sapless leaf
Guides o'er thy ocean by its compass brief.

Save one, whom often here glad Nature found
Seated beneath yon thorn, or on the ground

[349]

THOREAU

Poring content, when frosty Autumn bore
Of wilding fruit to earth that bitter store;
And when the building winter spanned in ice
Thy trembling limbs, soft lake! then each device
Traced in white figures on thy seamed expanse
This child of problems caught in gleeful trance.
   Oh, welcome he to thrush and various jay,
And echoing veery, period of the day!
To each clear hyla trilling the new spring,
And late gray goose buoyed on his icy wing;
Bold walnut-buds admire the gentle hand,
While the shy sassafras their rings expand
On his approach, and thy green forest wave,
White Pond! to him fraternal greetings gave.
The far white clouds that fringe the topmost pine
For his delight their fleecy folds decline;
The sunset worlds melted their ores for him,
And lightning touched his thought to seraphim.

   Clear wave, thou wert not vainly made, I know,
Since this sweet man of Nature thee could owe
A genial hour, some hope that flies afar,
And revelations from thy guiding star.
Oh, may that muse, of purer ray, recount,
White Pond! thy glory; and, while anthems mount
In strains of splendor, rich as sky and air,
Thy praise, my Henry, might those verses share.
For He who made the lake made it for thee,
So good and great, so humble, yet so free;
And waves and woods we cannot fairly prove,
Like souls, descended from celestial Jove.

With thee he is associate. Hence I love
Thy gleams, White Pond! thy dark, familiar grove;

Thy deep green shadows, clefts of pasture ground;
Mayhap a distant bleat the single sound,
One distant cloud, the sailor of the sky,
One voice, to which my inmost thoughts reply.

III

A LAMENT

A WAIL for the dead and the dying!
They fall in the wind through the Gilead tree,
Off the sunset's gold, off hill and sea;
   They fall on the grave where thou art lying,
   Like a voice of woe, like a woman sighing,
Moaning her buried, her broken love,
Never more joy,—never on earth, never in heaven above!

   Ah, me! was it for this I came here?
Christ! didst thou die that for this I might live?
   An anguish, a grief like the heart o'er the bier, —
Grief that I cannot bury, nor against it can strive, —
Life-long to haunt me, while breath brings to-morrow,
Falling in spring and in winter, rain and sleet sorrow,
Prest from my fate that its future ne'er telleth,
Spring from the unknown that ever more welleth.

   Fair, O my fields! soft, too, your hours!
Mother of Earth, thou art pleasant to see!
   I walk o'er thy sands, and I bend o'er thy flowers.
There is nothing, O nothing, thou givest me,
Nothing, O nothing, I take from thee.
What are thy heavens, so blue and so fleeting?
Storm, if I reck not, no echo meeting
In this cold heart, that is dead to its beating,
Caring for nothing, parting or greeting!

THOREAU

IV

MORRICE LAKE

(Written for E. S. Hotham.)

On Morrice Lake I saw the heron flit
And the wild wood-duck from her summer perch
Scale painted by, trim in her plumes, all joy;
And the old mottled frog repeat his bass,
Song of our mother Earth, the child so dear.
There, in the stillness of the forest's night,
Naught but the interrupted sigh of the breeze,
Or the far panther's cry, that, o'er the lake,
Touched with its sudden irony and woke
The sleeping shore; and then I hear its crash,
Its deep alarm-gun on the speechless night, —
A falling tree, hymn of the centuries.

No sadness haunts the happy lover's mind,
On thy lone shores, thou anthem of the woods,
Singing her calm reflections; the tall pines,
The sleeping hill-side and the distant sky,
And thou! the sweetest figure in the scene,
Truest and best, the darling of my heart.

O Thou, the ruler of these forest shades,
And by thy inspiration who controll'st
The wild tornado in its narrow path,
And deck'st with fairy wavelets the small breeze,
That like some lover's sigh entreats the lake;
O Thou, who in the shelter of these groves
Build'st up the life of nature, as a truth
Taught to dim shepherds on their star-lit plains,
Outwatching midnight; who in these deep shades

[352]

MEMORIAL VERSES

Secur'st the bear and catamount a place,
Safe from the glare of the infernal gun,
And leav'st the finny race their pebbled home,
Domed with thy watery sunshine, as a mosque;
God of the solitudes! kind to each thing
That creeps or flies, or launches forth its webs, —
Lord! in thy mercies, Father! in thy heart,
Cherish thy wanderer in these sacred groves;
Thy spirit send as erst o'er Jordan's stream,
Spirit and love and mercy for his needs.
Console him with thy seasons as they pass,
And with an unspent joy attune his soul
To endless rapture. Be to him, — thyself
Beyond all sensual things that please the eye,
Locked in his inmost being; let no dread,
Nor storm with its wild splendors, nor the tomb,
Nor all that human hearts can sear or scar,
Or cold forgetfulness that withers hope,
Or base undoing of all human love,
Or those faint sneers that pride and riches cast
On unrewarded merit, — be, to him,
Save as the echo from uncounted depths
Of an unfathomable past, burying
All present griefs.
          Be merciful, be kind!
Has he not striven, true and pure of heart,
Trusting in thee? Oh, falter not, my child!
Great store of recompense thy future holds,
Thy love's sweet councils and those faithful hearts
Never to be estranged, that know thy worth.

THOREAU

V

TEARS IN SPRING

THE swallow is flying over,
But he will *not* come to me;
He flits, my daring rover,
From land to land, from sea to sea;
Where hot Bermuda's reef
Its barrier lifts to fortify the shore,
Above the surf's wild roar
He darts as swiftly o'er, —
But he who heard that cry of spring
Hears that no more, heeds not his wing.

How bright the skies that dally
Along day's cheerful arch,
And paint the sunset valley!
How redly buds the larch!
Blackbirds are singing,
Clear hylas ringing,
Over the meadow the frogs proclaim
The coming of Spring to boy and dame,
But not to me, —
Nor thee!

And golden crowfoot's shining near,
Spring everywhere that shoots 't is clear,
A wail in the wind is all I hear;
A voice of woe for a lover's loss,
A motto for a travelling cross, —
And yet it is mean to mourn for thee,
In the form of bird or blossom or bee.

MEMORIAL VERSES

Cold are the sods of the valley to-day
Where thou art sleeping,
That took thee back to thy native clay ;
Cold, — if above thee the grass is peeping
And the patient sunlight creeping,
While the bluebird sits on the locust-bough
Whose shadow is painted across thy brow,
And carols his welcome so sad and sweet
To the Spring that comes and kisses his feet.

VI

THE MILL BROOK[1]

THE cobwebs close are pencils of meal,
   Painting the beams unsound,
And the bubbles varnish the glittering wheel
   As it rumbles round and round.
Then the Brook began to talk
   And the water found a tongue,
"We have danced a long dance," said the gossip,
   "A long way have we danced and sung."

"Rocked in a cradle of sanded stone
Our waters wavered ages alone,
Then glittered at the spring
On whose banks the feather-ferns cling ;
Down jagged ravines
We fled tortured,
And our wild eddies nurtured
Their black hemlock screens ;
And o'er the soft meadows we rippled along,
And soothed their lone hours with a pensive song, —

1 *One of the most labored pieces I ever wrote. But it was not helped by work. W. E. C.*

THOREAU

Now at this mill we're plagued to stop,
To let our miller grind the crop.

"See the clumsy farmers come
With jolting wagons far from home;
We grind their grist,
It wearied a season to raise,
Weeks of sunlight and weeks of mist,
Days for the drudge and Holydays.
To me it fatal seems,
Thus to kill a splendid summer,
And cover a landscape of dreams
In the acre of work and not murmur.
I could lead them where berries grew,
Sweet flag-root and gentian blue,
And they will not come and laugh with me,
Where my water sings in its joyful glee;
Yet small the profit, and short-lived for them,
Blown from Fate's whistle like flecks of steam.

"The old mill counts a few short years, —
Ever my rushing water steers!
It glazed the starving Indian's red,
On despair or pumpkin fed,
And oceans of turtle notched ere he came,
Species consumptive to Latin and fame,
(Molluscous dear or orphan fry,
Sweet to Nature, I know not why).

"Thoughtful critics say that I
From yon mill-dam draw supply. —
I cap the scornful Alpine heads,
Amazons and seas have beds,
But I am their trust and lord.
Me ye quaff by bank and board,

MEMORIAL VERSES

Me ye pledge the iron-horse,
I float Lowells in my source.

"The farmers lug their bags and say, —
'Neighbor, wilt thou grind the grist to-day?'
Grind it with his nervous thumbs!
Clap his aching shells behind it,
Crush it into crumbs!

"No! his dashboards from the wood
Hum the dark pine's solitude;
Fractious teeth are of the quarry
That I crumble in a hurry, —
Far-fetched duty is to me
To turn this old wheel carved of a tree.

"I like the maples on my side,
Dead leaves, the darting trout;
Laconic rocks (they sometime put me out)
And moon or stars that ramble with my tide;
The polished air, I think I could abide.

"This selfish race who prove me,
Who use, but do not love me!
Their undigested meal
Pays not my labor on the wheel.
I better like the sparrow
Who sips a drop at morn,
Than the men who vex my marrow,
To grind their cobs and corn."

Then said I to my brook, "Thy manners mend!
Thou art a tax on earth for me to spend."

[357]

THOREAU

VII

STILLRIVER, THE WINTER WALK[1]

THE busy city or the heated car,
The unthinking crowd, the depot's deafening jar,
These me befit not, but the snow-clad hill
From whose white steeps the rushing torrents fill
Their pebbly beds, and as I look content
At the red Farmhouse to the summit lent,
There, —underneath that hospitable elm,
The broad ancestral tree, that is the helm
To sheltered hearts, —not idly ask in vain,
Why was I born, —the heritage of pain?

The gliding trains desert the slippery road,
The weary drovers wade to their abode;
I hear the factory bell, the cheerful peal
That drags cheap toil from many a hurried meal.
How dazzling on the hill-side shines the crust,
A sheen of glory unprofaned by dust!
And where thy wave, Stillriver, glides along,
A stream of Helicon unknown in song,
The pensive rocks are wreathed in snow-drifts high
That glance through thy soft tones like witchery.

To Fancy we are sometimes company,
And Solitude 's the friendliest face we see.
Some serious village slowly through I pace,
No form of all its life mine own to trace;
Where the cross mastiff growls with blood-shot eye,
And barks and growls and waits courageously;
Its peaceful mansions my desire allure

1 *From Groton Junction (now Ayer) to Lancaster along the railroad.*

[358]

MEMORIAL VERSES

Not each to enter and its fate endure, —
But Fancy fills the window with its guest;
The laughing maid, — her swain who breaks the jest;
The solemn spinster staring at the fire,
Slow fumbling for his pipe, her solemn sire;
The loud-voiced parson, fat with holy cheer,
The butcher ruddy as the atmosphere;
The shop-boy loitering with his parcels dull,
The rosy school-girls of enchantment full.

Away from these the solitary farm
Has for the mind a strange domestic charm,
On some keen winter morning when the snow
Heaps roof and casement, lane and meadow through.
Yet in those walls how many a heart is beating,
What spells of joy, of sorrow, there are meeting!
One dreads the post, as much the next, delay,
Lest precious tidings perish on their way.
The graceful Julia sorrows to refuse
Her teacher's mandate, while the boy let loose
Drags out his sled to coast the tumbling hill,
Whence from the topmost height to the low rill,
Shot like an arrow from the Indian's bow,
Downward he bursts, life, limb, and all below
The maddening joy his dangerous impulse gives;
In age, how slow the crazy fact revives!

Afar I track the railroad's gradual bend,
I feel the distance, feel the silence lend
A far romantic charm to farmhouse still,
And spurn the road that plods the weary hill, —
When like an avalanche the thundering car
Whirls past, while bank and rail deplore the jar.
The wildly piercing whistle through my ear
Tells me I fright the anxious engineer;

[359]

THOREAU

I turn, — the distant train and hurrying bell
Of the far crossing and its dangers tell.
And yet upon the hill-side sleeps the farm,
Nor maid or man or boy to break the charm.

Delightful Girl! youth in that farmhouse old,
The tender darling in the tender fold, —
Thy promised hopes fulfilled as Nature sought,
With days and years, the income of thy thought;
Sweet and ne'er cloying, beautiful yet free,
Of truth the best, of utter constancy;
Thy cheek whose blush the mountain wind laid on,
Thy mouth whose lips were rosebuds in the sun;
Thy bending neck, the graces of thy form,
Where art could heighten, but ne'er spoil the charm;
Pride of the village school for thy pure word,
Thy pearls alone those glistening sounds afford;
Sure in devotion, guileless and content,
The old farmhouse is thy right element.
Constance! such maids as thou delight the eye,
In all the Nashua's vales that round me lie!

And thus thy brother was the man no less, —
Bred of the fields and with the wind's impress.
With hand as open as his heart was free,
Of strength half-fabled mixed with dignity.
Kind as a boy, he petted dog and hen,
Coaxed his slow steers, nor scared the crested wren.
And not far off the spicy farming sage,
Twisted with heat and cold, and cramped with age,
Who grunts at all the sunlight through the year
And springs from bed each morning with a cheer.
Of all his neighbors he can *something* tell, —
'T is bad, whate'er, we know, and like it well! —

MEMORIAL VERSES

The bluebird's song he hears the first in spring,
Shoots the last goose bound South on freezing wing.

Ploughed and unploughed the fields look all the same,
White as the youth's first love or ancient's fame;
Alone the chopper's axe awakes the hills,
And echoing snap the ice-encumbered rills;
Deep in the snow he wields the shining tool,
Nor dreads the icy blast, himself as cool.
Seek not the parlor, nor the den of state
For heroes brave; make up thy estimate
From these tough bumpkins clad in country mail,
Free as their air and full without detail.

No gothic arch *our* shingle Pæstum boasts, —
Its pine cathedral is the style of posts, —
No crumbling abbey draws the tourist there
To trace through ivied windows pictures rare,
Nor the first village squire allows his name
From aught illustrious or debauched by fame.

That sponge profane who drains away the bar
Of yon poor inn extracts the mob's huzza;
Conscious of morals lofty as their own,
The glorious Democrat, — his life a loan.
And mark the preacher nodding o'er the creed,
With wooden text, his heart too soft to bleed.
The Æsculapius of this little State,
A typhus-sage, sugars his pills in fate,
Buries three patients to adorn his gig,
Buys foundered dobbins or consumptive pig;
His wealthy pets he kindly thins away,
Gets in their wills, — and ends them in a day.
Nor shall the strong schoolmaster be forgot,
With fatal eye, who boils the grammar-pot:

THOREAU

Blessed with large arms he deals contusions round,
While even himself his awful hits confound.

Pregnant the hour when at the tailor's store,
Some dusty Bob a mail bangs through the door.
Sleek with good living, virtuous as the Jews,
The village squires look wise, desire the news.
The paper come, one reads the falsehood there,
A trial lawyer, lank-jawed as despair.
Here, too, the small oblivious deacon sits,
Once gross with proverbs, now devoid of wits,
And still by courtesy he feebly moans,
Threadbare injunctions in more threadbare tones.
Sly yet demure, the eager babes crowd in,
Pretty as angels, ripe in pretty sin.
And the postmaster, suction-hose from birth,
The hardest and the tightest screw on earth;
His price as pungent as his hyson green,
His measure heavy on the scale of lean.

A truce to these aspersions, as I see
The winter's orb burn through yon leafless tree,
Where far beneath the track Stillriver runs,
And the vast hill-side makes a thousand suns.
This crystal air, this soothing orange sky,
Possess our lives with their rich sorcery.
We thankful muse on that superior Power
That with his splendor loads the sunset hour,
And by the glimmering streams and solemn woods
In glory walks and charms our solitudes.

O'er the far intervale that dimly lies
In snowy regions placid as the skies,
Some northern breeze awakes the sleeping field,
And like enchanted smoke the great drifts yield

MEMORIAL VERSES

Their snowy curtains to the restless air;
Then build again for architect's despair
The alabaster cornice or smooth scroll
That the next moment in new forms unroll.

VIII

TRURO

I

TEN steps it lies from off the sea,
   Whose angry breakers score the sand,
   A valley of the sleeping land,
Where chirps the cricket quietly.

The aster's bloom, the copses' green,
   Grow darker in the softened sun,
   And silent here day's course is run,
A sheltered spot that smiles serene.

It reaches far from shore to shore,
   Nor house in sight, nor ship or wave,
   A silent valley sweet and grave,
A refuge from the sea's wild roar.

Nor gaze from yonder gravelly height, —
   Beneath, the crashing billows beat,
   The rolling surge of tempests meet
The breakers in their awful might. —

And inland birds soft warble here,
   Where golden-rods and yarrow shine,
   And cattle pasture — sparest kine!
A rural place for homestead dear.

THOREAU

Go not then, traveller, nigh the shore!
  In this soft valley muse content,
  Nor brave the cruel element,
That thunders at the valley's door.

And bless the little human dell,
  The sheltered copsewood snug and warm, —
  Retreat from yon funereal form,
Nor tempt the booming surges' knell.

II

THE OLD WRECKER

He muses slow along the shore,
  A stooping form, his wrinkled face
  Bronzed dark with storm, no softer grace
Of hope; old, even to the core.

He heeds not ocean's wild lament,
  No breaking seas that sight appall, —
  The storms he likes, and as they fall
His gaze grows eager, seaward bent.

He grasps at all, e'en scraps of twine,
  None is too small, and if some ship
  Her bones beneath the breakers dip,
He loiters on his sandy line.

Lonely as ocean is his mien,
  He sorrows not, nor questions fate,
  Unsought, is never desolate,
Nor feels his lot, nor shifts the scene.

Weary he drags the sinking beach,
  Undaunted by the cruel strife,

THOREAU

VI

MICHEL ANGELO—AN INCIDENT

Hard by the shore the cottage stands,
  A desert spot, a fisher's house,
  There could a hermit keep carouse
On turnip-sprouts from barren sands.

No church or statue greets the view,
  Not Pisa's tower or Rome's high wall;
  And connoisseurs may vainly call
For Berghem's goat, or Breughel's blue.

Yet meets the eye along a shed,
  Blazing with golden splendors rare,
  A name to many souls like prayer,
Robbed from a hero of the dead.

It glittered far, the splendid name,
  Thy letters, Michel Angelo,—
  In this lone spot none e'er can know
The thrills of joy that o'er me came.

Some bark that slid along the main
  Dropped off her headboard, and the sea
  Plunging it landwards, in the lee
Of these high cliffs it took the lane.

But ne'er that famous Florentine
  Had dreamed of such a fate as this,
  Where tolling seas his name may kiss,
And curls the lonely sand-strewn brine.

These fearless waves, this mighty sea,
  Old Michel, bravely bear thy name!
  Like thee, no rules can render tame,
Fatal and grand and sure like thee.

[368]

MEMORIAL VERSES

Alive, yet not the thing of life,
A shipwrecked ghost that haunts the reach.

He breathes the spoil of wreck and sea,
  No longer to himself belongs,
  Always within his ear thy songs,
Unresting Ocean! bound yet free.

In hut and garden all the same,
  Cheerless and slow, beneath content,
  The miser of an element
Without a heart,—that none can claim.

Born for thy friend, O sullen wave,
  Clasping the earth where none may stand!
  He clutches with a trembling hand
The headstones from the sailor's grave.

III

OPEN OCEAN

Unceasing roll the deep green waves,
  And crash their cannon down the sand,
  The tyrants of the patient land,
Where mariners hope not for graves.

The purple kelp waves to and fro,
  The white gulls, curving, scream along;
  They fear not thy funereal song,
Nor the long surf that combs to snow.

The hurrying foam deserts the sand,
  Afar the low clouds sadly hang,
  But the high sea with sullen clang,
Still rages for the silent land.

[365]

THOREAU

No human hope or love hast thou,
  Unfeeling Ocean! in thy might,
  Away — I fly the awful sight,
The working of that moody brow.

The placid sun of autumn shines, —
  The hurrying knell marks no decline,
  The rush of waves, the war of brine,
Force all, and grandeur, in thy lines.

Could the lone sand-bird once enjoy
  Some mossy dell, some rippling brooks,
  The fruitful scent of orchard nooks,
The loved retreat of maid or boy!

No, no; the curling billows green,
  The cruel surf, the drifting sand,
  No flowers or grassy meadow-land,
No kiss of seasons linked between.

The mighty roar, the burdened soul,
  The war of waters more and more,
  The waves, with crested foam-wreaths hoar,
Rolling to-day, and on to roll.

IV

WINDMILL ON THE COAST

With wreck of ships, and drifting plank,
  Uncouth and cumbrous, wert thou built,
  Spoil of the sea's unfathomed guilt,
Whose dark revenges thou hast drank.

And loads thy sail the lonely wind,
  That wafts the sailor o'er the deep,

MEMORIAL VERSES

Compels thy rushing arms to sweep,
And earth's dull harvesting to grind.

Here strides the fisher lass and brings
  Her heavy sack, while creatures small,
  Loaded with bag and pail, recall
The youthful joy that works in things.

The winds grind out the bread of life,
  The ceaseless breeze torments the stone,
  The mill yet hears the ocean's moan,
Her beams the refuse of that strife.

V

ETERNAL SEA

I hear the distant tolling bell,
  The echo of the breathless sea;
  Bound in a human sympathy
Those sullen strokes no tidings tell.

The spotted sea-bird skims along,
  And fisher-boats dash proudly by;
  I hear alone that savage cry,
That endless and unfeeling song.

Within thee beats no answering heart,
  Cold and deceitful to my race,
  The skies alone adorn with grace
Thy freezing waves, or touch with art.

And man must fade, but thou shalt roll
  Deserted, vast, and yet more grand;
  While thy cold surges beat the strand,
Thy funeral bells ne'er cease to toll.

MEMORIAL VERSES

OLD OCEAN

Of what thou dost, I think, not art,
  Thy sparkling air and matchless force,
  Untouched in thy own wild resource,
The tide of a superior heart.

No human love beats warm below,
  Great monarch of the weltering waste!
  The fisher-boats make sail and haste,
Thou art their savior and their foe.

Alone the breeze thy rival proves,
  Smoothing o'er thee his graceful hand,
  Lord of that empire over land,
He moves thy hatred and thy loves.

Yet thy unwearied plunging swell,
  Still breaking, charms the sandy reach,
  No dweller on the shifting beach,
No auditor of thy deep knell;—

The sunny wave, a soft caress;
  The gleaming ebb, the parting day;
  The waves like tender buds in May,
A fit retreat for blessedness.

And breathed a sigh like children's prayers,
  Across thy light aerial blue,
  That might have softened wretches too,
Until they dallied with these airs.

Was there no flitting to thy mood?
  Was all this bliss and love to last?
  No lighthouse by thy stormy past,
No graveyard in thy solitude!

[369]

THOREAU

IX

BAKER FARM[1]

Thy entry is a pleasant field,
Which some mossy fruit-trees yield
Partly to a ruddy brook,
By gliding musquash undertook,
And the small, mercurial trout
    That dart about.

Cell of seclusion,
Haunt of old Time!
Rid of confusion,
Vacant of crime;
Landscape where the richest element
Is a little sunshine innocent:
In thy insidious marsh,
In thy ancestral wood,
Thy artless meadow
And forked orchard's writhing mood, —
O Baker Farm!
There lies in thee a fourfold charm.

Alien art thou to God and Devil!
Man too forsaketh thee;
No one runs to revel
On thy rail-fenced lea,
Save gleaning Silence bearded gray,
Who frozen apples steals away,
Thinnest jars of Winter's jam,
Which he 'll with gipsy sugar cram.

1 *In 1848, when this poem was written, the retreat here celebrated was a most retired spot, the out-lands on Fairhaven Bay of James Baker's large farm in Lincoln, two miles southeast of Concord Village, and a mile or so from Thoreau's Cove and cabin, then standing and but lately deserted by Henry. It is now the frontage of C. F. Adams's villa. F. B. S., 1902.*

MEMORIAL VERSES

Thou art expunged from To-day,
Rigid in parks of thine own,
Where soberly shifts the play,
As the wind sighs a monotone;
But west trends blue Fairhaven Bay,
Green o'er whose rocks the white pines sway;
And south slopes Nobscot grand,
And north our still Cliffs stand.

And here a Poet builded
In the completed years;
Behold a trivial cabin
That to destruction steers!
Should we judge it built?
Rather by kind Nature spilt;
Henry, with his alphabet
Of the Past, this task could set.

Pan of unwrinkled cream,
May some Poet dash thee in his churn!
And with thy beauty mad,
Verse thee in rhymes that burn!
Railroad defier,
No man's desire;
Unspeculative place,
With that demurest face,
How long art thou to be
Absolute in thy degree?

I would hint at thy religion,
Hadst thou any, —
Piny fastness of the pigeon,
Squirrel's litany!
Here the cawing, sable rook

THOREAU

Never thumbed a gilt Prayer-Book
In this ante-Christian nook:
Set a priest at praying here,
He would go to sleep I fear.

Art thou orphaned of a deed,
Or title that a court could read?
Or dost thou stand
For that entertaining land
That no man owns,
Pure grass and stones,
In thy drying field,
And thy knotty trees,
In hassock and bield,
And marshes that freeze?

Simpleness is all thy teaching;
Idleness is all the preaching,
Churches are these steepled woods,
Galleries these green solitudes,
Fretted never by a noise, —
Eloquence that each enjoys.
Debate with none hast thou,
With questions ne'er perplexed;
As tame at the first sight as now,
In thy plain russet gaberdine drest.

Come ye who love,
And ye who hate!
Children of the Holy Dove,
And Guy Faux of the State;
Come, hang conspiracies
From the tough rafters of the trees!
One at a time, —
That is enough;

MEMORIAL VERSES

Two will not rhyme,
But make the roadway rough;
One at a time,
With interspace sublime, —
Before each of you go
A century or so!

Still Baker Farm!
So fair a lesson thou dost set,
With loving eyes
Commensurately wise, —
Lesson no one may forget.
Consistent sanctity, —
Value that can ne'er be spent,
Volume that cannot be lent;
Passable to thee,
And me, —
For Heaven thou art meant!

X

FLIGHT OF GEESE[1]

RAMBLING along the marshes
On the bank of the Assabet,
Sounding myself as to how it went, —
Praying I might not forget,
And all uncertain
Whether I was in the right,
Toiling to lift Time's curtain, —
And if I burnt the strongest light, —

1 *Written in 1848, but kept in manuscript for years by Emerson, as he told me, hoping to find the best word for the honking cry of the wild goose, to use as a chorus to each stanza. At last he printed it in his "Parnassus."*

THOREAU

Suddenly, high in the air,
I heard the travelled geese their overture prepare.

High above the patent ball
The wild geese flew;
Not half so wild as what doth me befall,
Or, swollen Wisdom! you.
Th' indifferent geese
Seemed to have taken the air on lease.

In the front there fetched a leader, —
Him behind the line spread out,
 And waved about;
For it was near night,
When these air-pilots stop their flight.

Southward went
These geese indifferent, —
South and south and south, —
Steered by their indifference, —
Slowly falling from their mouth
A creaking sense;
Still they south would go,
Leaving me in wonder at the show.
From some Labrador lagoon
They creaked along to the old tune.

Cruising off the shoal dominion
 Where we sit, —
Depending not on mere opinion,
 Nor hiving crumbs of wit,
Geographical by tact,
Naming not a pond or river;
Pulled with twilight down, in fact,
In the reeds to quack and quiver, —
 There they go,

MEMORIAL VERSES

    Spectators of the play below,
    Southward in a row.

These indifferent geese
Cannot stop to count the stars,
Nor taste the sweetmeats in odd jars,
    Nor speculate and freeze.
Raucous weasands needs be well,
Feathers glossy, quills in order;
Starts their train, — yet rings no bell, —
Steam is raised without recorder.

"Up, my merrymen, feathered all!"
Saith the goose-commander;
"Brighten bills and flirt your pinions!
My toes are nipt, — so let us render
Ourselves into soft Campeachy!
'T is too cold in brisk Spitzbergen,
And the waters are not leechy."

"Flap your wings, my stiff companions!
Air-sailors! clap your helm hard down!
Give one push, and we shall clatter
Over river, wood, and town!
By our stomachs do we know
Where we 'd best for supper go.

"Let 's brush loose for any creek
Where lurk fish and fly!
Condiments to fat the weak
Inundate the pie.
Flutter not about a place,
Ye concomitants of Space!"

    Creak away!
Start well in advance of Day!

THOREAU

Creak and clatter as you go,
Mortality sleeps sound below!
Mute shall listening nations stand
On that dark, receding land;
Faint their villages and towns
Scattered o'er the misty downs;
Named, divided, tethered cattle,
Dulled by peace, and spilt in battle.

As thus I stood,
Much did it puzzle me;
And I was glued
Speechless by this mystery;
How that thus from Labrador
Screeching geese flew south so far, —
How in the unfenced air
They should so nimbly fare,
Drawn along yearly in a narrow line,
The midst of an experiment? or the confine?

"How long?"
Never is that question asked,
While a throat can lift the song,
Or a flapping wing be tasked.
So long may be the feathered glee,
These geese may touch from sea to sea.

All the grandmothers about
Hear these orators of Heaven;
Then clap on their flannels stout,
Cowering o'er the hearth at even:
Children stare up in the sky,
And laugh to see the long black line on high.
Was it all
To make us laugh a little,

INDEX

INDEX

[It will be evident to any reader that an index of this volume, to be complete, must run to many more pages than are here allowed. What is now attempted is to give in the eight hundred and more titles, and more than three thousand page entries, the names of most authors mentioned, of towns, plants, etc., and a key to many of those expressions which these very original writers used. The towns named are in Massachusetts unless otherwise indicated. F. B. S.]

[381]

INDEX

INDEX

INDEX

[387]

INDEX

INDEX

INDEX

INDEX

[395]

INDEX